# The Los Angeles Agent Book

Get the Agent you need for the career you want

## K CALLAN

Eighth Edition
First Printing 2004

ISBN 1-878355-17-0
ISSN 1058-1928

Other books by K Callan

*An Actor's Workbook*
*The New York Agent Book*
*How to Sell Yourself as an Actor*
*Directing Your Directing Career*
*The Script Is Finished, Now What Do I Do?*
*The Life of the Party*

*Illustrations:* Katie Maratta
*Map:* Kelly Callan
*Editor:* Daniel Curran
*Photographer:* Don Williams

# ⚞ Introduction ⚟

Directors, producers, agents and civilians (people not in the business) frequently comment to me that my books about the entertainment industry follow a circuitous route. Actors never say that. They know the business is a circuitous route. You enter the circle anyplace and usually don't get to choose where.

The periods of heat in a career make an actor think he will never be unemployed again (no matter what he has witnessed or experienced before), the periods of unemployment produce a different agitated state: *I'll never work again. It was all an accident. Now they know I can't act. I just fooled them before.*

Some young actors waltz in, get attention, an agent and a job, and aren't seriously unemployed for ten or twenty years. When things inevitably slow down, they have to learn the business skills that other less fortunate actors began to learn on day one. There are no steps to be skipped as it turns out. We all just take them at different times. The purpose of this book is to identify and illuminate the various steps and help guide your journey through them on the road to a relationship with the best possible agent for you.

Self-knowledge is even more important than business skills. Although some actors never have to find a niche for themselves, most of us spend several years figuring out just what it is we have to sell. If you weigh five hundred pounds, it doesn't take a degree to figure out that you're going to play the fat one. If you go on a diet and become a more average size, casting directors will have a harder time pegging which one you are and so might you. This is not to say that if you are easily typecast your life is a bed of roses, but it can be a lot easier.

So, *Self-Knowledge* could be chapter one for one actor and the end of the book for another. An actor who already has an agent might feel justified in starting with chapter ten because he wants to change agents while a newcomer in town might feel that divorce is not the problem. At this point, all he wants is an agent. Any agent.

In fact, a beginning actor would gain insight from chapter ten. That information could alert him to potential warning signs when he is meeting with an agent and chapter two might prompt the seasoned actor to reexamine all the things his agent does do for him.

This book deals with all aspects of actor/agent relationships at various stages of one's career: the first agent, the freelance alliance, the exclusive relationship, confronting the agent with problems, salvaging the bond, and if need be, leaving the partnership.

There is information for the newcomer, help for the seasoned actor and encouragement for all. My consciousness has been dramatically raised as a result of meeting and interviewing over three hundred agents in New York and Los Angeles. The process was just like every other part of the business, sometimes scary, sometimes wonderful and sometimes painful, but always a challenge.

Mostly, the agents were funny, interesting, dynamic, warm and not at all as unapproachable as they seem when you are outside the office looking in.

Regardless of the circular nature of the business, my strong advice to you is to read straight through and not skip around. The first part provides background to critically understanding the information in the latter part of the book.

Fight the urge to run to the agency listings and read about this agent or that. Until you digest more criteria regarding evaluating agents you may find yourself just as confused as before.

If you read the agents' quotes with some perception, you will gain insights not only into their character but into how the business really runs. You will notice whose philosophy coincides with yours. Taken by themselves the quotes might only be interesting but considered in context and played against the insights of other agents, they are revealing and educational.

I have quoted a few agents that you will not find listed here because they are either from New York (Beverly Anderson), out of the business (Joanna Ross and Lynn Moore Oliver) or deceased (Michael Kingman, Barry Douglas). Even though you won't be able to consider them as possible business partners, I felt their insights were particularly valuable.

Check all addresses before mailing. Every effort has been made to provide accurate and current addresses and phone numbers, but agents move and computers goof. Call the office and verify the address. They won't know it's you.

Because I am asking the questions for all of us, if I've missed something you deem important, write to me at Kcallan@swedenpress.com or by snail mail at Sweden Press at the address on the back of the book and tell me and I'll try to deal with it in my next book. Be sure to write something in the reference line that identifies you as a reader; I dump a lot of junk mail.

K Callan, Los Angeles, California

# ⩕ Table of Contents ⩕

# ⚔ 1 ⚔

# Forewarned

The 7th edition of this book rolled off the presses in 2001 and in the meantime the world and the business continues to change.

Union issues cast a veil of uncertainty over the future of the Screen Actors Guild. Will SAG be able to forge an agreement with the Association of Talent Agents again? Will they merge with AFTRA? Was the commercial strike of 2000 a bad business decision? Does 9/11 play a part in what many perceive as a downturn in the business?

✦ *I think the business has changed, but not just because of 9/11 and the strike. It was changing before that. Today stars get everything, all the big roles, all the small roles, all the cameos. I keep hoping "stunt casting" is a phase but I'm afraid it isn't. As companies merge and wield broader power, the "safe" choice is treasured all the more.*

Dianne Busch/Leading Artists, Inc./New York

I agree with Diane, the business is merely reflecting the nation as a whole. We live in a corporate world leaving little room for all but big business.

Consider all the mom & pop bookstores replaced by Barnes & Noble, the neighborhood hardware stores erased by Home Depot. Log onto www.abc.com, www.nbc.com, www.cbs.com, etc. and check out the program schedule. The number of reality shows in one form or another is staggering. *Trading Spaces, Queer Eye for the Straight Guy,* and *Extreme Makeover* are just the tip of the iceberg.

Cheap to produce, topical, and growing in popularity, every time you see a time-slot filled with a reality show, that's an actor free time-slot. Not only that, shows that actually employ actors aren't hiring you and me.

Whenever you see Ann-Margret on *Law & Order: SVU*, Sally Field on *ER* and Sharon Stone on *The Practice*, you know two things: there's not that much other work for those actors to do and there's that much less work available for working actors.

✦ *It seems there are so many more people trying to enter "the business" these days as actors. Shows like "Entertainment Tonight," "Access Hollywood," etc. and the image of "Hollywood" lead viewers to think that the world of "showbiz" is all parties and Opening Nights, and in general, that there is a fabulous lifestyle waiting for them out here — without understanding the unfortunate realities of the business. They have no idea of the vast number of people trying to make a living as actors and how few succeed.*

*They have absolutely no idea of the vast avalanche of pictures and resumes received in the mail each day by agents and casting directors.*

*They assume that if they can get an agent, that agent has the power to get them appointments. If that were true, my office would look like New Year's Eve in Times Square. The unfortunate fact is that there are a vast number of people, all of whom think they are absolutely wonderful, competing for VERY few jobs. Look at the statistics. It's a very tough way to make a living.*

Eric Klass/Eric Klass Agency

✦ *This is not a good time to get into the business, nor a particularly good time for what used to be the solid class of "working actors."*

Dianne Busch/Leading Artists, Inc../New York

Bruce Smith from Omnipop just thinks things are not all that bad, it's a different way of doing business.

✦ *There is more opportunity now than ever. There are more outlets, more channels for an actor to work. With that good side comes the bad side which is that it takes so much more to become famous, to become recognizable, than it did years go.*

*When I was a kid, you'd be on "The Ed Sullivan Show" or "The Tonight Show" once and you woke up the next day and your entire career was changed. I haven't had a client on "The Tonight Show" for ten years whose career was changed by "The Tonight Show" in and of itself. Now, it's just another way to be seen. I'm afraid we all say it rather casually, but it's true, "Well, we got some good tape."*

*You use the tape to win the war. All the people who weren't watching "The Tonight Show" that night or "Friends" or weren't watching "Comedy Central," when your client was on, or "Everybody Loves Raymond." You go forth with that tape, that's what you use to break down barriers.*

*I'm afraid the truth is that it doesn't even really matter so much whether one million people are watching "Comedy Central" or ten million people are watching ABC. What matters is, "Are the people in Hollywood who make decisions about your career watching?" And very often what you find is that they went home and played with their children and just went to bed.*

Bruce Smith/Omnipop

As with any business, the way to survive and prosper is to see how you can use the energy of the marketplace to your advantage. If you were a saddle maker when automobiles were invented, you could whine and ask for a subsidy or you could figure out how to adapt your business to the new world.

That's what actors have to do now. Perhaps you'll be lucky and find a place in the marketplace without adapting, but maybe there is a way to make the current climate work for you.

Oprah Winfrey deviated from her original goal to be an actress and became a broadcaster. It was through that avenue that she was called to play Sofia which among countless other showbiz accomplishments, led her to an Oscar nomination for *The Color Purple*. You never know where your entrepreneurial talents will take you. The one thing we know is true is that an investment of positive energy always pays off.

## Forearmed

With that in mind, no matter where you are in journey whether you are just beginning, wondering what to do next, or reeling from an agent's rejection, take heart and take a big breath, anything is possible.

Let's begin.

*Change*

✓ continues
✓ sink or swim, it's up to you

## ⚥ 2 ⚥
# Avenues of Opportunity

Many actors regularly curse and malign agents. They either feel rejected that they can't get an agent to talk to them or frustrated once they have an agent simply because of unrealistic expectations.

You can save yourself a lot of heartache and ultimately move your career along faster by learning how the business really works and how agents do their jobs.

What is an agent anyway? What does an agent do? Where do I find one? Do I need one? How can I get one to talk to me? What would I say to an agent? Are there rules of behavior? How can I tell if someone is a good agent? When is the right time to look for one? If they all want to sign me, how can I choose the right one? Can I work without one? If no one wants to sign me, what will I tell my mother?

Let's dispense with the mother issue right off. Unless your mother is an actress, she is never going to understand. Those who have never pursued a job in show business(civilians and would-be actors who are still in school) can never understand what an actor goes through in pursuit of employment and/or an agent, so don't waste time on that conversation.

Just say: "Mom, I'm doing great. I'm unemployed right now and I don't have an agent, but that's part of the process. There are things I need to accomplish before it's time for me to look for an agent."

She can repeat that to her friends. She's not going to understand, but it will mean something to her that you have a plan.

## What Is An Agent?

Whether your agent fantasy includes the old-fashioned stereotype of cigar-chomping hustlers or the newer version of the cool customer in the expensive Armani suit, many actors fantasize that the right agent holds the secret of success. Joanna Ross was an agent at William Morris before she left the business and moved to Italy, but I'm still quoting her because her perspective on the actor/agent relationship is so insightful.

◆ *Actors feel that if they make the right choice the agent is going to make them a star and help them be successful, or they're going to make the wrong choice and that's it. And that's just not it. No agent can make anybody a star or make them a better actor than they are. Agents are only avenues of opportunity.*
Joanna Ross

That being the case, what do these "Avenues of Opportunity" do? The dictionary (which knows very little about show business) has several definitions for the word "agent." By combining a couple, I've come up with: "A force acting in place of another, effecting a certain result by driving, inciting, or setting in motion."

Huh?

In its simplest incarnation, the agent, acting on your behalf, sets in motion a series of events that result in your having a shot at a job. He gets you meetings, interviews and auditions. And he prays that you will get the job or at the very least make him look good by being brilliant.

When an actor is complaining that the agent is not getting him out, he seems to think the agent doesn't want him to work — completely forgetting that if the actor doesn't work, the agent cannot pay his rent. Not only that, the actor overlooks the fact that his part of the partnership is to get the job.

It should be simple to get the job, really. After all, you have spent years studying, perfecting your instrument, training your body, voice, craft and personality, and building a resume that denotes credibility.

Haven't you?

## An Agent Prepares

While you have been working on every aspect of your craft, the agent you want has spent his time getting to know the business. He's seen every play, television show and film. He's watched actors, writers, directors and producers birth their careers and grow. He's tracked people on every level of the business. He has networked, stayed visible and communicated. He's made it his business to meet and develop relationships with casting directors or CDs, as they are sometimes referred to throughout this book.

The agent you want only represents those actors whose work he personally knows so that when he tells a casting director that an actor is perfect for the role and has the background for it, the casting director trusts his word. That's the way the agent builds his credibility. It doesn't happen any faster than the building of the actor's resume.

In addition to getting the actor the appropriate audition, the agent has to be prepared to negotiate a brilliant contract when the actor wins the job. That entails knowing all the rules and regulations of the Screen Actors Guild, Actors' Equity, and American Federation of Television and Radio Artists, as well as having an understanding of the marketplace and knowing what others at similar career levels are getting for similar jobs.

He must then have the courage, style and judgment to stand up to the buyers in asking what is fair for the actor without becoming too grandiose and turning everyone off. And the agent must fight the temptation to sell the actor down the river financially in order to seal his own future relationships with the producers or casting directors.

## What Do Agents Think Their Job Is?

✦ *If you sign someone, if you agree to be their agent, no matter how big the agency gets, you've agreed to be there for them and that's your responsibility.*
Kenneth Kaplan/The Gersh Agency, Inc.

✦ *Actors expect their agents to make them stars, but that's up to the universe. Our job is to give them opportunities. Once we give them the opportunity, it's in the actor's hands to take it from there.*
Mimi Mayer/Angel City Talent

✦ *I feel that I'm responsible for my clients' attitudes and for their self-confidence.*
Kenneth Kaplan/The Gersh Agency, Inc.

✦ *Sometimes actors don't really consider all the work an agent may do for them that doesn't result in an appointment. The agent may have said your name many times to the casting director until the CD has heard it often enough that he begins to think you are actually working.*

*At that point, the actor happens to call the casting director himself and ends up with an appointment and subsequently a job. Now he calls his agent and says, "Well, hey. I got the job myself. Why should I pay you commission?"*

*In my head, I'm going, "Who sat down with you and told you how to dress? Who helped you select the photos you are using right now that got you that audition? Who helped you texture your resume? Who introduced you to the casting director? What makes you think you did that on your own?"*

*They don't see it. They don't see that like a manager, I have taken them from here to there. I set up the auditions. What makes them think they got this on their own? Most actors don't realize the initial investment we make, the time, the energy, the phone calls, the mail, the hours of preparing the actor and getting them to the right places. There is no compensation for that until maybe two years down the road.*

*At that point, you've made them so good that someone else signs them anyway. There's not a lot of loyalty among actors. They'll always want the person who gets them the next job. They don't comprehend what we go through to get them ready for that point where they can get a job.*
H. Shep Pamplin/Agents for the Arts, Inc./New York

Try to digest the truth of Shep's statement. It is an unusual person who arrives on the scene poised enough to handle himself in the audition room. That kind of poise usually cannot be acquired without going through the struggle time. An agent who invests his time and energy in the struggle time should be rewarded, not discarded.

✦ *I offer hard work and honesty and demand the same in return. If I'm breaking my ass to get you an audition, you better show up.*
Martin Gage/The Gage Group

Former agent Lynn Moore Oliver says actors need to raise their consciousness.

✦ *Actors don't have any idea what we do. They should each spend a week helping out at their agent's office. When anyone comes in here to help me, they are stunned to see how many submissions are made.*

*Actors also forget what we do for them. A client will say, "Oh, I know so-and-so..." and I'll say, "Well, I guess you do. I introduced you to him three years ago or five years ago."*

*They forget that all of these contacts they have are because someone introduced them. I'm in the business of introductions. And suddenly the actor just digests the contact without remembering where it came from, suddenly it becomes what have you done for me lately? And that comes from a lack of respect. The artist wants respect, but he sometimes forgets to give the agent his.*

*I consider our industry a collaborative effort. Agents are the only people left who invest in an actor's career. Most actors don't think about that. It costs me money to represent actors. Acting teachers, photographers, press agents, everybody else who provides the actor a service gets paid up front. The actor thinks nothing of it. Meanwhile the actor puts the most demands on his agent. He's the most critical of his agent and the agent is working on spec.*
Lynn Moore Oliver

✦ *It's not enough just to sit there and see who calls. Anybody can do that. Anyone can answer a telephone. You've got to actually solicit employment. You have to put rejection into its proper perspective for the actor. You can't allow the actor to take it personally. If the business were run solely on acting ability, it would be much easier. A lot of times you give the best reading, but they want to use Rin Tin Tin because he just did an ER.*

*One would think if you were casting that you would have people in and give them the opportunity to do their best work. What happens is, they say, "Let them get there early and look at the sides." So, they give you one sheet of paper. Unless you have the instincts of a migratory bird, you have no idea what is going on.*
Eric Klass/The Eric Klass Agency

✦ *If my job is to just get people a bunch of interviews and shuffle around a bunch of breakdowns, then I don't want to do this. I'm in this because I enjoy the fun of building a career, of bringing someone up, reviving a career, maintaining a career and promoting, finding innovative places for my talent.*
Lynn Moore Oliver

✦ *It takes a long time to know what you're doing. I've been an agent for 24 years and I'm still learning.*
Eric Klass/The Eric Klass Agency

✦ *I offer hard work and honesty and demand the same in return. If I'm breaking my ass to get you an audition, you better show up.*
Martin Gage/The Gage Group

And some agents leave the business because they feel the burden of their responsibility, as CAA's Jane Sindell said in an *Los Angeles Times* interview.

✦ *I don't want to be overly dramatic, but it means basically having to put food on someone's table. Even though someone is doing well economically, it's about getting their movies made, getting them marketed properly, getting them positioned. It's having to be absolutely on top of information before your competitor is.*
Claudia Eller, *Los Angeles Times*[1]

## Partners Not Pals

Although it might be nice to be pals with your agent, it is not necessary. One of the best agents I ever had never tried to help me feel good when all was dark. He did, however, initiate new business for me, was respected in the community, negotiated well, had impeccable taste as well as access to everyone in the business.

He also believed in me and did not lose faith when I did not win every audition. He gave me good notes on my performances, clued me in on mistakes I was making, and made a point of viewing my work at every opportunity.

Oh yes, and he returned my phone calls!

A friend of mine who toiled for many years on a well-regarded series was happy to be working, but felt her agent had not negotiated well. She changed agents and doubled her salary. A year later, she changed agents again: "They were good negotiators, but I couldn't stand talking to them."

You can't have everything.

Being a tough negotiator sometimes displaces graciousness. So maybe your agent won't be your best friend. He's not supposed to be, he's your business partner. You have to decide what you want and what you need.

✦ *I'm working on the belief that symbiotically we're going to build a career. While the actor isn't working, I'm paying for the phone, the stationery, the envelopes, Breakdown Service (which is expensive), the messenger service to send the pictures around, the rent, the overhead, stamps, all the things that one takes for granted in the normal turn of business. All this is coming out of my pocket working as an employment agent, because that is really what I am. The actor is making no investment in my promoting his career. If the career is promoted, we both benefit and I take my 10% commission.*

*Meanwhile the overhead goes on for months, sometimes years with no income. The first thing the actor is going to say is "Nothing's happening. My agent is not doing a good job."*

*What they forget is that I have actually invested money in their career and I've probably invested more money in the actor's career than he has, on an annual basis.*
Lynn Moore Oliver

If you think about what Lynn says, you will understand why credible agents choose clients carefully. Looking at your actor friends, are there any that you would be willing to put on your list and pay to promote?

Puts things more in perspective, doesn't it?

# Franchised Agents or Not?

The agreement between the Association of Talent Agents (ATA) and the Screen Actors Guild (SAG) have been in a state of flux since 2002 when SAG members voted down an new agreement proposed by the ATA. Since the agreement hasn't changed in forty years, it really is time for an arrangement reflecting the current marketplace that would give some assistance to smaller, mid-level agencies.

Although conglomerate agencies like The William Morris Agency, ICM, CAA, etc. that represent actors with million dollar paychecks have no problems paying their rent, the existence of agencies representing working actors is threatened.

Management's refusal to pay working actors much over scale, plus competition from managers who not only have the ability to produce, but can charge a higher commission, has put many smaller agencies out of business. It's possible that some restrictions will ease and that agents will soon be charging more than 10%.

Change is overdue. Agents deserve our support. Educate yourself so that you can make intelligent/unemotional decisions in the partnership between you and your agent. Focus on business.

✦ *Independent talent agencies (i.e., those agencies that are not affiliated with either the Association of Talent Agents [ATA] and/or the National Association of Talent Representatives [NATR] ) continue to be franchised and regulated by the SAG Franchise Agreement [or, Rule 16(g)], the Agreement that has regulated your relationship with your SAG agent for the last 63 years. Accordingly, so long as your agency abides by the terms and conditions of Rule 16(g), it may continue to represent you. Any standard SAG agency contract you sign with an independent agency may be filed with, and processed by, the Guild. If your independent agency chooses to surrender its franchise with the Guild, SAG will immediately notify you of that fact.*

*SAG's franchises with agents that are members of the ATA and/or NATR have ended. However, pending further review, SAG's National Board of Directors has temporarily suspended application of Rule 16(a) of the Rules and Regulations section of the SAG Constitution, which requires SAG members to be represented only by a franchised agent. Because of this temporary suspension, a SAG member may continue to be represented by one of these formerly franchised agents.*

*For those members who are contemplating signing new contracts with their ATA/NATR agents, you should insist, whenever possible, upon the standard SAG representation contract or a contract whose terms and conditions mirror those*

*in (or are better than) Rule 16(g).*
www.sag.org

If your agent hands you a General Services Agreement to sign, do take SAG up on their offer to go over it with you and offer advice. Most agents will not require that you agree with every single line in the contract.

At this point, the only thing the agent must do to operate legally is have a license to operate from the state. The license covers about 10% of the areas covered by the agreement hammered out by SAG. Just because an agent says, "Hey, we're fine, we're licensed by the state," doesn't constitute much protection for the actor. Neither this nor the old franchise agreement guaranteed the agent to be ethical, knowledgeable or effective. You'll have to check that yourself.

## Wrap Up

*Agent*

✓ a force acting in place of another, effecting a certain result by driving, inciting, or setting in motion
✓ no longer regulated by SAG

*Agent's Job*

✓ to get the actor meetings, interviews, auditions, and to negotiate salary and billing

# ⚞ 3 ⚟
# Before You Leave Home...
# and Once You Get to LA

The more background you have before you assault one of the major production centers, the better, so if you are still in a position to get yourself trained, there are better and worse ways to go about it.

Since I was a first generation college graduate in my family, I was lucky to get to go to a state school. Although I did yearn for a theater school I had read about, I was unaware of the politics of education or I might have made a different choice.

The addition of a celebrity school name on your resume can definitely enhance your career. If you can afford it and can gain admittance, by all means, do so.

These schools are not necessarily significantly superior to others, but are universally accepted as the most comprehensive training for young actors and whose cachet instantly alerts the antennae of buyers (casting directors, agents, producers, directors, etc.). This is where the creme de la creme of new young actors, the next Meryl Streep or Paul Newman, are coming from.

At one time there was an actual collective referred to as "The Leagues." That collective no longer exists, but the name, "League," has entered the vernacular as a handle for whichever theater school is currently considered prestigious.

Each of these schools have websites where you will be able to get an overview of the school, its curriculum, and sometimes, its graduates. Some of the websites are more user friendly than others, so be patient.

Whether or not a school is currently one of the favored ones depends on who you talk to. No one wants to take responsibility for saying one school belongs here and another one doesn't.

Andy Lawler was an agent at DGRW in New York before he left to become company manager at the Charlotte Repertory Theater but his words of wisdom are still golden.

# Andy Lawler's Words of Wisdom on Schools

✦ *The two best musical theater programs in the country belong to the Cincinnati Conservatory of Music and the Boston Conservatory of Music. Each year, these schools' industry showcases attract almost every agent and casting director in New York City. Their graduates probably have the highest employment percentage of ANY drama school, musical or otherwise, graduate or undergraduate.*

*Juilliard is, of course, one of the two or three best drama programs in the country, but does not specialize in musicals. Nonetheless many Broadway musical stars have gotten their start there, including Patti LuPone and Kevin Kline.*

*A number of other schools offer good programs as well, although they lack the prestige of the above mentioned three. Take a look at Carnegie Mellon, Northwestern, and to a lesser extent Michigan and NYU. Questions you need to ask of any program you attend are:*

*Does it offer a Bachelor of Fine Arts or a Bachelor of Arts degree? Aim for the BFA, as that's the sign of an actual professional training program. Does it offer a showcase in NYC or LA? There's little point investing in a degree if the industry doesn't see you at the end of it. What sort of performance options do you have? How recently have the faculty actually been participating in the biz?*

*A note of caution to close. Remember that everyone auditioning for these programs has been the star of their schools. Stature at your high school rarely guarantees success beyond. However, don't be intimidated by a lackluster resume either. What gets people into these schools is their audition and their look, and nothing else will really matter.*

Andy Lawler

## The Other Cool Schools

In addition to those schools, here is a list of other schools, based on hearsay and research that are thought to be the chosen schools at this moment in time. The best way to judge is to check out the curriculum as well as the track record of graduates via their web pages.

American Conservatory Theater, Carey Perloff
30 Grant Avenue, 6th Floor
San Francisco, CA 94108
415-834-3200
www.act-sfbay.org/conservatory/index.html

Carnegie Mellon, Drama Department/Elizabeth Bradley
College of Fine Arts/School of Drama
5000 Forbes Avenue, Room #108
Pittsburgh, PA 15213
412-268-2392
www.cmu.edu/cfa/drama

Columbia University in the City of New York, Kristin Linklater
305 Dodge Hall, Mail Code 1808
2960 Broadway
New York, NY 10027-6902
212-854-2875
www.columbia.edu/cu/arts

Harvard University, Richard Orchard
American Repertory Theater/Loeb Drama Center
64 Brattle Street
Cambridge, MA 02138
617-495-2668
www.amrep.org

Juilliard School, Kathy Hood, Director of Admissions
60 Lincoln Center Plaza
New York, NY 10023
212-799-5000 Ext. 4
www.juilliard.edu/splash.html

New York University/Drama Department
Arthur Bartow, Artistic Director
721 Broadway, 3$^{rd}$ Floor
New York, NY 10003
212-998-1850
www.nyu.edu/tisch

North Carolina School of the Arts, Gerald Freedman
Post Office Box 12189, 1533 Main Street
Winston-Salem, NC 27117-2189
336-770-3235
www.ncarts.edu

Northwestern School of Communications, Dean Barbara O'Keefe
Frances Searle Building
2240 Campus Drive
Evanston, IL 60208
847-491-7023
www.communication.northwestern.edu

State University of New York (at Purchase), Dean Irby
735 Anderson Hill Road
Purchase, NY 10577
914-251-6360
http://www.purchase.edu/academics/taf

Yale School of Drama, Yale University, Lloyd Richards
Post Office Box 208325
New Haven, CT 06520-8325
203-432-1505
www.yale.edu/drama

If you graduate from one of these schools, you are immediately thought to be the creme de la creme as far as NYC/LA are concerned. You probably will be better trained. Actors in these programs are courted by agents and some procure representation as early as freshman year. The career boost by the annual showcase of graduating students, produced specifically for an audience of agents and casting directors in New York and Los Angeles, is priceless.

✦ *Although the leagues may sometimes lead to auditions for immediate employment on a soap opera, in summer stock, in an off-Broadway play, more often it serves as a casting director's mental Rolodex of actors to use in future projects.*
Jill Gerston, *New York Times*[2]

All of the league schools offer excellent training, but they are hard to get into and expensive, so consider carefully and have a backup. This type of education requires a big commitment of time and money. Choose the school that is right for you.

Even if you are educated at the best schools and arrive highly touted with interest from agents, ex-William Morris agent Joanna Ross told me there is still a period of adjustment.

✦ *When you come out of school, you gotta freak out for a while. Actors in*

*high-powered training programs working night and day doing seven different things at once get out of school and suddenly there is no demand for their energy. It takes a year, at least, to learn to be unemployed. And they have to learn to deal with that. It happens to everybody. It's not just you.*
Joanna Ross

Even if you can't make it to a league school, all is not lost.

✦ *The truth is, a great performance in the leagues can jump-start a career, but if these kids have talent, they'll get noticed. They just won't be as fast out of the starting gate...they just have to do it the old-fashioned way by pounding the pavements, reading "Back Stage," calling up friends, going to see directors they know and knocking on agents' doors.*
Jill Gerston, New York Times[3]

## Market Research

Analyzing the marketplace and using that information wisely can save you years of unfocused activity. If you were starting any other kind of business, you would expect to do extensive research to see if there was a need for the product you had decided to sell. In addition to checking out actors, note who is working and where, and keep a file on CDs, producers, directors, and writers.

Note which writers are writing parts for people like you. Learn and practice remembering the names of everybody. Know who the critics are. Note those whose taste agrees with yours. Think of this educational process as your Ph.D.

If you want to be a force in the business, begin to think of yourself as such and assume your rightful place. Synonyms of the word "force" inspire me: "Energy, power, strength, vigor, vitality, impact, value, weight."

With each new detail about the business that you ingest and have ready at your fingertips, your vitality increases. With each play you read, see, rehearse, perform in and with each writer, actor, director, CD, costumer, etc. that you support, your power grows.

## The Unions

Beginning actors unduly focus on membership in the unions. Although routinely one-third of the 125,000 plus members of SAG make no money at all in a given year (and the numbers in Equity and AFTRA are similar), actors feel that membership in the unions will change their lives.

It will. It will make you ineligible to work in non-union films that can give you access to footage for your reel, as well as the many non-union theaters across the land that would give you a chance to sharpen your acting tools.

Becoming a member of the union is a worthy goal. I can remember the thrill when I got my Equity card (somehow that was the card that meant you were an actor), but I was far along in my resume before I joined. It makes sense to wait.

## Working as an Extra or Stand-In

While work as an extra gives you the opportunity to be on the set, unless you are looking for more extra work I would not list it on your resume. You want any agent, producer or casting director thinking of you for principal parts, so don't cloud his vision.

♦ *Working as an extra could be valuable for someone who has never been on a set. Working on a soap can help you become familiar with cameras and absorb information. It's not something that should be on your resume or even brought up to the agent.*
Flo Rothacker/DGRW

There are specific directors or producers for whom you might make an exception.

♦ *An extra job on a Woody Allen film could turn out to be a good job because Woody sometimes notices extras, gives them lines and you can end up working for weeks. You could end up getting upgraded or if you got a chance to work on a Sydney Lumet film as an extra, think of what you could learn.*
Marvin Josephson/Gilla Roos, Ltd.

If you plan to be a career extra, working as an extra makes sense. If your goal is to play principal parts, why amass a resume that advertises you in a different capacity? It's tempting to accept extra work to qualify for guild membership, pay rent, keep insurance active or get on a set. I understand that. So saying, the quote below speaks for itself.

I asked the agent if he had "John Smith" work as an extra, wouldn't casting directors and producers now only consider John to be an extra?

✦ *We all do. I spoke to a casting director the other day about an actor and that's exactly what she said. The actor has to learn where to draw the line and say, "Okay, I can't do this anymore."*
Anonymous Agent

A lot of people can't. They get used to the money and the insurance and their resumes reflect that they are full-time extras. This otherwise credible agent encourages actors to work as extras (after all, he is making a commission), expecting them to know when to draw the line at what is too much extra work.

To me it's like saying, "Here, these drugs will make you feel better. Just take them for a while, I know you will be able to stop in time." If you are not ready to get work as a principal on a regular basis, it may not be time for you to be in the union.

It would be more advantageous for you to work in some other capacity in order to pay your rent or observe the business from the inside. Become an assistant or work in production. You will see what goes on, make some money and you won't be fooling yourself into thinking you are really acting. You will be more driven to pursue work that will further your career.

## Now That You're in Los Angeles

First things first. If you've just arrived in Los Angeles, there are many things to confront before you start trying to find representation. It's hard to be patient, but there are things to consider.

If you are just a crazy person in general, don't even think about the business. This business takes even balanced people and chews them up and spits them out for breakfast unless they remain extremely focused and can provide another life for themselves.

If you are in an impossible relationship or if you have any kind of addiction problem, the business is only going to intensify things. Deal with these things first.

Even if you are in a good place emotionally, are tenacious, driven and talented, take time to get your bearings before you inflict yourself on the marketplace.

Before you look for an agent, you need a comfortable place to live and you need to know how the town works. Success is reached over time. Great success begins with a series of little successes that begin with getting settled and being financially secure. You don't have to be rich, but you must have a job and that job must allow for flexibility.

## Build a Support Group

Life is easier with friends. Begin to build relationships with your peers. There are people who say to build friendships with those who already have what you want. I understand the thinking, but it's not my idea of a good time. It's a lot easier to live on a shoestring and/or deal with constant rejection if your friends are doing the same thing.

If your friend is starring on a television show or is the king of commercials and has plenty of money while you are scrambling to pay the rent, it is going to be harder to keep perspective about your progress or lack of it. Remember, it takes different people differing amounts of time to make the journey. Having friends who understand that will make it easier for both of you.

I'm not saying you should dump your friends when they start working, but do know that you are going to have conflicting feelings about their success.

It's not easy to make friends in a new place, but it's not impossible. The easiest way, of course, is to join an acting class (Chapter Four). Working with scene partners can build rapport. If you don't have the money right now for classes, you can still access the people you want via bulletin boards at SAG, AFTRA, Equity, UCLA, USC and AFI (American Film Institute).

You don't have to be a member to put up a notice announcing that you are starting a weekly play reading group. State up front that you are limiting the group to ten. That way, if you get callers that don't appeal to you, you can say the group is filled. Be cautious and plan the first meeting at a public place until you know the people.

Whether or not you have weekly play reading groups, gather friends to do scenes on camera, or help paint somebody's apartment, stay focused on your goal: bonding and support. The activity is merely the method. Allow time for friendships to develop by making the effort to have coffee or food after your meeting.

## Attitude

One of the most valuable things you can do for yourself is to remain positive. Ruth Gordon's seventy-year career included an Oscar for acting (*Rosemary's Baby*), five Writers Guild Awards plus Oscar nominations for screenwriting *(Pat and Mike, Adam's Rib.)* In an interview with Paul Rosenfield, she spoke words to live by.

✦  *Life is getting through the moment. The philosopher William James says to cultivate the cheerful attitude. Now nobody had more trouble than he did except me. I had more trouble in my life than anybody. But your first big trouble can be a bonanza if you live through it. Get through the first trouble, you'll probably make it through the next one.*
Paul Rosenfield, *Los Angeles Times*[4]

There is no value judgment on how you spend your time. You can be happy or depressed. If you choose to spend your time being depressed (which takes more energy), that's your business. Do note, however, that this is how you choose to spend your time.

## Get a Place to Live

As actors, we are our own instrument. If the instrument is not in tune, it's impossible to play successfully. Living in a dump or out of a suitcase is like leaving your violin out in the rain. Give it a good home and polish it and there's a much better chance to make beautiful music.

The first order of business is to find a place to live and make it your own. If the place looks dingy, spend money on a coat of paint. Also, make sure there is plenty of light. You will need a place of shelter from the storms and good light will enhance your moods.

It can be a little overwhelming when you first get to Los Angeles. This is a big place. Where is the best place to live? What are the special routes between point A and point B? Where are the places people in the business congregate? Do you want to live there? Does it matter where you live?

Let's start off by organizing the place geographically. In this chapter you'll find a map showing where the major studios and networks are located. When looking for a place to live, keep those locations in mind. Although there are places with cheaper rents (West Covina, for example) and places with tempting features (the beach for example), these are not convenient locations for commuting to auditions and rehearsals.

Other areas, such as Hollywood, Silver Lake, Beachwood, Van Nuys, North Hollywood and Burbank offer much shorter commuting time, as well as bargains in rent.

When my daughter began editing *The Working Actors Guide,* I became aware of this great resource book. In addition to an amazing cross-section of information on the business, useful phone numbers and addresses of all kinds, it also includes another overview of different areas of the city and what each has to offer.

The bulletin boards of SAG, Equity and AFTRA are good sources for all kinds of information including apartment rentals and bargains in used cars. They don't check union cards at the bulletin boards, so you can access them even if you are not a member.

Some people actually get to auditions by bus. It can be done, but not easily. I don't recommend it. Check out Rent-A-Wreck, a place that not only rents second-hand cars, but has also become famous as the source of life long relationships formed by industry newcomers while waiting for their rental cars.

Many neighborhoods with cheaper rent are in high crime areas. When apartment shopping, try driving through the area at night. If you don't feel comfortable getting out of your car, don't rent there. The local police division can give you a good idea of the safety of a neighborhood. Call them.

No place is completely safe. I saw a robber jump in the back of a car stopped at a red light in Beverly Hills and hold a gun on the occupants. It's important to be alert, wherever you are. Los Angeles may look more benign, but it is every bit as dangerous as New York.

If you live in LA, you must own a copy of *The Thomas Guide, Los Angeles County Edition.* This book is more than a map book. In addition to listing every boulevard, street, nook and cranny in the county, the guide also has listings of emergency and hospital telephone numbers, a Zip Code directory, points of interest and just about everything else you will need to know to get around Los Angeles. To become acquainted with the city, you should learn some of the geographical landmarks and the relative location of different general areas.

The net is also helpful in providing maps from Point A to Point B, although I have to say that www.mapquest.com has sent me on some wild goose chases so cross reference your source and you won't be late to an appointment.

Assume Hollywood is the center of the universe. (Isn't it?) West is toward the ocean and east isn't. North are mountains. South are not. If you look north you will see the Hollywood Hills. These hills run east (Glendale) to west (Santa Monica Mountains). North of the Hollywood Hills is the San Fernando Valley (usually referred to as, simply, The Valley). The Valley is home to, east-to-west, Burbank, Universal City, Studio City, North Hollywood, Sherman Oaks, Van Nuys and Encino (plus a dozen more areas and cities).

On the Hollywood side of the Hollywood Hills, west of Hollywood, lies West Hollywood, Beverly Hills, Century City, Bel Air, Westwood, West LA and the beach communities (Malibu, Santa Monica, Venice and so on).

Southeast of Hollywood is downtown Los Angeles. East of Los Angeles is the San Gabriel Valley. South of Hollywood is South-Central LA and the South Bay. Almost all show business offices are in Hollywood, West LA or Burbank.

If you live in Hollywood, assuming traffic is normal you are within fifteen minutes of Sunset-Gower Studios, Paramount, Larry Edmunds Bookstore, Equity, AFTRA, Mann's Chinese Theater (in case you want to check out the footprints), Samuel French Bookstore, the Sunset Strip, KTTV, CBS, KTLA, KHJ, ABC and many casting people and agents.

If you live in the eastern Valley, you are within fifteen minutes of NBC, the Disney Studios, the Burbank Studios (Warner Bros.), Universal Studios (the studio and the tour), CBS Radford, Samuel French Valley Theatrical Bookstore and many agents and casting directors.

Commuting between the Valley and Hollywood is a nightmare during rush hour and merely a bad dream at other times. Plan on at least thirty minutes to travel over the hill in the best of situations. If it's rush hour or raining, be a good scout and be prepared.

Sony (Culver City) and Twentieth Century Fox (Century City) seem to me to be at least forty-five minutes from anywhere. Leave plenty of time to drive so you will not be late for an appointment. If you arrive early, you can relax and be at your best when your name is called.

## An Overview of Connecting Roads

There are four primary connector roads between the Valley and Hollywood. From east to west: The (101) Hollywood Fwy/Cahuenga cuts through the Cahuenga Pass connecting Burbank to Hollywood. Laurel Canyon links North Hollywood/Studio City to West Hollywood. Coldwater Canyon joins North Hollywood/Studio City to Beverly Hills. Beverly Glen connects Van Nuys/Sherman Oaks to Bel Air/Westwood.

Drive around while not under pressure and familiarize yourself with the surroundings. Los Angeles roads are the most clearly marked in the world and they are not as confusing as you may initially think. Don't worry, if I could figure it out, so can you. Following is a simple map designed to give you an overall understanding of where things are.

Key to Overview Map:

1. Larry Edmunds Theatrical Books
6644 Hollywood Blvd. (east of Las Palmas)

2. Academy Players Directory
1313 N. Vine St. (at Hollywood)

2. Sunset/Gower Studios
1438 N. Gower St. (at Sunset Blvd.)

3. Fox Television
5746 Sunset Blvd. (across from KTLA)

4. KTLA/Metromedia Studios
5800 Sunset Blvd. (at Van Ness Ave.)

5. The Lot (formerly Warner/Hollywood)
1041 Formosa Ave. (west of La Brea, south of Santa Monica Blvd.)

6. Hollywood Center Studios
1040 N. Las Palmas Ave. (south of Santa Monica Blvd., east of Highland Ave.)

7. Paramount Studios
5555 Melrose Ave. (south of Santa Monica Blvd., east of Gower St.)

8. Raleigh Studios
650 N. Bronson Ave. (south of Melrose Ave., west of Van Ness Ave.)

9. Samuel French Bookstore
7623 Sunset Blvd. (east of Fairfax Ave.)

## 10. Bo b Hope Health Center
335 N. La Brea Avenue (north of Wilshire Blvd.)

## 11. ABC/Prospect
4151 Prospect Ave. (east of Hillhurst Ave.)

## 12. Twentieth Century Fox Studios
10201 W. Pico Blvd. (at Motor Ave.)

## 13. Academy of Motion Picture Arts & Sciences
8949 Wilshire Blvd. (east of Doheny Ave.)

## 14. Center for Motion Picture Study/Margaret Herrick Library
Academy Film Archive/333 S. La Cienega Blvd. (south of Wilshire Blvd.)

## 15. Sony Pictures Entertainment
gate 1 — 10202 W. Washington (east 405/San Diego Fwy.)
gate 2 — 3970 Overland Ave. (south of Century City)

## 16. CBS/Studio Center/MTM
4024 Radford Ave. (east of Laurel Canyon, north of Ventura Blvd.)

## 17. Samuel French Bookstore - Valley
11965 Ventura Blvd. (south of CBS Radford)

## 18. Universal Studios
100 Universal City Plaza (north of 101/Hollywood Fwy.)

## 19. Warner Bros./Burbank Studios
4000 Warner Blvd. (Barham exit/Hollywood Fwy/101 or Pass from 134/Ventura Fwy)

## 20. Walt Disney Studios
500 S. Buena Vista Ave. (Buena Vista exit from Ventura Fwy/134 north of Riverside Dr.)

## 21. NBC Studios
3000 W. Alameda (north of Riverside Dr., or Buena Vista exit Ventura Fwy/134)

## 22. Raymar Studios
846 N. Cahuenga Blvd. (at Willoughby St.)

## 23. AFTRA/SAG/Equity/AFTRA SAG Credit Union
5757 Wilshire Blvd. (east of Fairfax)

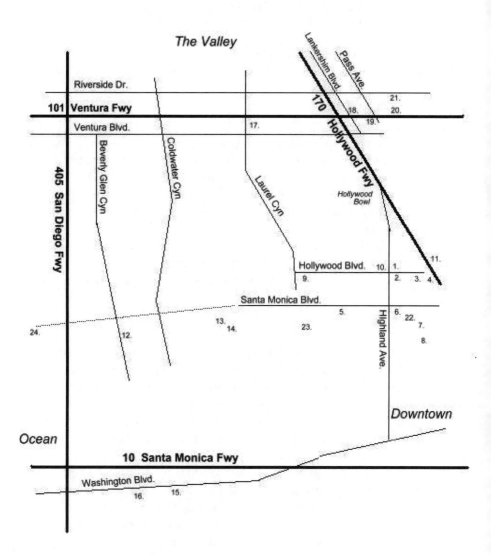

The Valley

Riverside Dr.

101 Ventura Fwy

Ventura Blvd.

170

Lankershim Blvd.

Pass Ave.

Hollywood Fwy

21.

18.    20.

17.    19.

Beverly Glen Cyn

Coldwater Cyn

Laurel Cyn

Hollywood Bowl

Hollywood Blvd.    10.  1.

9.    2.   3.  4.

11.

Santa Monica Blvd.

5.    6.  22.

13.    23.    7.

14.    8.

405 San Diego Fwy

24.    12.

Highland Ave.

Downtown

Ocean

10  Santa Monica Fwy

Washington Blvd.

16.    15.

## Los Angeles Overview Map

### 24. MGM

2401 Colorado Blvd. (west of 26th St./Cloverfield exit Santa Monica Fwy/10)

### 25. Westside Health Center

1950 Sawtelle Boulevard, #130 (west of 405/btwn Santa Monica & Olympic Blvd.)

### 26. Motion Picture Country Home
23888 Mulholland Drive (Ventura Freeway/exit Valley Circle/Mulholland)

### 27. Toluca Lake Health Center
4323 Riverside Dr. (Pass exit 134/Ventura Fwy., R on Alameda which becomes Riverside)

## Living Arrangements

When you are making living arrangements, consider getting a roommate. Not only is it cheaper, but you will have someone to talk to. If you don't want a roommate, get a pet.

When you move to a new area, it's important to make some new relationships as soon as possible, even if it is just with the grocer or the dry cleaner. Talk to them. Find out their names. Make sure they know yours. It's nice to have someone call you by name when you come in. It makes you feel like a member of the community. Furthermore, this is a business in which gregariousness pays off and this is good practice.

## Get a Job

Once you have a place to live, your next task is to find some way to support yourself. Even if you have money from home to keep you going, you should get some kind of job, preferably one in the business.

If possible, accumulate enough money so that when you get here, you can volunteer your time as an intern in an agent or casting director's office for three months. If you have a part-time job, then you could intern one or two days a week.

Having a job gives form to your life. It gives you a place to go every day, a family of people to relate to and helps you feel a part of the city much more quickly. Nothing feeds depression more than sitting at home alone in a strange city. Even if you know the city, you'll find, as time goes on, that activity is the friend of the actor.

Depression must not be allowed to get out of hand. You can't wait until you have eaten everything in the house and are thinking dire thoughts. It's much harder to turn those feelings around when you let things get too bleak. Take stock of yourself. Learn early signs and take action. If you allow yourself to be depressed, you are not only being self-defeating, you are being self-indulgent.

If you are fortunate and tenacious enough to get a job in the business, you will be that much closer to your goal. In addition to having a job, you will learn many things about the business and how it really works, i.e., who is having auditions, who you would like to work with, who are good teachers, who is a waste of time, etc. It's sort of like being paid to get an advanced degree in your field.

There is no way in the world you can learn what it's like to be in the business without being in the business. How nice to find a place to go every day and be with people who are interested in the same things that you are. You are furthering your process and getting paid for it.

More important than a job with contacts is a job with flexible working hours that enables you to get to auditions. If you look carefully and are lucky, you can find both. As soon as you are working in the business in any category (except as an extra), you are in the system and on your way. I don't want to imply that it is the easiest task in the world to come up with one of these jobs, but it is definitely worth the effort.

If you feel called upon to work as an extra once or twice to see what's it's like on a set, be my guest, but don't do it more than two or three times and don't talk about it. There is more discussion of the pros and cons of extra work on pages 17-18.

## Casting Society of America Job File

Sitting in an agent's office waiting for an appointment, I met a young actor who was manning the phones. He told me he has worked as a casting assistant in both Los Angeles and New York and had come to his present job by faxing his resume to the Casting Society of America job file.

The pay is very small, but as he pointed out, the access to the business was well worth it. He said he wouldn't trade the higher salary for the business maturity he had acquired. www.castingsociety.com

| Casting Society of America 606 N. Larchmont Boulevard, #48 Los Angeles, CA 90004-1309 323-463-1925 | Casting Society of America 2565 Broadway, #185 New York, NY 10025 212-868-1260 Ext. 22 |
| --- | --- |

As soon as you are working in the business in any category, you are in the system and on your way.

## Encountering Agents

Before your resume is ready for you to be interviewing agents as possible business partners, you may find yourself encountering them either in your work or on a social level. Just as doctors don't like to listen to your symptoms at a party, an agent wants to party in peace. Be a professional and talk about something other than your career. Agents prefer to do business in their offices.

If you detect signs of interest from anyone: directors, producers, etc. follow up on it. Ask if there is anything you can do to help with a current project. It's unlikely anything will come of that meeting, but at the very least, you should go home and put the name of the person you spoke to in your Rolodex (you do have one, don't you?). You should have another log where you note the date, where you met and what you talked about. Add subsequent meetings to the log — you're compiling your own personal showbiz database of people you are meeting in the business. You should have sections for agents, casting directors, producers, directors, writers and other actors. Add any other categories that are meaningful to you. You will meet these people again and your database will become invaluable.

## Emergencies

If an emergency comes up, call one of the unions if you are a member. SAG, Equity, and AFTRA all have some kind of financial assistance available to members in need. If you are not a member of a union, talk to your acting teacher and ask for advice.

There are city agencies equipped to help people with problems. There is low-cost counseling available. Look for this information in the front of the white pages of the phone book under government and city agencies or call UCLA or USC for referrals. Don't be afraid to ask.

## Invaluable Trade Papers/The Trades

*Ross Reports Television & Film* (*Ross Report*) is a monthly publication that prints contact information on agents, casting directors, networks, unions, advertising agencies, NYC and LA series, talk shows, soaps, and production facilities, as well as New York, Los Angeles, San Francisco and San Diego casting news and credits of casting directors. There is also a section on films in development and in preparation.

In addition to the reference information, *Ross Reports* regularly focuses on a particular topic in depth, such as "Talent Agencies," "Comedy Casting Guide," "USA Talent Directory," "Film's Top 20 Casting Directors," "Personal Managers Directory," etc. A single copy costs $6.95 on newsstands with a year's subscription of ten issues going for $59. The magazine is available at Samuel French Book Store or Larry Edmunds, at most good newsstands or directly from the publisher. RR also publishes stand-alone books: *Film Casting & Production Directory*, *Television Commercial Casting & Production Directory*, and other guides.

In the last edition of *The Los Angeles Agent Book*, I reported that *RRT&F* was in the process of creating its own website with a projected launch date of summer 2001, but since it's already 2004 and there's no website, I wouldn't hold my breath.

If you type in www.rossreports.com all you get is *Back Stage* and an ad for *RRT&F* since both publications are owned by the same publisher.

*Ross Reports Television & Film*
770 Broadway
New York, NY 10003
800-817-3273
www.backstage.com/backstage/rossreports/index.jsp
e-mail: rossreports@rossreports.com

*Back Stage West*, Los Angeles' weekly showbiz newspaper ("trade") is a rich resource of casting information for non-union and union theater, film and television.

*BSW* states that they have not checked the veracity of the ads and suggests caution and skepticism. Some ads will be scams but most of the castings, teachers, photographers, etc. are on the level. Just do your homework and don't be needy.

Many agents and managers advise clients to use the paper as an information source but to skip placing ads for their work. They say the prices are exorbitant and that it's unlikely that a casting director is going to view work from an ad in anything but *Variety* or *Hollywood Reporter*.

The weeklies are available at newsstands. *Back Stage West* is also available at www.backstage.com.

*Daily Variety* and the *Hollywood Reporter* are dailies that publish showbiz information ranging from the grosses of the latest movies to actors' obituaries. There is no casting information as such, but each paper runs a weekly listing of film and television productions of every kind for networks and cable.

The *Hollywood Reporter's* film production chart seems a little more comprehensive and easy to decipher. Subscriptions to both *DV* and *HR* are expensive, but you can pick up single copies at any newsstand or visit any library and read them for free.

Check to see which day the production notes you are interested in appear and pick up that one. *Daily Variety* also lists cable production notes weekly.

The various unions have bulletin boards listing classes, housing, reduced or free theater tickets and sometimes, casting notices. Although you have to be a member to obtain many services, check to see what you can get.

The unions also have free listings of agents posted on their websites: www.sag.org, www.aftra.org, and www.actorsequity.org.

The Reference Supplement for *The Academy Players Directory* is a free source of current phone numbers and addresses for agents and casting directors. The Academy will mail you a copy if you call and ask. Their number is 310-247-3000 or drop by their new offices at Hollywood and Vine (1313 N. Vine St.) and pick up a copy. Consult your map for particulars.

## Joining the Unions

Do not join SAG, Equity or AFTRA before you have to. There are already well over 112,000 members of SAG, 85% of whom are unemployed on any given day. If your career is not far enough along that someone is asking you to do a union job, then don't go through the backdoor of joining via being an extra. SAG is currently working to tighten requirements for membership anyway, but for your own sake, don't take yourself out of the running for the non-union films and commercials that will build your skill and your resume.

When you are far enough along in your growth to warrant membership, some agent or producer will have found you and will help you not only get your card, but a nice SAG job at the same time.

Once you are a member of SAG and you do non-union work, the union will find out (they always do) and you will be brought up on charges before a room full of your peers, relieved of all the money you made and possibly suspended. The experience is heartbreaking and humiliating for both your fellow actors who exact the punishment and for the scab, for that's what you would have become.

Thoreau says: *If one advances confidently in the direction of his dreams and endeavors to live the life which he has imagined, he will meet with success unimagined in common hours.* The experience of my own life supports this.

We are all embarked on an exhilarating adventure. Some of us are farther down the road than others and we all travel at differing speeds. It's important to enjoy the journey. From the perspective of time, I look at my life and realize that the times of great struggle were frequently the most rewarding.

## Wrap Up

*Personal Resources*

✓ form a support group
✓ interact with family
✓ ask your teacher for advice

*Geographical Resources*

✓ don't forget phone books
✓ own a copy of *The Thomas Guide, Los Angeles County Edition*
✓ learn the lay-of-the-land as soon as possible

*Professional Resources*

✓ consult with the unions
✓ read theatrical publications
✓ get a job in business
✓ join a good acting class

# ⚐4⚐
# Your First Agent & His Tools

There's good news and bad news. First the bad news: you're probably going to have to be your own first agent until you can make yourself into a marketable product. Now, the good news: nobody cares more about your career than you do, so your first agent is going to be phenomenally motivated.

✦ *Don't look for an agent too quickly if you are brand new in the business. It's not necessary to work right away. It's more important to study and be ready to get an agent. A lot of people aren't ready to audition yet. They've never auditioned and they wouldn't know what to do if they went into an audition room.*
Arthur Toretzky/Paradigm

✦ *Some people come to LA and they think they must have an agent in order to get work. No. You must get work to get work. An agent follows the work. A casting director who hires you might find you an agent. Even when you do have an agent, don't sit around expecting it to be in the hands of the agent.*
*Don't limit your mailings to agents, contact casting directors.*
Sheba Williams/*Agency West Entertainment*

Your focus at this point has to be a day job so you won't feel poor and desperate. Next you need credits, a good acting class, and a professional audition tape.

✦ *Make sure you have enough money to enter the business. If you don't have money for pictures or resumes or to get your hair professionally done, wait. If you need to get your teeth fixed, get that done. Get everything ready before you assault the business.*
Sheba Williams/*Agency West Entertainment*

This book is focused on those who are already entrepreneurial, but if you need help in that department, my marketing book, *How to Sell Yourself as an Actor* will give you some ideas.

In order to attract an agent, you have to have something to sell. No matter how talented you are, if you don't have some way to show what you've got, you're all talk. Working up a scene for the agent's office will work for a few agents, but basically, it's not enough.

I know what you are thinking: "Swell. How am I going to amass credits and put together a professional tape without an agent? How am I ever going to get any work?"

## First Steps

First of all, action. Inaction is a killer. You must start doing something even if you change direction later. Get into an acting class. Pick up *Back Stage West* or *The Ross Reports* for casting information. Once you are involved with other actors, you will begin to hear about student films or plays that are casting, but be selective.

✦ *Don't do just an independent film, try to get into a thesis film at USC, AFI or UCLA.*
John Lyons/The Austin Company

Join a theater group. Produce your own play. That's exactly what Carol Burnett did when she first got to New York. Her autobiography, *Just One More Time*, is filled with inspiration for actors just starting out. Check it out of the library and begin to see what others in your situation have done.

## Get Into an Acting Class

When choosing an acting class, shop around. The *Working Actors Guide* (a good bible for actors) and *Back Stage West* are good places to start because you'll see ads for many of the acting teachers in town. Another way to investigate is to start checking out the local theater companies by viewing their shows.

Afterward, if you like someone's work, go backstage and compliment him and in the conversation, mention that you are new in town and trying to research acting teachers, does that person have a good referral?

Whether you choose a list of prospective teachers from ads in the guides or from a referral, do audit some classes to give you a feel for the class. You'll not only see which teacher appeals to you, but another deciding factor, the caliber of the students you would have to work with.

There are some excellent teachers like Anita Jesse, Larry Moss, and

Susan Batson who won't allow audits because they don't want to expose their students to outside eyes while they are in a creative stage and at their most vulnerable.

If you can't check the class out in person, you really need personal feedback from someone in the class or from an actor whose work you respect.

Once you get on a teacher's mailing list (from auditing the class, perhaps) you may get phone calls trying to sell you the class. That doesn't necessarily mean the teacher is not credible, it may just mean he is hungry. In any event, please don't get talked into anything. Part of being a good actor is learning to listen to your own inner voice.

Any teacher is in a powerful position over a student. The teacher is there to lead and you are there to follow. An acting teacher is more powerful than any other teacher because in order to act well, the acting student must be particularly exposed and vulnerable.

Since most of us think there is something mystical about the process, it's tempting to believe that someone really holds all the answers and thus all the keys to fame, fortune and happiness. The only person who holds all those keys, however, is you. All the information must be filtered through you. Don't blindly follow anyone. I don't care who it is.

## Acting Classes/Teachers/Studios

Combining personal experience and interviews with agents and friends in the business, I have come up with a list of people who are credentialed and respected. There are other fine teachers around, these just happen to be the ones I personally know about and feel comfortable vouching for. Fees printed here are subject to change, so check prices when you call.

*Allan Miller* is a wonderful actor, director and teacher. He was Barbra Streisand's first teacher and continues to act, direct and coach top stars as well as teach his private classes. His classes meet in Van Nuys, are ongoing, meet once a week for two hours and cost $120 every four weeks. 818-907-6262 or allan.miller@sbcglobal.net.

I am particularly taken with Allan's ability to open you up so that you can do your best work. Both his book *A Passion for Acting* and his videotape *Audition* are excellent. I've been in his classes and he's directed me in a couple of plays. He always makes me better.

I was aware of *Larry Moss* way before Hilary Swank, Michael Clarke

Duncan and other Oscar winners were thanking him in their acceptance speeches. Larry taught at Juilliard and Circle in the Square, where he was musical director for eight years. When Moss moved to Los Angeles in 1990 he founded The Larry Moss Studio which is now in residence at the Edgemar Center for the Arts in Santa Monica.

The new facility combines many disciplines teaching everything from scene study to mask and clown workships that meet once weekly for twelve weeks.

Larry is so busy right now directing and teaching that his classes are sporadic, but partner Michelle Danner is also an excellent and talented teacher/director/actor.

New students meet at the facility at 2437 Main Street on Fridays for an informational session. 310-392-0815. www.edgemar.com/index1.htm. There's an interview with Larry online at www.yelba.com/interview_moss.htm that's worth checking out.

I haven't experienced *Bernardo Hiller*'s classes, but his website www.berniehiller.com makes me want to. He's teaching a Master Class at the Moscow Art Theater for heaven's sake. Bernie teaches everything from acting to dialects to career guidance. His six-week acting classes costs $375 a three-hour class. He is highly recommended as a private coach at $75 an hour. I can't begin to do him justice here, so check the web or call 818-781-8000.

New York guru *Susan Batson* comes to Los Angeles several times a year and teaches at her studio, Black Nexxus. Nicole Kidman and Tom Cruise are only two of her high profile private students. She's only in Los Angeles from time to time and classes are $50 on a per class basis.

Black Nexxus has other teachers (Corey Parker, Natasha Goss, Jimmy Antoine, Kadeem Hardison, Greg Braun) who have all studied with Susan. Check out BN's website www.blacknexxus.com for a description of classes that include Scene Study, On-Camera, Sensory, Develop Your Own Method and Ex-Er. Classes by staff members are all $40 per class on a class by class basis, no ongoing commitment.

Black Nexxus
6363 Sunset Blvd., Ste. 910
LA Film School Bldg. (near Vine)
Hollywood, CA 90028
323-467-9987
www.blacknexxus.com

*Robert Carnegie* and *Jeff Goldblum* founded Playhouse West in 1981. Their prices are phenomenal since $180 monthly buys you two three-hour classes per week. The classes are limited to fifteen people so that each student works in every class. Classes are taught mornings, afternoons and evenings, seven days a week. You can audit a class for free on Tuesdays at noon or Thursdays at 7 PM.

A training ground for actors, writers and directors, PW students are featured in plays directed by PW staff members and other students. Their film activities include film production from features to shorts. *Little Surprises*, directed by Jeff Goldblum, was nominated for an Oscar. PW member Henry Barrial's *Some Body* was a finalist at Sundance in 2001. An annual three-day film festival features projects that Playhouse West has had a hand in generating.

*Playhouse West*
4250 Lankershim Boulevard
North Hollywood, CA 91612
818-881-6520
www.playhousewest.net

Like all gifted teachers, *Anita Jessie* wants her students to learn everything. To that end, in addition to her highly recommended acting classes, students are now creating their own short films. Although they may write, direct, star, and edit their own films. Anita encourages her students to network with writers, directors and editors and engage in joint ventures. Anita says, "It's not a filmmaking course. It's a course in networking and learning what you can do if you put your mind to it." Budgets range from $150 to $3000, all paid by the students. She tells her students, "These are not showcases for your work, they are your laboratory to learn."

Her classes meet twice weekly from 7:30-10:30 PM. The eighteen students who are admitted work out twice nightly. The fee is $270 per month. Students must interview and audition for acceptance. Her number is 323-876-2870/818-767-4576. www.anitajessiestudio.com

You will gain insight into her process by checking out one of her books, *Let the Part Play You* and *The Playing is the Thing*. Other classes at her studio are taught by Jim Ingersoll. His students work out twice one night a week and audit Jessie's class once a week. Those classes are limited to fourteen people. The fee is $180 monthly.

*Millie Slavin* was on Broadway when I first got to New York. She continues her acting work and is also known as a terrific acting teacher and coach. She teaches an ongoing weekly scene study/monologue class that costs $200 for the month. Her private coaching and Private Technique Classes each cost $75 hourly. 310-582-3485.

There is a list of teachers, coaches and photographers for young actors in Chapter Thirteen.

Improv guru *Gary Austin* (one of the founders of The Groundlings) also teaches all over the country. His classes range from Improv Technique to Characters to Acting Technique/Making Choices. He works with students on an ongoing basis to create their own material. Classes have different prices relative to content and time but average about $25 hourly. Details at www.garyaustin.org or call 800-DOG-TOES.

Screaming Frog Productions bills itself as Chicago Style improv. SFP members teach four different levels of improv. Aa free workshop evaluates where you belong. The eight week classes are $225 and limited to ten students. wwwjscreamingfrog.com

# TVI

Gee, how to write about TVI without looking like I'm on their payroll? At first glance, TVI looks like one of those places I tell actors to stay away from. They offer classes, casting director workshops, advice, and they charge a membership fee. They want to be your mother offering a home away from home.

Now, having visited TVI, I cannot think of a single bad thing to say. It is a club for actors. TVI provides computers, help texturing your resume (they'll even keep it in their computer and update it for you at no charge), free industry mailing labels, rehearsal space even if you are working on something in no way related to the club, a research gallery of photographers' work (no kickbacks), a place to hang out with fellow actors and various other perks.

Started in New York in 1986 by ex-commercial agent Alan S. Nusbaum (Cunningham, Escott & Dipene), and joined soon after by his wife and partner, Deborah Koffler, the organization has thrived because the goal has been not only to teach business skills to actors, but to help them translate those skills into jobs by providing access to all the necessary tools.

The annual membership fee is $450 (about $38 a month) payable in two installments. Classes cost extra but are discounted for members.

While waiting to meet with Nusbaum, I encountered an actor at the bulletin board who said he was a former member. I asked if he had had a good experience. He was unhappy because none of the casting director workshops resulted in a job or an interview. I'm not a fan of casting director workshops because I think casting directors should see you for free. I asked Alan about the actor's complaints.

Alan told me (and I saw all the posted disclaimers) that TVI explains to actors that no casting is done through the casting director workshops and that they are an opportunity for actors to ask questions about the casting process from an industry professional.

Hope springs eternal, though. No matter how many times anyone tells that to an actor, in the actor's heart of hearts, he secretly thinks that the act of just being in the presence of a CD, agent or director, is going to result in stardom — or, at the very least an audition.

TVI isn't going to get you any work, but their club/family atmosphere might really help you feel less isolated and will definitely give you access to other people in the business. You can upgrade your business skills in a protected environment created by someone who actually worked successfully in the business and, in addition to making money from his work, appears to me to really have the actors best interests at heart.

TVI Actors Studio
14429 Ventura Blvd. #118
Sherman Oaks, CA 91423
818-784-6500
www.tvistudios.com

## Pictures and Resumes

Be honest about both, no matter what anybody else tells you. Agents and casting directors all tell me you had better look just like your picture when you walk in or you've blown it. If you look prettier than the picture, they don't want you and vice-versa. They've asked to see the person represented by the picture. If they wanted someone prettier or uglier, they would have called someone else.

✦ *I brought in two people off blind submissions and did not sign either of them. One of them did not look at all like the picture. I thought I was bringing in a teenage leading man and got a mid-twenties actor.*
Mitchell K Stubbs/Mitchell K Stubbs

Learn to judge what a good picture is by spending time looking through the *Academy Players Directory*. Notice what is common in the pictures your eye is drawn to. What grabbed your attention?

Interview several photographers before choosing. Look at their work. Show them pictures of yourself that you like and those you don't like. Let them know the parts you go up for so that they can be sure to feature that in the photos. Don't act for the camera. Be natural.

I admired a photo by *John Galucci* at an audition and immediately asked for his phone number. The Los Feliz resident asks you to arrive at the shoot with a clean face, looking just like you look every day. He shoots a few shots of you *au naturel* because that's really what casting directors want to see. You'll have ample opportunity to change your look for other pictures during the session.

Because the way the light hits your face is so important, John does your base himself and leaves everything else to you. For men, he applies base and a little bronzer to get the look he's after.

His fee is $350 for three to four rolls of thirty-six exposures and three 8x10s (additional prints $18 each). John's pictures are appropriate for both commercial and theatrical portfolios. 323-953-3622.

*Timothy Fielding* in North Hollywood is high on everyone's list. He has never advertised because casting directors, agents, and managers are so crazy about his work that they are constantly recommending him. If you are looking for help to figure out "which one you are," Timothy will be a big help. He has a great eye and now has a side business of makeovers, helping actors focus on their uniqueness. His portfolio features the actor's old picture alongside the new one. Like many photographers, he shoots digitally now. His fee is $295 until he's finished. You'll get the disk as well as two 8x10s ready for reproduction. 818-760-6630.

*Alan Weissman* shoots celeb photos for American Movie Classics, HBO and Fox, of people like Anthony Hopkins, Jack Lemmon, Angelina Jolie, Diane Keaton and Gregory Peck, so if you think you would like to join their company, at least in Alan's portfolio, he charges $360 for two rolls of film. For that you get one 8x10. Additional 8x10s are $17 each. His website, www.alanweissman.com will give you a good idea of his work. 818-766-9797.

*Carrie Cavalier* will do some great pictures for you at $150 (one roll) and up. She gives you the negatives and a proof sheet. 8x10s are extra at $16 each. 818-556-8291/840-9148. Check her work at her website: www.cavalierphotography.com.

*Ken Weingart* has relocated his studio from New York to Los Angeles. He charges $175 for one roll/$250 for two rolls then add $100 for each extra roll of thirty-six pictures.

Negatives, or all digital files burned to CD, are included with each package. If needed, a personal website or web gallery for one month of viewing, a set of proof sheets is included with each package. A post session consultation to review images is included with each package. 310-395-4613. www.kenweingart.com.

A friend's stunning 8x10 sent me to the net for photographer *Laura Burke*. Her site says she "photographs not only your essence but your spirit too." Pretty lofty aspirations, but when you check out the images, she may just be right.

An agent in New York at Lester Lewis years ago, a chance meeting with a camera sent her to LACC to study photography, Laura charges $375 for three roles. Add $25 per roll for color. 818-759-6767. www.lauraburkephotography.com.

If a photographer suggests a hair/makeup artist, that doesn't mean you have to go for it. My own feeling is that I need to be able to recreate the look myself for auditions. Since the makeup artist is not going to take up residence at my house, I'd better do it myself.

Manager Robbie Kass was still an agent when he gave me advice on pictures.

✦ *I think the important thing is a nice straightforward picture. Something that looks like you and doesn't cost over $300.*

Fees for good pictures go from $150 to $500 and beyond. Be circumspect. After you pay the photographer, it still costs another $100 or so to get prints made. These are not the last pictures you will ever have made, so don't spend every last cent on them.

The photographer should shoot several rolls for his fee and provide you with at least two 8x10s that you will take to a good duplicating house to have copies made.

When I'm at an audition and I see actors handing out color shots, I'm always impressed and want to get color, too. My agent tells me it's a waste of money. He says many times, they are faxing pictures and the color won't show and that it doesn't matter anyway. I still think it's a good idea, particularly if you have interesting coloring.

## Close-ups/Bodies/Borders

Whichever photographer you choose, looking through their portfolio will begin to give you an idea of what kind of shots appeal to you. Though you will surely want to include some of today's popular ¾ body shots, you really should have one good close-up. If you have representation, be sure to ask your agent for his input as to how you should present yourself in the pictures.

SAG disapproves of agents recommending photographers because they fear kickbacks, but if you have a credible agent who is getting you work, you're safe in at least asking which photographers they think are good. You'll make your own decision, but it's nice to have a professional opinion.

It costs more to have pictures copied without borders, but it's a classy look. You'll see pictures with much larger borders, jagged, thin, all kinds of options, but before you fall in love with a look, weigh how it's going to balance with your picture.

## Copies

There are many excellent duplicating services in Los Angeles. One of my favorites is *Duplicate Photos*. Prices vary relative to how many copies you have made and what kind of paper, and there is a charge to print the negative first if you don't already have one, but basically you can get 100 borderless 8x10s for seventy cents each. Borders are much cheaper at 55 cents each if you buy a hundred. The smaller the quantity, the higher the price and vice versa. If you are on the net and want to check out their prices, their website is www.duplicate.com. They have a branch in Hollywood at 1522 N. Highland. (323-466-7544) and in the Valley at 12606 Ventura Boulevard, across from Jerry's Deli in Studio City (818-760-4193).

I also like *Custom Print Shop* at 1759 Las Palmas in Hollywood. They run test printings and will give you pearl finish for the same price as glossy, but their copies are $80 for 100 prints. 323-461-3001.

*Reproductions* at 3499 Cahuenga Boulevard near Universal, gives you color for the same price. www.reproductions.com. 323-845-9595.

# Resumes

A resume (a listing of your theatrical work and training) is sent along with your 8x10 glossy or matte print. Your resume should be stapled to the back of your picture so that as you turn the picture over side to side, you see the resume as though it were printed on the back of the photo. The buyers see hundreds of resumes every day, so make yours simple and easy to read.

When prospective employers see too much writing, their eyes glaze over and they won't read anything. Be brief, it's not necessary to list every job you ever worked. Even though I know you are proud of it, it's not necessary to list union affiliation (SAG, AFTRA, Equity) on your resume.

There are many ways to organize resumes. Many agents prefer the work listed in categories beginning with your most prestigious credits on top. In Los Angeles that means film, if you've done any. Next, television and theater. List the film, show, or play. Some people list the director. Some list their character name. If they played with a star, some mention that. Once you get a body of work in television episodes, just list titles under Most Recent Television Episodes.

I list the name of the director on my resume instead of anything about the size of the part, but if you are just beginning and no one knows you, the casting director and/or agent will want to know something about the size of the role you played.

If you played Blanche in a production of *A Streetcar Named Desire* , by all means say so. If you were a neighbor, say that. The CD or agent wants to know how much work you have actually done; if you have "carried" a show, that's important.

Misrepresenting your work on a resume is self-destructive. Not only do you run the risk of being caught and never trusted again, but actually playing a big role anyplace does help you grow as an actor. If you haven't had that experience, you are inviting yourself to be judged more harshly than you deserve.

Choose the most impressive credits and list them. There is an example on the previous page to use as a format guide. Adapt this example to meet your needs. If all you have done is college theater, list that. This is more than someone else has done and it will give the buyer an idea of parts you can play.

Note that you were master of ceremonies for your town Pioneer Day Celebration. If you sang at The Lion's Club program, list that.

Accomplishments that might seem trivial to you could be important to someone else, particularly if you phrase it right. If you are truly beginning and have nothing for your resume, at least list your training and a physical description along with the names of your teachers. Younger actors aren't expected to have a lot of credits.

---

# John Smith/818-555-4489

6'2" 200 lbs, blonde hair, blue eyes

*Theater*

*Defying Gravity* . . . . . . . . . . . . . . . . . . . directed by Jenny Sullivan
*Who's Afraid of Virginia Wolff* . . . . . . . . . . . directed by Allan Miller

*Film*

*School of Rock* . . . . . . . . . . . . . . . . directed by Richard Linklater
*Radio* . . . . . . . . . . . . . . . . . . . . . . . . directed by Michael Tollin
*Mystic River* . . . . . . . . . . . . . . . . . . . directed by Clint Eastwood

*Television*

*Carnivale* . . . . . . . . . . . . . . . . . . . . . directed by Rodrigo Garcia
*JAG* . . . . . . . . . . . . . . . . . . . . . . . . . directed by Bradford May
*West Wing* . . . . . . . . . . . . . . . . . . . . . . directed by Paris Barclay

*Training*

*Acting* . . . . . . . . . . . . . . . . . Larry Moss, Anita Jessie, Allan Miller
*Singing* . . . . . . . . . . . . . . . Eric Vetro, Robert Edwards, John Peck
*Dance* . . . . . . . . . . . . . . . . . . . . . . Joe Tremaine, Anna Cheselka

*Special Skills*

guitar, horseback riding, martial arts, street performer, Irish, Spanish, British, Cockney, & French dialect, broadsword, fencing, certified Yoga instructor, circus skills, etc.

---

If you are also using this picture and resume for commercials, it's wise to list a few. Not too many. You don't want them to think you are overexposed.

My name is on my resume on the back of my picture, but I also pay more to have it printed on the front because I want them to associate my name with my face instantly.

The most important thing on your resume is your name and your agent's phone number. If you don't have an agent, get voice mail for work calls. Don't use your personal phone number, it's more professional and it's safer to list a different number.

As I discussed on page 17, don't list extra work on your resume.

## Audition Reels/Tapes

There are many places to get your tapes edited and copied. I have always used Rick Phazel. An actor who started a niche business, he has kept up with all the technology and doesn't charge an arm and a leg. I select my tapes and cue them to the proper place before I get there so I don't have to waste time with the clock running for something I can do at home.

Rick recently moved and since his rent is now less, he has done the unheard of thing of passing along the savings and has lowered his prices! Cost for linear editing is now $50 an hour instead of $60 and digital editing has gone from $80 per hour to $60.

Rick Phazel/Phase-L Productions
7220 Woodman #201
just N of Sherman Way on the E side of street
818-782-4700

### 99-Seat Theater

If you just got to town and have done at least some work in college or in your own home town, pick up *Back Stage West* and look for a play to audition for. Your soul and your resume both dictate that you should get involved in the theater scene in town as soon as possible. Although 99-Seat Theater doesn't pay you, they must adhere to Actors' Equity Rules in their treatment of actors and if nothing else, they do have to give you transportation money.

The real pay, of course is in getting a chance to work, grow and hopefully be seen by someone who has another job to give.

Here's a list of 99-seat theaters that casting directors might actually visit, particularly if you get good reviews and send them a postcard with your reviews and offer to set them up with tickets.

| | |
|---|---|
| The Actor's Gang<br>6029 Santa Monica Blvd.<br>www.theactorsgang.com | Founded by Tim Robbins Original and well received work. |
| The Black Dahlia Theater<br>5453 W. Pico Boulevard<br>www.thedahlia.com | Does terrific original work. Good actors. Good material. |
| The Blank Theater Company<br>6500 Santa Monica Blvd.<br>www.blank.com | Artistic Producer<br>*ER* star Noah Wylie |
| The Cast Theater<br>809 E. El Centro Ave.<br>www.thetheatredistrict.com/Cast_Theatre_History.htm | Famous for showcasing the plays of LA's Justin Tanner |
| Circle X<br>No resident space<br>www.circlextheatre.org | Many Ovation Award nominations |
| Deaf West Theater/NoHo<br>5112 Lankershim<br>www.deafwest.org | Featuring deaf actors with hearing actors in double parts |
| East West Players in Little Tokyo<br>120 N. Judge John Aiso Street<br>www.eastwestplayers.org | Always interesting Asian Pacific/American Company |
| The Hudson Guild/Hollywood<br>6539 Santa Monica Boulevard<br>www.hudsontheatre.com | Consistently gaining attention and awards |
| The Road Theater/NoHo<br>5108 Lankershim Boulevard<br>www.roadtheatre.org | Consistently gaining attention and awards |

| | |
|---|---|
| Actors Alley/NoHo<br>5269 Lankershim Boulevard<br>www.1bc.com/vtl/Sched2.htm | Consistently gaining attention and awards |
| Tiffany Theater/Hollywood<br>8532 Sunset Boulevard | A theater for hire that always gets press attention |
| The Matrix Theater<br>7657 Melrose | Company of working visible actors |
| Odyssey Theater/West LA<br>2055 S. Sepulveda Boulevard<br>www.odysseytheatre.com | Established award winning theater |
| Coronet Theater/LA<br>368 N. La Cienega Boulevard | Another theater for hire that always gets press attention |
| InterAct Theater/NoHo<br>5215 Lankershim Boulevard<br>www.interactla.org | Consistently good work good theater company |
| Pacific Resident Theater<br>703 Venice Boulevard<br>www.pacificresidenttheatre.com | Well thought of theater run by actress, Marilyn Fox |

### Drawing the Attention of Casting Directors

Though a prestigious place to work, South Coast Repertory in Costa Mesa is not a favorite with busy casting directors without the time to make the 100-mile round-trip to check out actors. You will do good work, you will be paid, and you will be growing as an actor, but it's unlikely casting directors will see your work. If the show gets some great reviews, that may draw them, but it's tough.

Basically, casting directors and agents are most impressed with resumes listing work at The Mark Taper Forum and The Dorothy Chandler Pavilion in downtown Los Angeles. The work is not necessarily one bit better than the work in 99-Seat Theater, but not only do they pay you in money, you'll get respect as well.

### The Actor's Job: Looking for Work

✦ *As a beginning actor, you can't expect people to come to you. You've got to go to every open call. You've got to audition for everything you can get your hands on because the bottom line is what you're trying to do is get the parts. The bonus result is that you are getting the life experiences of the actor you are sitting next to. I went to an audition at King Studios in New York. I was sitting next to this woman who was on of the leads in this Equity Tour of "Showboat."*

*Since I wasn't Equity yet, and non-Equity people are seen after all the Equity people, I was waiting for four hours at an Open Call and I asked this woman questions and got to absorb all her years in the business. I did that over and over again. I used every connection I had.*

*Whenever I met a casting director through a connection, I didn't expect a job or a reading, I expected them to spend some time with me...for us to get to know each other as people. We talked about the person who was our connection, how do you know so-and-so, etc., discussed the plays I saw, that they saw.*

*All this got us out of the casting director/actor relationship. You conduct the interview. Obviously, there are a lot of jerks out there who are not going to like that. There are a lot of people in this business. All you need are a couple who are going to help you. One casting director can be very influential in your career because he can introduce you to all the agents in town...and can cast you and can get his friends to cast you. You've got to be a person, not an actor and get to know people.*
Jim Weissenbach/Weissenbach Management

✦ *Learn the totality of the business. Read the trades. If you get "Back Stage West," read all the articles. Train yourself to be multidimensional. It's your job. Be professional. It's a business. Your job is to get the job. Anything you can do to get that job, you should do. Plan. Prepare. Train.*
Sheba Williams/Agency West Entertainment

In order to agent yourself, you will need to do everything we talked about agents doing on Chapter Two. Check the paragraph titled "An Agent Prepares" on page 5. It's not easy to meet agents, but as you make friends with others in the business on your level, one thing leads to another.

Becoming an actor is not an overnight process. Don't equate being paid with being an actor. A large part of being an actor on any level is looking for work.

You are already an actor. Even if you are a student actor, you're still an actor and you actually have your first assignment: get a resume with decent credits. This will not only begin to season you as an actor, but if it's on film, you will be able to start building an audition tape.

What denotes decent credits? Although agents are happy to see school and hometown credits on a resume so they know you've actually had some time onstage, those credits not only don't mean much in the marketplaces of Los Angeles/New York/Chicago, they don't constitute an arena for the agent to see you in action first hand.

If, on the other hand, you are appearing in a decent venue where he can drop by or, if he is canvassing the town on his own, discover you, then you have the possibility of becoming a marketable commodity.

When you can also deliver an example of your work on tape, you are in business. The audition tape is a video usually no longer than six minutes that shows either one performance or a montage of scenes of an actor's work. It is better to have just one good scene from an actual job than many short moments of work or a scene produced just for the reel.

Don't show several scenes from the same performance. Agents and casting executives view tapes endlessly and can tell quickly if you interest them. It's always better to leave your audience wanting more.

Agents and casting directors prefer to see tapes featuring professional television or film appearances though some will look at a tape produced solely for audition purposes.

If you can't produce footage that shows you clearly in contemporary material playing a part that you could logically be cast for, then you aren't far enough along to make a tape. Better to wait than to show yourself at less than your best. Patience.

✦ *No tape is better than bad tape.*
John Lyons/The Austin Company

✦ *We will look at actor produced tapes, but make sure there is good light and sound. Otherwise it is distracting from the actor's performance. We can't see them well or hear them well.*
Ginger Lawrence/House of Representatives

## Everybody Was New Once

The most successful people in any business are smart, organized, and entrepreneurial, but almost no one starts out that way. We all stumble in the beginning, just as when we were learning to walk. This is just another learning curve.

As you continue reading agents' remarks about what successful actors do, you will begin to develop an overview of the business that will help you in the process of representing yourself. It's essential to stay focused and specific and give up the urge to panic and think all is lost.

Bring the same creative problem-solving you use in preparing a scene to the business side of your career and you will not only be successful, you will begin to feel more in control of your own destiny.

Don't rush out and take just any agent. Have a sense of yourself. You are a commodity to be reckoned with. You're not nothing. If you know that, then other people will know it, too.

## Wrap Up

*Tools for First Agent*

✓ decent credits
✓ acting classes
✓ audition tape

# 5
## Self-Knowledge

Buckminster Fuller says that if you took all the wealth of the world and redistributed it equally, in twenty-five to fifty years there would be the same distribution of wealth we have today. It's a law of physics.

That same law applies to actors. Let's just say we'll give all the actors the same amount of talent and training. Nothing would change. Some actors will be business-like and work-oriented and others will be self-destructive and lazy. Some don't care if they are late. Some like to be organized. Some think the world owes them a living.

So, when people talk about all the starving actors and the fact that there are only five agents and one part it doesn't really matter. A large percentage of those actors won't be business-like, motivated and/or trained. Even if there are only five agents and one part, as long as you get the agent and the part, the rest is immaterial.

When I asked agents, during our interviews, what information they wanted to impart to actors about the craft or their relationship with their agents, the most prevalent answer was some version of: "Know which one you are." Don't expect to play Brad Pitt's parts if you look like Billy Bob Thornton.

Develop your own taste. Study. Not just acting. Study art. Go to the museum. Learn how the masters perceived love, anger, despair. The more you perfect your own personhood and trust your own instincts whether it is for what constitutes a really great pair of socks or what is a superb jump shot, the more you become the one you are.

When I first left Texas, I did everything I could to make sure I wouldn't be mistaken for the middle-class lady from Texas I was. I wanted so badly to be a New York lady. What I didn't realize, Texas accent not withstanding, was that my very middle-classness is what I have to sell. Yes, I can (and have) played ladies who went to Vassar, but, more often, they can (and will) get a real lady from Vassar for those parts.

I am an authentic lady from Texas who has raised three children alone and had all the unique adventures that have gone into creating who I am. There is nobody else who has all my components. I must prize what is uniquely me and find a way to tie that to a universality of the life experience.

+ *When I got off the boat from Georgia, I thought everyone was just going to find me the funniest thing that they ever saw. You have to do the work and you have to break the ego down and find out who you are.*

*Know what type you are. Know what your tools are. If you're the character guy and you are not going to be asked to remove your shirt and kiss the girl, don't waste time trying for those parts.*
Mitchell K. Stubbs/Mitchell K. Stubbs

+ *Successful actors have an accurate image of what they sell. Unsuccessful actors don't have an accurate image of what they sell. That's the sign. If you're going out and you're getting the job, then you know who you are. If you're going out and you're not getting the job, then something is wrong.*

*And you can't say it's talent. In this town, talent doesn't mean a lot. If you are the right type, you will get the job. I'm not saying you are going to get "Hallmark Hall of Fame," signed contract, but you will be getting work.*
Martin Gage/The Gage Group

Martin's New York counterpart, Phil Adelman talked to me about the importance of self-knowledge and illustrated it with this story:

+ *I had a funny-looking lady come in, mid-30s, chubby, not very pretty. For all I know, this woman could be brilliant. I asked her what roles she could play; what she thought she should get. She saw herself playing Michelle Pfeiffer's and Sharon Stone's roles.*

*I could have been potentially interested in this woman in the areas in which she could work. But it was a turn-off because, not only do I know that she's not going after the right things, so she's not preparing correctly, but she's not going to be happy with the kinds of things I'm going to be able to do for her. So, I wouldn't want to commit to that person.*
Phil Adelman/The Gage Group New York

+ *You do need to find your unique genetic makeup as an actor and understand it. You have to "dance with the one that brung you." Once you have been in the business for a time, you can start to stretch. If you're twenty-two years old, fresh off the boat from Kansas, you're going to play that stranger from "Picnic."*

*Why would you try to stretch to play Quentin Tarrantino characters? At the beginning of one's career, you need to do what is most easily done. If you are Susie Sunshine, be Susie Sunshine and understand who that is.*
Mitchell K. Stubbs/Mitchell K. Stubbs

✦ *You must always show the most commercial quality. They may or may not be buying it that day, but one day they will and they will have already seen the one person who could do this better than anyone else in the world.*

*I didn't want Geraldine Page to do "The Pope of Greenwich Village." It was a tiny part. I said, "Geraldine, why do you want to do this?" She said, "Because I know how to do this part better than anybody." She got an Academy Award nomination for it. Here's an example of the actor knowing better than the agent.*

Martin Gage/The Gage Group

✦ *Although the business has changed a lot over the past few years, what has not changed is that talent will win out. Talent wins. From a marketing standpoint, however, "you gotta have a gimmick." You must have a specific look or a specific personality and channel that.*

*Even if you haven't had the classic training that other actors have, that look or that personality or that sense of humor or whatever it is that sets you apart, if you've got the hook and middle America buys into it, you can write your own ticket.*

Mitchell K. Stubbs/Mitchell K. Stubbs

All this is good, but how do you go about finding out who you are?

✦ *Anything you can do to give you more of an idea who you are, whether it's therapy, talking to people or looking in a mirror, that's valid. There's an exercise I used to give my class when I taught actor therapy. I would tell them to get stark naked in front of a mirror and sit and look at themselves for an hour. Just sit and look at yourself. Talk to yourself. Look at how you look when you talk. When you cross your legs. When you move. Look at how your face changes. Look at how your body moves.*

*Think of all your competition. Think of what is unique about each of them. Think about what is different in you that is not in them. Watch what you do with your hands. Watch yourself. See yourself. You may have to do it for a year. For three weeks. Who knows for how long until all of a sudden you see something that is accessible that people will buy.*

*The smart actor will study himself until he can see what he has that is unique, special, commercial, saleable, acceptable that he can develop and magnify and use better than anybody else.*

*Think of you and your four closest competitors. If someone sat and talked to each of you for twenty minutes, what would they see that was different? What is it about you? Why should they hire you instead of the other one? She may have more credits or make more money. Why should I hire you? You have to go in with the qualities that are the most accessible of you to make those people buy you.*

*When you walk in a room, you have about four seconds while people decide to*

*hire or not hire you. It's your vibes. They may call it your nose, but it's your vibes. You have to go in with the qualities that are the most accessible of you. You've got to get those people to buy you.*
Martin Gage/The Gage Group

✦ *I believe every person on the face of the earth is unique. I believe that if I had a set of identical twins who were in touch with their uniqueness, I could sell them separately because, once they are in touch with their own uniqueness, there is no such thing as competition. Because, if you are in control of your uniqueness and you are centered, you take that into a room and, if someone chooses not to use it, you can't feel negative. It simply meant they didn't want to use that uniqueness. You are not in competition with anybody else.*

*A person's ideas dictate his uniqueness. What I believe about homosexuality or what I believe about any major subject is my uniqueness because it comes from my experience of it. So, you can't compare it. Many times you will be in the minority. The greatest people in the world have normally been in the minority.*
John Kimble

✦ *What kinds of parts do you want to play? You have to develop your skills, your vocal talent, your physical body, you have to develop yourself to be able to market yourself as the product to go get those roles that you want.*

*So many people don't understand who they are. They're forty-two and expect to get the part of a twenty-one-year-old.*
Mitchell K. Stubbs/Mitchell K. Stubbs

✦ *This is what I am. This is what they want me to be. Can I put them together and find out what I am capable of being? They want me to be a nerd. I want to be sexy. Maybe I can be a sexy nerd. Then, you have to convince your agent that that's what you are, because if your agent doesn't see it you're out again.*

*If the agent sees you and thinks he can make money on you, but not in the same way you think, then you have a problem. You and the agent must have the same vision. You might change his vision or he might change yours. If you both have the same vision, you can't be unsuccessful. The level of success may vary, but if you know who you are and the agent knows it, accurately, that's the recipe for success.*

*And remember, what you are at twenty-five is not what you are at thirty-five. Things change and your perception of yourself must change, too.*
Martin Gage/The Gage Group

Part of self-knowledge includes realistically evaluating the marketplace.

✦ *Look at the business: half-hour comedies, a number of magazine shows, reality shows, news shows that don't use actors. Sitcoms use only one or two guest stars and now they are usually all name actors. The amount of money available to the community is somewhat diminished.*

*What you have is a number of people who were able to make a living who can no longer make a living. The movies are all youth-market movies with sixteen-to seventeen-year-old kids. Once they're twenty-three and can no longer play a senior in high school, the business slows down for them.*
Jimmy Cota/The Artists Agency

✦ *The actor has got to have the creative energy juices flowing and have the right mind-set and the right attitudes to have the wins come to him. He needs to have an angle on the role that's going to be different and maybe the director is going to say, "That's interesting." If he's not in his most creative time, he's going to miss some things. He's going to walk out of the audition and say, "Damn, I should have put this twist on it," or "I don't know why I did that, it's so obvious."*

*If an actress' energies are in the theater, and she hasn't done a play in a year, it's going to drain her and she needs to be filled up and dealing with what to do about that. Whether it's working at a 99-seat theater, scene study, comedy workshop. There are lots of choices other than just sitting home and staring at the bare walls.*
Ann Geddes/Geddes Agency

Elinor Berger was an agent at Irv Schechter when she told me:

✦ *It's also a question of the competition. You can send a girl in who's very pretty, does a great reading, but somebody else will come in that happens to be a friend of the producer or a nephew of the director or somebody that somebody wants to go to bed with. Or whatever. There's 20,000 reasons why you're not going to get the part. And it's not necessarily that you are without talent. It's because there is so much competition.*

*When I think about it, when I look at the end of the week and I see all the people I've gotten out on appointments, I say to myself, It's amazing that I did that. I'm just one little person. When I think about all the agents and all the actors, I think we're lucky to get people out on the appointment.*

## Get a Grip

Insecurity is not appealing. There is too much money at stake. Some actors speak of being so frightened at an audition that they didn't do their best. Frightened of the buyer? The only thing you have time to focus on is the work. And if you are focused on the work, fear will not be able to pierce your consciousness.

A radio psychiatrist I used to listen said: "Decide to give up whatever is making you crazy. Get over it." It works.

Driving away from yet another rejection, a friend of mine started to totally lose it. He was frightened. He would never work again. He had never been talented in the first place (every actor's secret fear). Finally, he stopped the car and said to himself, "Wait a minute. I'm not starving to death. Me and my family are in good health. Your children are not dope addicts. Are you going to pieces here just because you don't work every day? Who does?" "I'll make a deal with you. Three years from now, all your dreams are coming true. In the meantime, you are going to continue being a working actor. So, start enjoying your life. Go back and take some classes again and become more assured. Take the dialect class you always wanted to take. Lose that ten pounds. Do all the things you don't have time to do when you are working."

Whether his predictions come true doesn't matter. When he gave up playing the "I'm not okay unless I'm chosen" game, his life changed.

Recently, I sat in on an acting class taught by Milton Katselas, who is not only a well-regarded director, but a highly respected teacher in Los Angeles. A working actor was complaining that he just had to keep it together a little longer because the payoff was just around the corner. Milton stopped him, "What's just round the corner?" The actor said, "The payoff." "No," Milton responded. "The payoff is now."

All you have is now. If you are not fulfilled by the now, get out of the business. If the payoff for you is the big bucks, the Tony or the Oscar, change jobs now. You will miss your whole life waiting for the prize. If you are unlucky enough to get the prize with this mind-set, you will not only be the same unhappy person, but you will now have an Oscar. And if you had thought getting the award was going to "fix" you, you'll be even more depressed.

✦ *Too many people forget that we're supposed to be here to do something good. It just becomes about who's making the most money and the person making the most money is supposed to be the smartest. He's the genius and the person who isn't is not.*

*We all know that's not true.*
Bruce Smith/Omnipop

## Why Are You Here?

Actors are drawn to the business for many reasons. They only stay if those reasons are being satisfied. Some people are drawn to the suffering, some to the big pursuit. The work that takes more time than anything else is the job of looking for and winning the work.

Even two-time Oscar winner Sally Field says it isn't like she thought it would be. She's constantly reading scripts, looking for things. Then, when there is a good project, she still has lots of competitors. That's depressing, isn't it? It never lets up. I think sometimes that, if they just gave me all the jobs, I might lose interest
and leave the business. I certainly wouldn't mind putting that one to the test. Another Oscar winner, Sissy Spacek, says she lives out of state so she won't be depressed all the time seeing all the work that others are getting.

## Assess Yourself & the Marketplace

Begin to assess which one you are: Are you a young character actor? A juvenile? Someone who is right for a soap? Check out every possible place where you might conceivably work whether it's film, televison, cable, the school system, service clubs, cruise ships, conventions or the local mall presenting plays geared to popular holidays.

Notice who is like you and who is not like you. Keep a list of things you have seen that you realistically think you would have been right for. What are the most successful parts you have done? What's the same about them? View theater, film and television at every opportunity. What parts would you have been right for? Why?

As you become smarter about the business, you will begin to perceive that casting directors cast essence. More important than the look is the essence. The essence of Robert De Niro that shines through his many diverse roles is his strength of spirit.

Practice thinking like a casting director. Consider Hugh Jackman, Nicolas Cage, Jim Carrey, and Frances McDormand. Figure out what their essence is. Cast them in other people's roles. How would Julia Roberts' part in *Erin Brockovich* have been if Emma Thompson played it? What if Brad Pitt played Sean Penn's part in *Mystic River*?

Thinking like a casting director will help you understand why you will never be cast in certain roles and why no one else should be cast in your parts.

Work on your appearance. Another responsibility you have is to be the best-looking you that you can be, given what you came with. That doesn't mean that appearance is more important than the work; it's not, but it's a large part of it. The business gravitates toward prettier people just as in life. Getting upset about that fact is like throwing a fit because the sun shines in your window every morning and wakes you up. Get a shade. If you are not pretty, be clever.

Ruth Gordon says beauty is nice, but courage is better.

✦ *Two things first. Beauty and courage. These are the two most admired things in life. Beauty is Vivien Leigh, Garbo; you fall down in front of them. You don't have it? Get courage. It's what we're all in awe of. It's the New York Mets saying, "We'll make our own luck."*

*I got courage because I was five-foot-nothing and not showgirl-beautiful. Very few beauties are great actresses.*
Paul Rosenfield, *Los Angeles Times*[5]

## Making It

✦ *Nobody changes the rules. What you can do is play the game for what you want or at least toward your ends. Nobody will force you to do work that you find insulting or demeaning. You have to know the rules in order to play the game. You have to assess what is a variable and what's not. If actors would take the time to put themselves in the shoes of the people they're dealing with, they would quickly figure out what's reasonable and what's not.*

*It's not like there's some arbitrary system where God touches this person and says, "You get to audition," and you (the untouched person) sit there wondering why God didn't smile at you.*

*If you think about a director casting a play and you understand what he will have to do to cast it as well as possible, at least you know what you're up against. It's not some vague, amorphous obstacle. It's not fair but at least it makes sense.*

*What you know is never as bad as your imagination. If you know what you're up against, it can be difficult, but at least it's concrete. What you don't know, your imagination turns into "Everyone in the business knows I shouldn't be doing this. I'm just not talented." It's like conspiracy theories.*

*Careers are like pyramids. You have to build a very solid base. It takes a long time to do it and then you work your way up. No single decision makes or breaks a career. I don't think actors are ever in a position where it's the fork in the road or the road not taken and it's "Okay, your career is now irrevocably on this course. Too bad, you could have had that."*

*If an actor looks at another person's career and says, "I don't want that," he doesn't have to have it. People do what they want to do. It's like people who are on soaps for twenty years. Well, it's a pretty darn good job, pays you a lot of money and if you're really happy, great. But if you're an actor who doesn't want to do that, you won't. Nobody makes you sign a contract. Again. And again. And again.*

*Every decision you make is a risk because it's all collaborative and it can all stink. Every play at The Public is not a good play. Every television series isn't a piece of junk. People make decisions based on what price they want to pay, because there is a price.*

*If you don't want to work in television, there's a price. If you want to work in television, there's a price. If you want to work in New York in theater, there's a price. You have to decide if that's worth it and it's an individual decision, not a moral choice. It shouldn't be something you have to justify to anybody but yourself.*

*It's not about proving to your friends that you're an artist. It's about what's important to you at that moment. People can do two years on a soap and that can give them enough money to do five years of theater. And that's pretty important. It depends on why you're doing it and what you're looking to get out of it, what is the big picture. And nobody knows it but you.*

Tim Angle/Don Buchwald & Associates, Inc.

I found New York agent Beverly Anderson to be candid, entertaining and helpful. When I asked for her best advice, she thought for a moment, fixed me square in the eye and said:

✦ *Be smart. Don't be naive. If you're not smart, it doesn't make any difference how much talent you have or how beautiful you are. You're dead. In all my experience of twenty-nine years, all the people that I can sit here and say, "They made it," they did not make it because they were the most talented or the most beautiful or even the best organized or the most driven.*

*They made it because they were basically extremely smart human beings. It has nothing to do with the best looks and the best talents, the best voice or the best tap dancing ability. It's being smart. Donna Mills is smart. Alan Alda is smart. Johnny Carson is smart. Barbara Walters is smart. They made it because they're smart not because of talent. Talent is just automatic in this business.*

*Who's to say that Barbra Streisand has the best voice in the world? I mean, let's face it, she sings well and has gorgeous styling and she makes a great sound, but who's to say if she has the best voice? I think the one ingredient that counts the most in this business is smarts. You could be talented and be sucked in by some agent who signs you up and never sends you out and you sit there for five years and say, "Well, I thought they were going to get me a job." Is that smart?*

*To be smart is the best thing. Talent is like a dime a dozen out the window.*
Beverly Anderson/Beverly Anderson New York

We're back to Buckminster Fuller. Them that has gets; them that don't, won't. It's up to you and your smarts. Will you make positive choices? Will you refuse to be depressed and take positive action?

## Wrap Up

*Analyze*

✓ how the business works
✓ the marketplace
✓ who gets hired
✓ who hires and why
✓ what do they have that you don't have?
✓ which actor is getting your parts?
✓ your strengths
✓ your weaknesses

*Important*

✓ focus on the process not the goal
✓ study
✓ nourish your talent
✓ be organized
✓ acquire business skills
✓ be smart

# ⚔ 6 ⚔
# Research and Follow-Through

Unfortunately, agents do not send out a resume in search of clients. Even if they are looking for clients (and they are all looking for the client who will make them wealthy and powerful beyond their dreams), agents don't send out a list of their training, accomplishments and/or a personality profile.

Beyond their list of clients (which is not, by the way, posted on their door), there is no obvious key to their worth; therefore, it is up to you to conduct an investigation of your possible business partners.

You have taken your first step. You bought this book. I have already done lots of research for you by interviewing agents, asking about their background, looking at their client lists and engaging in conversations with anyone and everyone in the business who might have something informed to say about theatrical agents. I've also read everything that I could get my hands on regarding agents and the way the business is conducted.

You should begin to have agent-conversations with every actor you come in contact with. If you are just beginning in the business and your actor contacts are limited to your peers, they will probably be just as uninformed as you. Never mind, ask anyway. You never know where information lurks.

As I said in the Introduction, read this entire book before you make any judgments about your readiness to attract an agent or about what kind of agent you seek. Your understanding of various bits of information is enhanced by an informed overview, so make sure you have one. Analyze how the business really works. What do really have a right to expect of an agent? What does your agent have a right to expect of you?

Prepare yourself as an artist and as a business person so that you can operate on the level to which you aspire. If your work and presentation are slipshod, what kind of agent is going to want you?

## Get On With It

After you've digested this book once, read the agent listing section of the book again taking notes. You'll learn their lineage, education, credits (clients), the size of their list and get some idea of their style.

If there is someone that interests you, check the index to see if the agent is quoted elsewhere in the book. Those quotes can give you further clues as to how the agent conducts business, views the world, and how compatible you might feel with him.

If you read his dossier and don't recognize any of the clients' names, don't just assume the actors don't have careers. Perhaps the client listed is a respected working actor whose name you don't happen to know.

Ask questions. Perhaps it's an up-and-coming actor whose work you have not seen. If all the agent has is stars and you are just beginning, that means this agent is too far along for you.

If the agent has bright-looking actors whom you have never heard of, he is building his list. If you fit that category of client, perhaps you and the agent can build credibility together. It's worth a shot.

When you have a list of agents you want to research, visit the Margaret Herrick Library at 333 South La Cienega, south of Wilshire in Beverly Hills. Spend an afternoon leafing through the *The Academy Players Directory* and raise your agent-consciousness, viewing the names and faces of clients of various agents.

Look for those agents you have chosen. See who their clients are. You'll see famous actors with famous agents, but also some well-known clients represented by agents you might not have considered like Mitchell K. Stubbs or IFA.

If you are an actor of stature, you will be looking for an agent that lists some of your peers. Some fine agencies have opened in the last two or three years whose names may not be as well-known as older agencies, but who nonetheless are quite important. Usually they are agencies started by agents who interned at larger offices, learned the business, groomed some clients and left the agency (frequently with some of the agency's choicest clients).

If you are a member of SAG, go to their offices and check out the current client list of any agent you are considering. There is a code delineating theatrical or commercial representation. Make sure you are checking the theatrical list if that is the representation you are seeking. Also note the size of the list.

If you have access to both the SAG Agency Lists and *The Academy Players Directory*, check both. SAG's list will give you a quick overview of the size of the list and names of the players. Names of actors might not be enough, faces might be more revealing, so *APD* is invaluable.

Because the *APD* doesn't have the actors listed by agent, it's difficult to get as focused a picture of a particular agency.

As you look at these lists, you are having fantasies about the large conglomerate agencies, I know. Be sure to check out the following chapter before you form your final opinion. You'll see that there are pros and cons to star representation at various levels of one's career.

Remember, while you are salivating, that most stars come to star agencies after a struggling independent agent helped the actor achieve enough stature and access of his own that the conglomerate agent felt his interest was financially justified.

William Morris, ICM, CAA, APA, UTA and Endeavor do not offer career building services. These large corporations are there to cash in on the profits. Although it is true that star representation enhances some careers, it is not true in all cases.

In making agent selections, be sure you are seeking an agent you have the credits to attract. Nicole Kidman's agent is probably not going to be interested.

Make sure other clients on the agent's list are your peers. It's all very well and good to think big, but, remember, you must walk before you can run.

Don't expect an agent who has spent years building his credibility to be interested in someone who just got off the bus. Remember, you must effectively agent yourself until you are at a point that a credible agent will give you a hearing.

I met a young actor when he had just arrived in town. Because he had lots of chutzpah, he was able to hustle a meeting with an agent far above him in stature. The agent asked if there was an audition tape available. Although he had none, the actor said his tape was in New York and that he would send for it.

He kept putting the agent off and finally volunteered to do a scene in the agent's office. He ended up getting signed. After he was signed, he confessed there was no tape.

A year, few interviews, and no jobs later, the actor angrily left the agent. Interestingly, it had not occurred to the actor that he was just not ready for representation on that level.

I'm sure he will manage to waste even more time before it occurs to him to spend the energy studying and doing plays instead of squandering himself trying to trick an inappropriate agent into signing him.

## Agent Looking Season

There are better and worse times of the year to call agents in Los Angeles. The first of January to the first of May is pilot season and any agent with entrée is frantic either all the time or sporadically enough to make it difficult for them to focus on new clients. Many agents take a much needed vacation around the first of May to recuperate.

By the first of June, they are back in their offices waiting for the season to begin and are more amenable to being approached. Many of them weed out their lists at this time. Actors who were marginal were kept on during pilot season in the hopes they could be sold, but now the sale is over and those who haven't performed well are reevaluated.

It's during this Spring housecleaning season that agents are most accessible. Many set aside time just for meeting prospective new clients. Mid-week and mid-afternoon are the best times to contact them.

One of the assistants in my own agent's office called and asked me to please tell actors everywhere, whether you are a client or looking for an agent, "Don't call an agent before noon." Up until that time, most agencies are in chaos as agents rush to read "The Breakdown" and submit pictures and resumes.

Unless you are calling to cancel or change an appointment for that day, do yourself a favor and wait until after the agents have had a time to collect themselves. They will be able to hear you better and will definitely be happier to speak with you.

### Who Do You Love?

As you begin to have some idea of which agents appeal to you, start making a list. Even if you know you are only interested in Martin Gage or Marc Chancer, target five names. You can't make an intelligent choice unless you have something to compare. You don't know that you like Agent A best unless you have seen Agent B and Agent C.

✦ *Find a way to get your work seen. Actors just starting out need to be their own first agent. Somebody's got to see you. Some casting directors have offices that are accessible and once one casting director falls in love with you and keeps bringing you in, you're on your way.*
Mitchell K. Stubbs/Mitchell K. Stubbs

Now's the time to ask advice from any casting directors with whom you have formed relationships. A casting director who has hired you will probably be pleased that you asked his opinion. Tell him you are agent shopping and that you would like to run a few names by him.

Also ask for any names he might like to add to your list. Listen to the casting director's opinion but remember, he has a far different relationship with an agent than you will have. Make your own decision.

At this point your research is based on style, stature, access, size of list, word of mouth and fantasy. Now, with research complete and a list in hand, your next goal is to get a meeting.

## Getting a Meeting

The absolutely best way to contact anyone is through a referral. If you know someone on the agent's list who would act as a go-between, this is good.

If a casting director whose advice you have sought offers to call, this is better. Don't put the casting director on the spot by asking. If you ask for advice about agents and he feels comfortable recommending you, he will suggest it. If he doesn't, be thankful for the advice. If you are creative and have been doing your homework, you will be able to find someone who knows someone.

✦ *If an actor can't figure out how to get a referral to see an agent, then maybe he isn't ready to seek representation.*
Chris Barrett/Metropolitan

Winning an Oscar, a Tony, or an Emmy is a great door opener. What else?

If you are Young and Beautiful, just drop your picture off in person looking as Y&B as possible. It is sad (for the rest of us) but true, that if you are really Y&B and can speak at all, few will require that you do much more. May as well cash in on it.

If you are smart, you will study while cashing in since Y&B doesn't linger long and you may want to work in those grey years of your thirties and beyond.

You're not Y&B? Me neither. So this is what I suggest. If you are just starting in the business or you don't have any strong credits, concentrate on classes, showcases and writing notes to casting directors asking for meetings. It's a 9-to-5 job every day. Studying, showing, meeting.

If you have graduated from one of the league schools and/or have some decent credits and/or an audition tape and have a clear idea how you should be marketed, it's time to begin.

I always think it's best to send a letter that precedes a picture and resume by a couple of days. Letters get read; pictures and resumes tend to sit on the as-soon-as-I-get-to-it stack.

Make sure your letter is typed or beautifully written on good, heavy, expensive stationery. That makes an unconscious impression even before they open the envelope. State that you are interested in representation. Say that you are impressed with the agent's client list (make sure you know who is on it) and that your credits compare favorably. If you have a particularly impressive credit, mention it.

I've been asked to provide an example. Please don't use it verbatim or every agent in town will get identical letters. This is just to stimulate your thinking.

Dear Mary Smith:
I've just moved to Los Angeles from Timbuktu. Although I am new to town, I have a few credits. I worked two jobs through John Casting Director, *Hello Everyone* and *It Pays to Study*. The parts were small, but it was repeat business and I'm compiling an audition tape. It's not long, but it's a chance to see me on film.

I'm dropping (or mailing) my picture and resume by your office on Thursday. I'll call on Friday to see if you have a few minutes. I'm looking forward to meeting you.
Sincerely,
Hopeful Actor

If you've just graduated from one of the league schools, mention this and some roles that you have played. Make sure your picture and resume tell the truth and arrive when you promised them.

If your letter has piqued interest, your picture will be opened immediately. Make sure your letter doesn't get there on a Monday. Most actors send their pictures out over the weekend and they all come in on Monday and Tuesday. If you send yours on Wednesday and it comes on a Friday, yours might be the only one on the agent's desk.

When you call, be dynamic and be brief. Be a person the agent wants to talk to. If he doesn't want a meeting, get over the disappointment and get on to the next agent on your list.

If you want an agent on a higher level who doesn't seem interested, don't be deterred; there are many other agents on that level. If they all turn you down, then perhaps you are not as far along as you think.

Maybe you need to do more work on yourself until you are ready for those agents. If you feel you really must have representation at this time, you may need to pursue an agent on a lower level. Try to set up meetings with at least three agents and plan all the details of the meeting.

For starters, be on time and look terrific. This is a job interview, after all. Choose clothing that makes you feel good and look successful and that suggests you take pride in yourself. Bright colors not only make people remember you, but they usually make you feel good, too. Remember, in today's world, packaging is at least as important as content.

◆ *When an actor comes to interview with me in flip flops and being all rowdy, how do I know he won't go into an audition with producers looking and acting the same way? You should be camera ready when you go to see agents and producers.*
Sheba Williams/Agency West Entertainment

Go in and act like yourself. Be natural and forthright. Don't bad-mouth any other agents. If you are leaving another agent, don't get into details about why you are leaving. If he asks, just say it wasn't working out. Agents are all members of the same fraternity. Unless this agent is stealing you away from someone else, he will be at least a little anxious about why you are leaving. If you criticize another agent, the agent is wondering, subconsciously at least, when you will reject him.

In general, don't talk too much. Give yourself a chance to get comfortable. Adjust to the environment. Notice the surroundings. Comment on them. Talk about the weather. Talk about the stock market, the basketball game, or the last film you saw. That's a great topic. It gives you each a chance to check out the other's taste.

Don't just agree with him. Say what you thought. If you hated it, be tactful, just say it just didn't work for you. Remember, this is a first date. You are both trying to figure out if you are interested in each other.

If you've seen one of his clients in something and liked it, say so. Don't be afraid to ask questions, but use common sense. Phrase questions in a positive vein. Discuss casting directors that you know and have worked for. Ask what casting directors the office has ties with. Tell the agent what your plans are. Mention what kind of roles that you feel you are ready for and that you feel you have the credits to support. Ask what he thinks. Are you on the same wavelength? Don't just send out, make sure you are also receiving.

◆ *Tell the agent your strengths and weaknesses. Ask the agents about his.*
Buzz Halliday/Buzz Halliday and Associates

Find out how the office works. If you are being interviewed by the owner and there are other agents, ask the owner if he will be representing you personally. Many owners are "closers" who dazzle the talent into signing, but are not actively involved in agenting.

Find out office policy about returning phone calls. Are you welcome to call? Does the agent want feedback after each audition? What's the protocol for dropping by? Will they consistently view your work? Will they consult with you before turning down work? Explore your feelings about these issues before the meeting.

If you need to be able to speak to your agent regularly, now's the time to talk about it. Does the office have a policy of regularly requesting audition material for their actors at least a day in advance of the audition? Let him know what you require to be at your best. If these conversations turn the agent off, better to find out now. This is the time to assess the chemistry between you.

✦ *First meet with them. See what the rapport is. The most important thing is check around. Call casting friends. Go to SAG. Look at the client list. See who they handle. How many. I always tell people to check me out. I'd rather somebody do that.*
Eric Klass/The Eric Klass Agency

During the meetings, be alert for those intangible signs that tell you about a person. Note how he treats his employees. Whether he really listens. Body language. How he is with people on the phone. If he's interested in you, he'll probably show off a little. Resist the temptation to reciprocate. Keep checking for how you feel when he's speaking to you. What's the subtext?

Craig Wyckoff of Epstein/Wyckoff/Corsa/Ross & Associates says actors rarely ask questions. He suggests asking what roles the agent might cast you in, not just physically, but whether he sees you as a lead, second lead, day player, etc. The agent may ask the actor the same question and the actor should have a clear, realistic answer.

The agent will want to know the casting directors with whom you have relationships. Make sure this information is at your fingertips so that you can converse easily and intelligently. Even if your specialty is playing dumb blondes (of either sex), your agent will feel more comfortable about making a commitment to a person who is going to be an informed business partner.

✦ *Morgan Fairchild came in early in her career. Out of the hundreds and hundreds of actresses and actors that I have seen and had appointments with, I've never been literally interviewed by an actress, "Okay, What have you done? Where are you going?"*

*Incredible. She interviewed me. Yes, I was turned off to a degree but, I was so impressed by her brilliant mind and her smarts that I thought to myself, gal, even without me, you're going to go very far. She came in here and she knew where she was going and she interviewed me and I thought, "that's fantastic."*
Beverly Anderson/Beverly Anderson Agency

Now that you have met the agent; given focus to him and his accomplishments, his office and personnel; impressed him with your punctuality, straightforwardness, drive, resume, appearance and grasp of the business and your place within it, it is time for you to end the meeting.

Make it clear that you are having such a good time you could stay all day, but you realize that he is busy and that you in fact have a voice lesson (dialect coach, dance class, whatever) and must be on your way.

Suggest that you both think about the meeting for a day or two and set a definite time for when you will get back to him or vice versa. If he asks if you are meeting other agents, be truthful. If he's last on your list, mention that you need to go home and digest all the information.

He will probably have to have a meeting with his staff before making a decision. Let him know you were pleased with the meeting. Even if it was not your finest moment or his be gracious. After all, you both did your best.

My advice is to hurry home and write down all your feelings about the meeting and put them away for twenty-four hours. Then write your feelings down again and compare them. When I was interviewing agents for this book, I wanted to sign with most of them on the spot. They are salesmen and they were all charming. The next day I was more circumspect. By then, the hyperbole seemed to have drifted out of my head and I was able to hear more clearly what had gone on.

If the agent elects to call you and doesn't, leave it. There are others on your list. If he forgot you, do you want him as your agent? If he is rejecting you, don't insist he do it to your face.

Remember, you are choosing an agent. The qualities you look for in a pal are not necessarily the qualities you desire in an agent.

## Making the Decision

Mike Nichols gave an opening night speech to his players: *"Just go out there and have a good time. Don't let it worry you that the "The New York Times" is out there, every important media person in the world is watching you, that we've worked for days and weeks and months on this production, that the investors are going to lose their houses if it doesn't go well, that the writer will commit suicide and that it will be the end of your careers if you make one misstep. Just go out there and have a good time."*

I think that's the way many of us feel about choosing an agent. When I was in New York, I freelanced long past decision time because I felt this momentous verdict would have irrevocable consequences on my career. Make a decision. If you are wrong, you can change. No decision means standing still.

# Wrap Up

### Research

✓ peruse *The Los Angeles Agent Book*
✓ check SAG Agent/Client Lists
✓ study the *Academy Players Directory*
✓ consult casting directors
✓ don't underestimate word of mouth
✓ have face-to-face meetings

### Tools to Set Up Meetings

✓ referrals
✓ good credits
✓ good reviews
✓ awards
✓ beauty
✓ youth
✓ audition tapes
✓ perfect letter
✓ picture & credible resume
✓ creativity
✓ energy

### The Meeting

✓ be punctual
✓ be smart
✓ be sure to dress well
✓ be focused
✓ know what you want
✓ ask for what you want
✓ end the meeting
✓ set up definite time for follow-up

# 7
# Conglomerate Agents to the Stars

So we're all dreaming of advancing confidently to William Morris and CAA, right? Julia chose ICM, should you? Are star agencies the goal? Where does power lie?

◆ *The new power elite, the people who really decide what projects get made and at what price, consists increasingly of the handlers and gatekeepers of top actors and filmmakers. In short, the power of the studio exec is dwindling, even though studios hold the purse strings and thus technically control the game. When I'm putting together a project, the only 'yes' I need is from one of seven or eight agents. If I get their support I know I can set up a deal anywhere in town, asserts one of the town's top drawer directors.*
Judy Brennan & Andy Marx, *Daily Variety*[6]

The question of whether the large star-level conglomerate agency is the best place to be is an endless debate. Stars large and small leave the large conglomerate agencies daily looking for more personal attention and most independent prestigious agencies have at least one star in residence.

As in all other important decisions (who to marry, which doctor or lawyer to choose, whether or not to have elective surgery, etc.), you can only collect data and using your research and instincts, make a decision.

CAA, ICM, William Morris, UTA, APA, and Endeavor have the most information and the best likelihood (if they want to) of getting you in for meetings, auditions and ultimately jobs depending on where you are in your career.

I was lucky enough to interview Steve Tellez just as he was leaving APA to join CAA. As an agent who has trekked from a prestigious, small, independent agency (Fred Amsel) to CAA, his remarks are the most articulate I've encountered regarding the part the agency plays in our identity. I asked Steve the biggest difference he has discerned during his journey.

◆ *The level of buyers that you deal with. Two and three man operations can be very effective for the people they represent. I think the danger is when you get into quantity vs. quality situation. Too many clients for too few agents. You can't possibly cover the whole town and/or list that way.*

*There are respect levels in the industry that benefit the agent and the client. Fred (Amsel) was respected. He was known as having good actors and for being effective with casting directors especially on the television side. When I went with David (Shapira), it did elevate me and my clients because David was getting into packaging and more into writers and trying to become a full service operation as opposed to just theatrical.*

*That raises your level in the industry and it also raises your expertise. It also elevates the clients. It's information flow. You get more information when you are talking to producers and executives at the studios to try and package. It gives you more access. Shapira had more clients that were packagable or that would drive a project. He turned careers around. Amsel was more on an individual basis. Shapira was more a packaging situation. When you represent directors and writers, that gives access. When you start representing other elements in addition to actors, it broadens your base.*

*From there to here (APA),\* it opened up the feature side. I had done features before, but now I was doing them on a different level. Full service makes a big difference not only to the agent, but to the client. Full service literary, producers, writers, directors, books, plays, actors, personal appearance, music artists, soundtracks, comics, comediennes, concerts, college tours, a New York office (not an affiliation but your own), that just gives more opportunity for cross-over for the client who wants to direct or write. There are more opportunities of every kind.*

Steve Tellez/CAA

\*Since this interview, Tellez has joined CAA

## Distinguished Independent Agents

What about the agent who helped make it happen for you? Not every star is at CAA, ICM, William Morris, UTA or APA. Jack Nicholson is still with Sandy Bresler.

What about actors who leave the agent who engineered the big break for the big conglomerate agencies? I met a well known actress at a party. She works a lot, mostly in films. Lately, she had been doing theater, something not particularly interesting to conglomerate agencies in Los Angeles as there is little money involved. This actress got her break while she was at a prestigious mid-level agency and moved to ICM. Now she's back at her old agency: "It's too much trouble to keep up with all those agents. They won't all come see your work. Who needs it?" Would she return to the big conglomerate if she got hot?

"I was hot when I was at the smaller agency. My name was on everybody's list anyway. I didn't need to have a big office behind me. The only way I'd go back to the big agency would be with a very strong manager who could call and keep up with all those agents."

Scott Manners' plea makes a great deal of sense.

✦ *Respect effort. If I don't take care of you on that level, then leave me.*
Scott Manners/Stone Manners Talent Agency

Gene Parseghian has now departed William Morris, but was an independent agent who climbed the ladder with his clients. He and his partners formed their own mini-conglomerate, Triad, which was so distinguished, it was acquired by William Morris.

✦ *We had a number of actors who were playing significant roles in features at that point, to whom the packaging arguments of the large agencies were suddenly making sense and we had to be able to provide a wider range of services for our clients. I think what pleased me about each of these steps was that I always paralleled the growth of the clients. It doesn't work if the client takes off and the agent isn't growing as well. I'm still learning stuff. So are my clients. You've got to grow with them.*
Gene Parseghian

## Power, Information, So What?

So the conglomerates have more power and information. Will they use it to help you? Do power and information compensate for lack of personal attention?

The power of the large agencies comes from the actors. When you have Cameron Diaz or George Clooney and hundreds of other big names on your list, you have the attention of the buyers. The Catch 22 is, if you are Cameron or George, you really don't need those agencies because you are the power and if you're not Cameron or George, you are mainly filler.

I heard a story about a big star who was in the final stages of closing a deal on a big movie. A bigger star at the same agency (who gets even more money) decided he was interested in the project. The original plans were immediately shelved and the bigger star did the movie. The agency made a better deal for themselves. No matter who handles you, there is a bigger star someplace. It just might be nicer if that bigger star were not at your agency, serviced by someone who knows your price, your projects and has the ability to pull such a switch.

John Kimble traveled the same route at Gene Parseghian. Although no longer an agent, while at William Morris he voiced his support for a simpler style of representation.

✦ *When I was in a one-room office on 57th Street in New York, I was as powerful as anyone if I believed in someone. I could get them in anyplace, because I wouldn't take no for an answer. I believe if someone works out of a phone booth on Hollywood and Vine, if they believe in you, they can get you in as quickly as the strongest agent in town.*
John Kimble

I don't actually believe that, but I get John's point. Margie Clark was an agent and then a casting director. Her perspective is worthwhile.

✦ *I think it's wrong for any actor to think, "Well, I'm going with William Morris or CAA or ICM, and to think that that alone will make a difference." I think they are all very fine agencies, but it's more important to consider who your responsible agent is. Being with the tiniest agent who will pick up the phone and call twenty people to find out what's going on is preferable to being with the most prestigious agent who does nothing. You need the one agent who says to you, "I think you are talented. I want to help you." No matter where you are, large or small agency, you need that one person who will work for you.*
Margie Clark

Chris Knight was a successful actor on *The Brady Bunch* before becoming a casting director. Chris isn't casting anymore either, but his insight made an impression on me.

✦ *When I was an actor, I didn't pay much attention to stature; to the fact that the kind of appointments that the agent is going to get you out on is completely related to the power and stature of that agency. I wouldn't ignore that information today, as I once did. I used to think, "Oh, it doesn't matter how small they are. If they're a hard worker and you get along with them, they'll do just fine."*

*I now realize that some agents are limited and they are never going to have stature, for God knows what reason. I used to think that I would always stay with the same agent out of loyalty. I now realize that that could hurt me in the long run.*
Chris Knight

There are some prestigious independent agencies who have had a shot at the big time and chose to go back to a more intimate way of doing business. Sandy Bresler, a very successful, distinguished agent (Jack Nicholson and Randy Quaid are clients) left William Morris to form The Artists Agency. When it got too big for him, he left and started his own smaller office again. Of course, he took his own glittering client list with him.

I know another agent who has groomed several stars. As those stars became more and more important and demanded more and more time, the agent just wasn't interested in assuming those new responsibilities. I don't think he even minded when the actors went to William Morris or ICM. It just wasn't the type of service that he wanted to provide.

When Gene Parseghian was still at William Morris, he confessed to me that there are days he wished he still had a small office with three or four people and twenty clients.

I kept hearing agents saying over and over, "I got this person started. Just when it was all paying off, CAA or ICM (or whoever) came with the limos, the flowers. The actors left. Why?"

I understand the agents' feelings. They did do the developmental work. They introduced the actor to their contacts. They held the actor's hand when he was frightened and/or depressed.

What they don't understand is that actors dream of CAA or ICM as they dream of winning an Oscar. "CAA wants me. I'm nominated for an Academy Award. I'm validated!"

Not everyone wants/needs that validation, however, and it's expensive. Big conglomerates do introduce you at a higher level as Steve Tellez points out, but they are also going to be less impressed with you. They don't know you as well. And they don't call them corporations for nothing; this is business.

The current climate finds the conglomerates courting those actors fortunate enough to land lucrative series destined to stay on the air. Although the agent who booked the show in the first place still gets commission on the job he booked for the first five years, after that period of time, when the hit series comes up for lucrative renegotiation and those million dollar salaries are passed out, the original agent is cut out of the deal.

The powerful conglomerate agent does negotiate that big salary for the actor, but the roots of the deal have been set by the original agent setting the wheels in motion for the actor to score the job at all.

Leaving the agent out in the cold guarantees that the supply of independent agents will continue to dwindle.

An actor in this position has the power to negotiate with the new agent, demanding that the old agent be cut in for 2½ or even 5% of the new contract. If the conglomerate agent balks at that, one has to wonder if he really feels he will be able to get the actor work beyond the series or is just there to cash in on the current job.

When you slip from favor (and everyone does), it's unlikely the corporation will be looking for ways to revive and resuscitate your career. It is there to cash in on your success, not create it or revive it.

The quintessential story illustrating this painful point concerns Burt Reynolds. Burt has had a long and fluctuating career. He was on the top ten list of bankable actors for many years and as that period drew to a close, he was interviewed by *Playboy Magazine* where he discussed the fact he was no longer able to get studio heads or his important agents on the phone. "I thought they liked me," said the disappointed Reynolds.

## So, Who's the King?

✦ *Twenty-five years ago, a clutch of agents left the William Morris Agency to form CAA, forever changing the way tenpercenteries conduct business. Many are speculating that Jim Wiatt's first year at William Morris may have the same impact.*

*William Morris's new prexy and co-CEO is turning things upside-down. After twenty-two methodical years at ICM, Wiatt quickly pulled the plug on William Morris' costly London office, severely curtailed its NY motion picture staff and, most controversially, began getting rid of senior agents with older clients.*

Dan Cox and Claude Brodesser, *Variety*[7]

Until recently, ICM was considered on both coasts to be far and ahead of William Morris, which has gone through some lean times over the recent past as top Los Angeles agents Toni Howard, Elaine Goldsmith and Risa Shapiro defected to ICM in 1992 because women agents at William Morris were not promoted.

But in 1999, William Morris managed to lure ICM co-chief Jim Wiatt as their president and co-CEO. When that happened, many star agents were not far behind, trailing with them their impressive client lists.

Now that CAA has moved to New York and spirited away William

Morris' star theater agent George Lane, William Morris may not be the most coveted place for a theater actor to be. Julia Roberts just chose CAA over ICM when her agent left to head Roberts' production company. The landscape continues to change but basically, these huge corporations have their fingers in every pie around. If you are big enough to go to any one of them, you can't go wrong.

✦ *For decades, the Hollywood pecking order was clear. There was always one agency that was dominant, though the top dog shifted over the years: William Morris, MCA, CMA, then CAA.*

*But in a "Variety" survey, dozens of top studio execs and producers say something strange has emerged in the agency biz — parity. Newish tenpercenteries are hitting their stride as once indomitable firms hit some speed bumps, creating a competitive, nearly equalized environment.*

*"Variety" asked a substantial sampling of studio execs and producers, who spoke under condition of anonymity, to rate the five major agencies in five categories. Of those answers, there were only four "C" grades and one "A"; nearly everyone scored in the "B" range.*

*That's good news for most of the agencies, but may be unsettling for those agents who thought that their company was head and shoulders above the competition.*

*In a tight race, CAA came out slightly ahead, followed by Endeavor, UTA, William Morris and then ICM. Overall, on a four-point scale, only one-half point separated No. 1 and No. 5.*

Claudia Brodesser, *Variety*[8]

Supposedly CAA's strength is the best actor client list and the strongest management team while ICM's lies in its stars, directors and lucrative television packages. William Morris holds the keys to television and music.

Collect data and then use your research and instincts so you can make an informed decision based on what is important to you. When all is said and done, limos not withstanding, do you want a family member or do you want a corporation?

You'd probably be thrilled to be in the company of the names on the list of any large conglomerate agency. The casting people do say they call them first because the CD is looking for a star to front a project.

But Mitchell K. Stubbs; The Gage Group; Bauman, Redanty, & Shaul Agency; The Gersh Agency; and other independent agents, also have star clients and the access that goes with big names.

The *Los Angeles Times* on August 10, 1999 placed ICM at #2, but I'm not sure that order still holds.

◆ *# 1 Creative Artists Agency (CAA)*
*Agents: approximately 125; clients: about 1,200*
*Major strength: Best client list; strong management team.*

*#2 International Creative Management (ICM)*
*Agents: 124; clients: 3,400*
*Major strength: Big movie stars and directors and lucrative television packages.*

*#3 William Morris Agency (WMA)*
*Agents: 235 worldwide; clients: 4,000*
*Major strength: television and music.*
Claudia Eller and James Bates, *Los Angeles Times*[9]

In addition to Wiatt's departure, ICM faces another hurdle.

◆ *United Talent Agency, which has signed Harrison Ford, Kevin Costner, Madonna, Barry Levinson and Claire Danes, among others, is making a strong play to displace ICM in the top three.*
Dan Cox and Claude Brodesser, *Variety*[10]

Harrison Ford had not had an agent for many years, preferring to be repped by his former agent, now manager, Pat McQueeney, but he and McQueeney recently chose UTA in order to have access to the new young filmmakers.

◆ *"...It's likely that the agency with the best stable of writers and directors will land Ford. In a world of moviemaking as we know it today, studio films are only one part of the equation," McQueeney said. "There is another segment of the industry emerging and that is new writers/directors that are bringing a fresh vision and an exciting voice to their own material."*

*"While studio pictures have been and will always be very important to us, I want to take advantage of these opportunities for Harrison, and I feel the need for some help — some arms and legs, if you will — to cover that all-important and new avenue of film production."*
Michael Fleming, *Daily Variety*[11]

## Bigger is Better?

You'd probably be thrilled to be in the company of the names on any of the lists of any of the conglomerate agencies. Casting directors, looking for stars to front their projects, say they do call CAA, William Morris, UTA, ICM, APA and Endeavor first.

Since what agents have to sell is their access and information, the conglomerates obviously have more in-house facts than an enterprising one-man office. But if the big agency with lots of information isn't motivated to use it for you, you'd be much better off with a resourceful independent agent who is so enthusiastic about you that he uncovers just the information needed to get you a great part.

## Substance or Style?

Like many people, I am easily impressed by style, lots of scripts, limos, candy and flowers. All that stuff appeals to me. In a few days or weeks, I come to my senses and see past seduction to content, but it requires real strength of character.

When all is said and done, limos notwithstanding, you're going to have to make your decision based on what is important to you. Do you want a family member or do you want a corporation? My final vote is for a prestigious, successful, tasteful mid-size agency.

Of course, no one has plied me with limos and flowers either.

## Wrap Up

*Conglomerates*

✓ have more information
✓ command more power
✓ have access to more perks
✓ can package effectively
✓ may give less personal attention
✓ may provide less support in times of duress
✓ their advice is usually more corporate, less personal
✓ may well lose interest when you are not in demand

## *Distinguished Smaller Agencies Offer*

✓ possibilities of more respect
✓ more personal attention
✓ more empathy
✓ more freedom to experiment
✓ might be more motivated
✓ freedom for career fluctuations
✓ no limos
✓ no flowers
✓ no candy

# ⇥ 8 ⇤
# What Everybody Wants

Assuming you have your life somewhat balanced, an apartment, are in class, have some decent credits, are involved with other actors, and have analyzed the marketplace in a meaningful way, it's time to confront the next hurtle. What kind of agent will you want? What kind of relationship will you require?

If you could sign with any agent in town, who would you choose? Would CAA be right for you? Maybe TalentWorks? Could Buzz Halliday be the answer? Maybe Paradigm? These agencies are prestigious, but that doesn't necessarily mean acquiring A instead of B would be the best move. Before we start looking for the ultimate agent, consider what the agents are looking for.

## The Definitive Client

✦ *I want to know that they work and make a lot of money so I can support my office or that the potential to make money is there. I am one of the people who goes for talent, so I do take people who are not big money-makers, because I am impressed with talent.*
Martin Gage/The Gage Group

✦ *I'm looking for brilliant actors that I think can break. Who either have hopes of breaking or who come very close to breaking.*
Scott Manners/Stone Manners Talent Agency

✦ *I like clients that challenge me as an agent, as they are not easily typeable. I think they end up having more range. Although it may be more difficult sometimes to get them seen, it's more rewarding because it's more creative for you as an agent. If you look at my list, you would notice that I tend to choose actors who aren't very "straight on."*
Peter Strain/Peter Strain & Associates

✦ *I want an actor with the ability to get a job and pay me a commission.*
Beverly Anderson/Beverly Anderson New York

✦ *Real theatrical credits get my attention. There was an actor whose look I liked*

*and then when I saw the resume, I wanted to see him, but I just didn't have room on my list for someone like him. I have to be loyal to my long time wonderful clients.*
Mitchell K. Stubbs/Mitchell K. Stubbs

✦ *Someone who is talented, someone you believe and whose work moves you. Aside from that, the intangible part, there is clearly a physical attraction. I mean that whether they are character people or leading ladies or men. There is something that you see when you sit with them and talk with them, when you look at them, that you think is special in some way. It's interesting.*
Nina Pakula/Pakula/King & Associates

✦ *When I was an actor, I wish I had understood the value of focus. Actors come in and read for me all the time and haven't made a 100% clear choice. I want an actor who can make a choice. A bad choice is better than none. That shows me you have guts. You make a choice and you go with it.*
Nikkolas Rey/Carlos Alvarado Agency

✦ *I look for talent and something that is interesting to me that lights my passion to run to the phone and call ten people. And equally important, I don't want to want "it" for the client more than he wants it for himself. I provide scripts for my clients. It is frustrating to me if an actor has the access for a script and they don't take the time to read it. That doesn't happen twice.*
Mitchell K. Stubbs/Mitchell K. Stubbs

✦ *There are too many people in the industry to be lazy. When I look at a prospective client, I'm asking, "Do they have the passion? Are they taking the steps to prepare? Are they going to be persistent and hang in for the long haul?*
Sheba Williams/Agency West Entertainment

✦ *Reciprocity. I represent you as a talent, you represent my agency, so be professional and be prepared.*
Kim Dorr/Defining Artists Agency

✦ *I want people who are willing to start at the bottom and work their way up. I'm not interested in people who want to start at the top and work their way down.*
Sheba Williams/Agency West Entertainment

✦ *We are really into team effort. We consider ourselves career facilitators and we look for actors who are going to participate in facilitating their own careers. We are not good at working with people who just sit by the phone and wait for us to call. We like "hands on" and we like to know that actors are doing something too: studying, getting the pictures, actively pursuing their career. A lot of actors say they*

*are, but they aren't.*
Mimi Mayer/Angel City Talent

✦ *Training is the most important thing. I get very annoyed with people. Someone is attractive, so people say, "You should be in television, and then the actor just thinks that's going to just happen.*
J. Michael Bloom/Meridian Artists

✦ *Never quit training. The benefits of training and learning your craft will eventually always pay off.*
Joel Kleinman/Baier/Kleinman International

✦ *It is difficult to take someone who has spent their entire career doing regional and start a career for them at the age of forty-five. They are competing with people who have done so much more who have credits and the community already knows them.*

*It is a business and you look at it and say, "Is this person marketable?" "Do I respond?" "Are they talented?" "Can I go to the wall for them?" Your agent should be so passionate about you that in the crunch, they will go to the wall for you.*
Nina Pakula/Pakula/King & Associates.

New York agent Beverly Anderson told me a great story about meeting a prospective client and her reaction to her.

✦ *Sigourney Weaver asked to come in and meet me when she was with a client of mine in Ingrid Bergman's show, "The Constant Wife." She's almost six feet tall. I'm very tall myself and when I saw her, I thought, "God, honey, you're going to have a tough time in this business because you're so huge."*

*And she floated in and she had this big book with all her pictures from Bryn Mawr or Radcliffe of things she had done and she opened this book and she comes around and drapes herself over my shoulders from behind my chair and points to herself in these pictures. She was hovering over me. And I thought, "No matter what happens with me, this woman is going to make it." There was such determination and strength and self-confidence and positiveness.*
Beverly Anderson/Beverly Anderson/New York

Sigourney is the daughter of *The Today Show* producer, Pat Weaver. Surely, some of her strength came from having an awesome role model.

✦ *...From my father, I learned that business was not fair; I knew that things did not happen in any kind of logical, nice way. I didn't believe that people necessarily*

*got what they deserved. Knowing that the business was unfair helped me.*
Scott Poudfit, *Back Stage West*[12]

I asked agents what it is that attracts them to an actor and in a hundred different ways, they all said, "I don't know. You just like them. You just look at them. You just want to be their friend. They have an innate likeability." And then inevitably, they spoke the word; charisma. I decided to look that word up in the dictionary: "a spiritual gift or personal magic of leadership arousing a special popular enthusiasm."

The late Michael Kingman, a New York agent of great originality and verve, said it concisely, "An actor must have contagious emotions. Whatever he feels, the audience feels."

✦ *There's something going on there that doesn't fade into the woodwork. If you spark to that person, you hope that when you send them into a casting room to meet with producers and directors, that they will respond the way you respond. That's the only thing you can go by, your gut reaction to somebody. Some people have charisma.*

*When we first started our business, we met an actor who had just one little piece of independent film that no one was probably going to see, but he filled up the room, charmed us, attracted us in some way and we said, "We're going to take a shot."*
Nina Pakula/Pakula/King & Associates

There do seem to be people who appear blessed by the gods; you just can't take your eyes off them. I asked Nina if actors without that kind of charisma have a chance.

✦ *There are actors that you can't send for a meeting because they are too frightened, so they get shy and they hide. Even someone like that might have something really interesting to bring to a part.*
Nina Pakula/Pakula/King & Associates

So, although charisma would be nice, talent and a unique persona can fill that gap.

## What to Look for in an Agent

If agents are looking for actors who get the job and make money for them, I think the actor has to be primarily looking for an agent who can get him the audition. That sounds pretty simple, doesn't it? Maybe, but listen to one of my favorite New York producers, Marvin Starkman.

✦ *If the actor/agent relationship were based on getting auditions for everything, then the agent would have a right to say that you must get everything I send you out on. If you don't get everything I send you on, then we have a one-sided relationship.*

*Getting an audition isn't necessarily the most important thing either. Is he sending you on the right auditions? Does he see you accurately? Do you both have the same perception regarding the roles you are right for?*
Marvin Starkman

When I asked agents what qualities they would seek if they were choosing agents, they cited integrity, enthusiasm, taste, communication, client list, size and background.

✦ *Don't be wowed by the size of an agency and its client list. That is often the recipe for getting lost. If you find a person who is really enthusiastic and willing to work for you, treasure them, work with them and stick with them.*
Joel Kleinman/Baier/Kleinman International

✦ *An actor should look for the agent who sees the career path in the same way as the actor, who can visualize the roles the actor is right for. The key is passion. There are wonderful agents and wonderful actors and sometimes they are mismatched.*
Mitchell K. Stubbs/Mitchell K. Stubbs

✦ *Look for honesty, complete integrity, and someone who is passionate about selling you.*
Kim Dorr/Defining Artists Agency

Mark Litwak's penetrating book, *Reel Power,* is an excellent resource for information about the film and television businesses. Here's a little of what Mr. Litwak reports on what it takes to be an agent.

✦ *First, an agent must have the stamina to handle a heavy workload and be able to endure the frenetic pace in which business is conducted. "It's like working in the commodities pit," says William Morris agent-turned-manager Joan Hyler. "It's hectic," says agent Lisa Demberg, "because you can't do your job unless you're always on the phone, always talking to someone, or socializing with someone or trying to do business, or following up on the projects you've discussed."*

*"Great agents," says agent-turned-executive Stephanie Brody, "have enthusiasm and tireless energy. And they must be efficient. The agent is juggling thirty phone*

*calls a day. He has to send out material and follow up. You have to be extremely well-organized."*

*Second, agents must be able to cope with the vicissitudes of the business. "In a certain sense it's like 'Dialing for Dollars,'" says William Morris agent Bobbi Thompson. "Each call may be the big money. You never know. It's all a roulette wheel." Third, an agent must be an effective salesman. Fourth, agents must be able to discern talent.*

*Many top agents are very aggressive in their pursuit of deals, some would say ruthless. Says a former CAA agent, "In order to be an extraordinarily successful agent you can't have any qualms about lying, cheating, stealing and being totally into yourself."*

Mark Litwak, *Reel Power*[13]

I was particularly struck by what Joan Hyler said about agenting being like working in the commodities pit. Frequently there is no tangible reason why the commodities market goes up or down, just as there is frequently no tangible reason why one actor gets a job and the other one doesn't, or why one actor is singled out by the public and another one isn't. It really is "Dialing for Dollars."

✦ *Agenting is a demanding business that can burn out even the profession's toughest practitioners. Historically, many prominent agents have left the field at the top of their game, including [Jane] Sindell's own former bosses, CAA founders Michael Ovitz and Ron Meyer.*

Claudia Eller, *Los Angeles Times*[14]

An article in *The New York Times* featuring Jeff Berg, the chairman of ICM, made me think agents may have it worse even than actors. After all, if we get rejected fifty times a year, they surely get rejected hundreds of times more.

✦ *I'll tell you what I like about agents. I like the fact that agents look to make it happen. And a good agent can't take "no" and expect to support himself. Agents have to develop a kind of resistance to rejection. I think it makes you stronger and I think it makes you better.*

Bernard Weinraub, *The New York Times*[15]

## Ratio of Clients to Agents

Another important consideration in overall agent effectiveness is size. The number of clients is meaningless. What is important is the ratio of agents to actors. One person cannot effectively represent a hundred clients. That's like going to the store and buying everything you see. You can't possibly use everything, you're just taking it out of circulation.

Having an agent may feed your ego (I have an agent!) but it also takes you out of the marketplace. Better to wait until you have the credits to support getting an agent with more manpower, than to sign paper with someone who doesn't have the personnel to represent you effectively.

Many agents believe a good ratio is one agent to twenty or twenty-five clients. An agency with four agents can do well by a hundred or even a hundred and forty clients, but that really is the limit. Look closely at any lists that are extravagantly over this size. It's easy to get lost on a large list.

It's valuable to have stamina, taste, a short list and be a great salesman. Actually, I take those as a given for an agent. There are two other attributes, however we would all like to have in our agents.

## Access and Stature

The dictionary defines *access* as "ability to approach" or "admittance." Because the conglomerate agencies have so many stars on their lists, they have plenty of ability to approach. If the studios, networks and producers do not return those phone calls, they might find the agency retaliating by withholding their important stars.

Stature, on the other hand, is different entirely. That word is defined as "level of achievement." So, Kim Dorr and Martin Gage surely have more stature than some lowly agent at William Morris, but possibly not as much access.

There's also the question of style. An actor friend had a great agent whose liability was his penchant yelling at casting directors and the client. He was effective, but the client left just because he didn't want to be represented that way.

## Commercial Agents

Relationships with commercial agents are quite different than those with theatrical agents. Although this book is really focused on relationships with agents who submit actors for film and television, I would like to focus on one particular aspect of the commercial agent/actor relationship that can be related to theatrical representation.

Not all agents are franchised (have contractual agreements) with all the unions or even have every agreement with every union. An agent may have an agreement for commercials or theatrical or both.

When you sign, you must pay attention to what specific union agreements you sign. Because commercials are so lucrative (and theater is not), some agents require your name on the dotted line on a commercial contract before they will submit you theatrically, particularly in New York.

If that is the deal someone offers you, be wary. If they had confidence in their ability to get you work in the theatrical venue, they would not require commercial participation.

Many actors who become successful in commercials find it difficult to cross over into film or television and sign joint agreements only to find that they are never submitted with the agency's theatrical clients.

## Commercial vs. Theatrical Success

Frequently, commercial progress comes swiftly and the actor finds he hasn't had time to build the same credibility on the theatrical level as he has commercially. He doesn't realize that the agent does not feel comfortable sending him on theatrical calls because of the disparity between his theatrical and commercial resume.

Until the actor addresses this disparity, signing across the board is not a good business decision. There are many reasons, not the least of which is the contractual commitment.

Paragraph 6 of the old SAG/ATA agreement allowed either the actor or the agent to terminate the contract if the actor has not worked for more than a certain number of ninety-one days within a prescribed time period by sending a letter of termination. The actor could void his contract with an agent simply by sending a letter to the agent plus copies to all unions advising them of Paragraph 6.

Since the defeat of a referendum to change the agreement with the Association of Talent Agents (ATA) and SAG regarding proposals allowing agents to produce as well as share ownership with advertising agencies, there is actually no formal agreement between SAG and ATA members. Many agents are honoring the old agreement until a new one is agreed upon but many are asking their clients to sign a new General Services Contract that utilizes all the proposals the agents were asking in the referendum which changes the time to four months. This is something you might want to negotiate if you are presented with such an agreement.

If you have been working commercially, but are not sent out theatrically, you might want to find a new theatrical agent. Since you have been making money in commercials, you cannot utilize Paragraph 6 to end your relationship assuming you are still working under the old contract which is undoubtedly no longer legally binding.

On the other hand, if you have a successful theatrical career going and no commercial representation and your theatrical agent has commercial credibility and wants to sign you, why not allow him to make some realistic money by taking your commercial calls?

Think carefully about your commitments when you sign. I know actors who got out of their contracts easily, but I also know actors who had to buy their way out.

People win commercials because they are blessed with the commercial look of the moment. It's easy to get cocky when you are making big commercial money and think you are farther along in your career than you are. What you really are is momentarily rich. Keep things in perspective. Thank God for the money and use it to take classes from the best teachers in town.

Cultivate theatrical casting directors on your own. Some are very accessible. When you've done a prestigious waiver show or managed to accumulate film through work via casting directors, theatrical agents will be more interested.

Be patient. It's all a process. The central issue is this: Who will provide the best opportunity for you to be gainfully employed in the business?

## Wrap Up

*The Ideal Client*

✓ has talent
✓ possesses contagious emotions
✓ displays a singular personality
✓ exhibits professionalism
✓ manifests self-knowledge
✓ shows drive
✓ is innately likeable
✓ maintains mental health

✓ is well trained
✓ boasts a good resume

*The Ideal Agent*

✓ is aggressive
✓ has stature
✓ has access
✓ is enthusiastic
✓ has the same goals for the actor
✓ has an optimum ratio of actors to agents
✓ has integrity
✓ has done the time

# ⚞ 9 ⚟
# Everybody's Responsibilities

Once you have made a decision to sign with an agent, there are many things to do. If you haven't notified your old agent, do so now. Do it in person and do it with style. Say you're sorry it didn't work out. Make it a point to speak to, and thank all your agents and everyone else in the office for their efforts, pick up your pictures, tapes, etc., and leave. Buy your agent a drink if that's appropriate. If the parting is amicable, maybe you'll want to send flowers. Send the necessary letters to the unions.

## Setting Up Shop

The next stop is your new partner's office to sign contracts and meet (and fix in your mind) all the auxiliary people who will be working for you. If there are too many to remember on a first meeting, make notes as soon as you leave the office as to who is who and where they sit. Until you become more familiar with them, you can consult the map before each subsequent visit.

Leave a supply of pictures, resumes, videocassettes (not too many, bringing more is always a good excuse for dropping by). Also leave lists for each agent of casting directors, producers, and directors with whom you have relationships. Alphabetize them if you ever want them used. Also leave lists of your quotes (how much you were paid for your last jobs in theater, film and television) plus information about billing. The more background you give your agent, the better he can represent you.

Now the real work begins. Remember the agent only gets 10% of the money. You can't really expect him to do 100% of the work.

## How Do We Really Get Work?

How many of us have resented our agents when we have been requested for a job and all the agent had to do was negotiate? In fact, if all our jobs were requests, would we just have a lawyer negotiate and do away with the agent altogether? Or is the support and feedback worth something? And as Lynn Moore Oliver said in Chapter Two, what about all the times he may send our picture and/or talk about us and not get an appointment so we never knew about it? And all the appointments we went on and didn't get the job? That costs him money that we frequently don't consider when we're whining about his shortcomings.

Maybe our whole thought process about agents is incorrect. In our hearts, we really think the agent is going to get us a job. Based upon my years in the business and my research, I finally know that the agent does not get me work, he gets me opportunities. I get my own work. By my work. Not only by my ability to function well as an actress, but also by my ability (or not) to be who I am.

The times I have not worked as steadily have been directly connected to my rise and fall as a person. I went into a terrible depression when my children left home. I willed myself to be up, but it was just a loss that I had to mourn, and while I was mourning, I was not particularly attractive to casting directors (or anybody else). You can change agents or mates or clothes sizes to try to make yourself feel better, but none of those things will change the fact that we all have to experience our lives in order to move through them.

These changes are reflected in our work and enrich us as performers. If one can remember to commit to experiencing the evolutionary process instead of fighting it, the pain dissipates much faster.

Although we can hope that agents are going to initiate work for us and introduce us to the casting directors, producers, directors, etc., what they are really going to do (over the span of a career) is negotiate for us, initiate meetings, arrange appointments when we are requested, and, hopefully, be supportive in our dark moments and help us retain our perspective in our bright moments. Notice I say moments. Neither state will last as long as it seems.

## 90%/10%

Although I've always been business oriented about my career, I never really thought about the ramifications of 90%/10% until I began doing the research for my books. When I finally signed with an agent in New York after successfully freelancing for a long time, I really did think that my hustling was over. Knowing what I know now, I realize all the ways I might have contributed to my career if I had agented more myself or at the very least paid closer attention.

✦ *I own 10% of the business. I don't work for the actor. I'm on the board of directors with him. My function is to maintain the stock and bring it up. That's the way I look at the function. I am there to maximize the positive and minimize the negative. Advise. Help. Guide.*
Scott Manners/Stone Manners Talent Agency

Since we own 90% of the stock and get 90% of the money, we really have to give up being cranky when we realize we are going to have to do 90% of the work.

✦ *Don't make the mistake of thinking that upon signing with an agent (particularly if it's your first agent), that it means your work is done. You need to do every bit, if not more, than the agent does, to open doors and create opportunities. You have to help your agent by being aggressive and getting yourself out in the film and theater community, getting your work known and your face seen. The worst thing that happens to people is that they get an agent and then they just sit home waiting for the phone to ring.*
Joel Kleinman/Baier/Kleinman International

I know actors who are angry when they have to tell their agents how to negotiate for them. They feel the agent is not doing his job if he has to be reminded to go for a particular kind of billing or per diem or whatever.

What's the problem here? We all bring whatever skills we have to every relationship and hope the result is synergistic. If you are better at negotiating, you're both lucky. If you're fearless you give your agent more power. If the agent has it all together and does everything perfect, great.

But it's your career and since you own 90% of the stock, you're the senior partner. It's up to you to know not only what the union minimums are, but also how to go about getting more money and who might be getting it. It's up to you to figure out the billing you want and to help the agent get it. Not only is it your responsibility, it's a way for you to be in control of your destiny in a business where it is too easy to feel tossed about by the whims of the gods.

# Other Things the Actor Can Do

✦ *I'm someone who encourages people to keep working. Not only on their craft, but just as a person. I think I've always been drawn to people who are, let's call them, "slightly neurotic about growth." I'm a growth-oriented person.*

*I like that people have interests other than just being insulated in the business, I guess that's because I think acting is about what you bring from your own life experience. You can see from the really great careers that they are people who have a lot going on.*

*I do have a couple of clients once in a while that I have to get out of the rut of sitting and waiting for the phone to ring. Some of them have to get into a class situation. They'll feel better in class; scene study, audition classes, working with coaches. They need to keep moving.*
Peter Strain/Peter Strain & Associates

✦ *The media has made pursuing an acting career seem easier than it is, so a lot of people come out here and they give it a shot and sometimes they succeed and most of the time, they don't. Some succeed for a little while and then, they don't and they go back home.*

*It's always hard getting in and staying in. The arts demand that you constantly study and constantly look out for the next job.*
Mimi Mayer/Angel City Talent

Put yourself in the agent's position. Every actor in town is trying to get his attention. The people who are already his clients and the people who are not. What would get your attention if you were the agent?

✦ *Continuing the process of what you were doing as a beginning actor. Being in acting class. I don't understand why all actors are not in class or doing plays at all times, no matter how successful they are. Doing play readings. Because that means more actors, more directors, more people to see you. Even if it is something bad, you will learn something from it.*

*We have all been in terrible productions, and we all came out of it with great friends. As Arthur Stortz said, "If you could be in a good play, with a good situation, a good director, and with good actors, you'll get it once in your lifetime, that's it. You'll get it once in your life. Don't expect it every time."*
Jim Weissenbach/Weissenbach Management

✦ *The actor's responsibility is to take whatever material he is given and make it come alive. If you want to be a writer, go write. That's another craft based on an art. You have chosen as a communicator to society to be an actor, not a writer, not a*

*saxophone player, but to be an actor.*
Scott Manners/Stone Manners Talent Agency

Your energies should be spent toward moving yourself into the system. Whether it's classes or a job, make sure you are dealing with people who are already working in some part of the business. Choose a teacher who works or has worked extensively, or a class where casting directors, directors and/or writers either sit in or are fellow students.

When you get a day job, if possible, get a showbiz related one. Sell tickets at the theater, or wait tables at Spago. There are endless possibilities. If you are going to succeed in this business you will need to use your research ability and your creative talents as extensively off stage as on.

✦ *Do your homework. Keep studying. Keep working out. Like an athlete does calisthenics, the actor should keep studying. Keep working. Learn who else is in the business. Watch TV. Go to the movies. What we do for a living is what the rest of the country does for dessert.*
Eric Klass/The Klass Agency

✦ *The first thing an actor should do when he gets into town is get involved with the acting community. Checking out acting classes and theater possibilities in town. Although Los Angeles seems less formal than New York, relative to the business, it is more formal. You cannot freelance or do some of the things you can do in New York. You need introductions. Whether it's through some form of theater or showcase or seeing what casting people are willing to meet new actors, whatever it takes, the actor must do the work.*
Nina Pakula/Pakula/King & Associates

✦ *I had one client who came in to me and said, "I need more interviews." I said, "No, you don't need more interviews, you need a class. When I send you out, no one calls me later and tells me you're brilliant. They call me back and tell me he's a good looking guy and he gave me an okay reading. You need to get to class and study and make yourself a good actor." He went to Diane Hardin's adult class and studied and now he's on an important series.*
Judy Savage/The Savage Agency

✦ *There are many things an actor can do and needs to do for himself; he should stay active in the theater, do independent films, get involved in a student's master thesis, do mailings to casting people and knock on doors in offices.*

*I'm opposed to the Showcases where actors pay to meet agents and do a scene for them, and yet, a client of mine has gotten three guest starring roles through this. He is quite different because he is Welsh and has an accent, so maybe that's it. If you are special, it might be an opportunity to be seen.*

*When I go to these Showcases, I am usually lulled to sleep by the mediocrity, but when someone special appears, they stand out and I say to myself, "This is why I am here tonight, to meet this actor."*
Joel Kleinman/Baier/Kleinman & Associates

Just because you get into the system, doesn't mean you will automatically remain there. Treat Williams and Mickey Rourke are only two of many actors who have been their own worst enemies. This first quote is from Treat Williams and the second from Mickey Rourke.

✦ *My career came to me very young and I assumed it would always be easy, as do most young actors, so I burned lots of bridges during a certain period. I didn't know then that word gets out if you're not sharp, and that this is a competitive and unforgiving industry driven by money.*
Kristine McKenna, *Los Angeles Times*[16]

✦ *I came out of the Actor's Studio and took acting very seriously. I wasn't educated to realize that filmmaking was business and politics as well as an art. I didn't listen when people told me that things I said and did prevented me from working. There were no business courses at the Actor's Studio.*
Eric Gutierrez, *Los Angeles Times*[17]

✦ *If you're not working because you are in your mid-life crisis, divorce, whatever, you may not be able to readily fix it, but it's up to you to assume you have a problem and set out to fix it.*
Martin Gage/The Gage Group

## Networking

I know that networking is a dirty word to many of you. "Oh, I'm not good at all that. I don't want to get a job just because I know someone. I'm here for art, not for commercialism, etc." Forget it. Come on, wouldn't you really rather work with people you already know? Someplace where you feel comfortable? With a director you already know you can trust? Management feels the same way and their money is on the table.

I've frequently had a hard time behaving naturally around management, because I was so afraid they would think I was talking with them because I wanted a job. I hear Laurence Olivier used to ask anyone working on a project whether there was anything in it for him. If Lord Olivier could do it, am I going to pretend I don't want to be employed?

✦ *Relationships are key. Be nice to everyone because you never know who is where at what point in his life. Always research people so you know who you are talking to or talking about. Learn the business. Start with an internship somewhere. You never know where the networking opportunity is, so always be on cue. It takes time and it's a process. Be persistent and don't give up until you reach your goal.*
Holly Davis Carter/Relevé

## Actors' Responsibilities

Most actors would be happy to shoulder their responsibilities in their actor/agent relationships if they only knew what the agents expected, so I asked agents what they wanted.

✦ *My job is to get the appointment. Your job is to show up, sell yourself and do your thing.*
Martin Gage/The Gage Group

✦ *You're not going to get every part you go in for. You're not going to get nearly every part you go in for. But what I never want to hear is, "He was late." "It was a slovenly audition." I don't even mind hearing, "She didn't do well." What I don't ever want to hear is, "He didn't pick up the sides." "She was ten minutes late."*
*All those things eventually hurt. Be prepared. If I'm putting my reputation on the line to get you the appointment, then put your reputation on the line enough so that I'm not looking like a fool for sending you in on it.*
Alan Willig/Don Buchwald & Associates/New York

Alan puts it in perspective, doesn't he? In every audition, the agent is putting his reputation on the line by sending you in and you are putting your reputation on the line by the quality of your work.

## Important Details

☎ Have a pen and paper in your hand when you return your agent's call.

☎ Check in often.

☎ Return calls promptly.

☎ Take picture and resume to audition.

☎ Get call-waiting to make sure your agent never gets a busy signal.

☎ Consider getting a beeper.

☎ Keep lines of communication open.

☎ Trust your agent and follow his advice from picture and resume to what kinds of shows to audition for.

☎ Make sure your picture is in the current edition of the *Academy Players Directory*

☎ Provide agent with ample supplies of pictures, resumes and videotapes without being reminded.

☎ Pick up the script before the audition.

☎ Arrive on time and be well-prepared for the audition.

☎ Don't try to date the receptionist.

## Agents' Responsibilities/What the Actor Has a Right to Expect

As I discussed in Chapter Two, all we want an agent to do is get us meetings for projects we are right for. This very simple thing we are asking agents to do involves all the things I just mentioned that actors need to do: be informed and professional, network, stay visible, and communicate.

As we maintain our credibility by giving consistently good readings, the agent maintains his credibility every time we make a good showing. The agent has to build trust with the buyers so that when he calls and says, "See K Callan, you won't be sorry," the casting director will go for it. Then, if K Callan gets the job, the agent has got to be ready to do a wonderful job of negotiation, one that will make the actor (and the agent, he does get 10%) happy and at the same time make the casting director feel he got a bargain.

The agent has all our responsibilities and more. Essentially the agent must maintain relationships with all the buyers and with his clients and must make each feel he is in their corner.

It's not the agent's duty to empathize with you, but it certainly impresses me when he does.

✦ *I take this business very personally. I'm not selling Cadillacs. I'm selling human beings, I'm selling artists' souls.*
Scott Manners/Stone Manners Talent Agency

Although the agent's commitment is to get you appointments and negotiate, you also have a right to expect him to consistently view your work and to consult with you before turning down jobs. His advice regarding career moves is one of the things you are paying for. The agent is a conduit to and from the casting director and, as such, should convey feedback honestly about the impression you are making.

Make it clear you are ready to hear the bad with the good, but that you would prefer he express it in a constructive manner. Not "You did lousy," but "You were late," "You were unprepared," or something else specific. Sometimes we need help to assess our auditions accurately.

Some agents like to give advice about pictures, resumes, dress, etc., but, unless you are just starting in the business or have just come to Los Angeles, established agents assume you have those things under control. Since pictures and audition tapes are the agents' sales tools, they might want a voice in what they are sending out, but your relationship will suffer if the agent feels you are asking for time in other matters that are basically your responsibility.

Many agents will be amenable to your dropping by, using the phone, and visiting with the secretary, etc., but it's best not to take these things for granted. After all, you want these people to be free to be doing business for you.

## What the Actor Doesn't Have a Right to Expect

✍ It is not okay to call your agent at home other than in an emergency.

✍ It is not okay to drop by the office at any time and expect the agent to be available to talk to you.

✍ It is not okay to expect your agent to deal with your personal problems.

✍ It is not okay to arrive late (or very early) for your meetings.

✍ It is not okay to expect to use the agent's phone for personal calls.

✍ It is not okay to hang around with the agent's auxiliary people when they are supposed to be working.

✍ It is not okay to bad-mouth the agent to others in the business. If you've got a gripe, take it up with the agent.

✍ It is not okay to interview new agents while your old agent thinks your relationship is swell.

✍ It is not okay to call and say: "What's happening?"

✍ It is not okay to expect the agent to put all the energy into the relationship.

A successful actor/agent relationship is no different than any other relationship. No one likes to be presumed upon.

If I were writing a book I thought agents would read, I would suggest that periodically they call the actor in (whether the career is going well or not) and ask the actor to rate the agency. Is the actor feeling comfortable? Cared for? Serviced properly? An annual mutual rating wouldn't be a bad idea. Is the actor doing his part? Is feedback good? Pictures and/or resume need updating?

At contract renewal time, perhaps the agent himself (instead of an assistant) would call and say, "K, how are you? It's contract renewal time, I'd love to have you stop by and have a cup of coffee with me (lunch?) and have us talk about our relationship. We're still happy, we hope you are, but I'd like to get some input from you on what kind of job we're doing. Come in. We'll talk. We'll celebrate your contract renewal."

If I were suddenly a hot commodity, it would sure be a lot harder for me to think about leaving that agent for the attentions of ICM because I had been made to feel valued by the agent before the big break.

## Emotionally Prepared to Audition

If you are not feeling confident about yourself, go to class, talk to a friend, a shrink, whatever, but don't burden your agent with that information. Will he feel like using up his credibility calling casting directors and telling them that you are the best actor since Meryl Streep when he knows you can't even get out of bed?

And if you are not up to auditioning well, tell your agent you are sick and postpone or cancel the audition. In the meantime, get help. If your marriage is over or your loved one just died, you may as well take the time off and grieve (assuming you're not in the middle of a big movie or a regular on a series). You are not only not going to be performing well enough to get the job anyway but people will lose confidence in you and it will be harder to get the buyer to see you next time.

## Staying in Touch

+ *Be seen visually by your agent on a regular basis.*
John Kimble

Many agents believe actors should make it a point to be seen by their agents once a week, although most of them won't say it out loud, and actors by and large haven't a clue as to how to keep in contact with their agents in a constructive manner. Agents say that they hate getting phone calls that ask "What's going on?" They translate that into "Where's my appointment?"

It's kind of like when you were little and your mom said, "What are you doing?" when she meant "Is your homework done?"

If you think about it from that perspective, perhaps you can find a way to have a conversation that does not make the agent feel defensive. If you are calling to say you've just gotten a good part in a Waiver play or just begun studying with a new teacher, or "Hey, did you see the new play at The Matrix? It's great, don't miss it," the agent is going to be a lot happier to hear your voice or see your face.

There are many constructive ways to keep in contact with your agent, from dropping off new pictures and resumes to calling and asking the assistant when the agent would be available for you to get his opinion on your new pictures or resumes.

Maybe you'll just be in the neighborhood and drop by to show a new wardrobe, haircut, whatever. Then be sure to do that; just poke your head in and show it. Don't sit down unless asked and, even if asked, stay no more than five minutes. Be adorable and leave. If you just need to bond with your agent, call ahead and see if your agent has time for you. Suggest a cup of coffee after work.

Suggest a snack in the middle of the afternoon and bring goodies. It's amazing how happy people are to see free food. Particularly free homemade food.

It takes two energy-expending components to make any merger work. The agent must work hard for you all the time and you need to deliver every time. If you don't stay abreast of what's in town, what shows are on television that might use your type, what you got paid for your last job, which casting directors you have met and who your fans are, and if you are late to appointments and ill prepared, the agent is going to get cranky. If he doesn't drop you, he'll stop working for you. Worse, you'll get work anyway and he won't feel able to drop you; he'll just hate you.

If you are diligent and do everything you can do for your own career and consistently give your agent leads that he doesn't follow up on, then you're going to get cranky and leave.

It takes two.

## Wrap Up

*Upon Signing*

✓ officially notify former agent that you are leaving
✓ send necessary letters to unions
✓ take pictures, resumes, tapes, quotes, billing, etc., to new agent's office
✓ meet everyone in the office, make map of where everyone sits, note who they are and what they do

*Actor's 90%*

✓ stay professionally informed
✓ network
✓ follow-through
✓ communicate
✓ make informed suggestions
✓ get in a good acting class
✓ have call-waiting, dependable machine or service
✓ check in and return calls promptly
✓ stay visible
✓ be loyal
✓ pick up the sides
✓ do great auditions
✓ be punctual
✓ give and get feedback

*Agent's 10%*

✓ arrange meetings
✓ arrange auditions
✓ negotiate
✓ network
✓ maintain credibility
✓ communicate
✓ make informed decisions
✓ stay professionally informed
✓ return phone calls promptly
✓ guide career

# ⚔ 10 ⚔

# Divorce

Searching for a new agent requires a whole different mindset than the quest for first time representation. But before we deal with the search, let's deal with the situation. Either you are dumping your agent or you are being dumped. If you are leaving your agent of your own accord, please tell me in one sentence why you are leaving and don't just say it's because you are not working. There may be many reasons why you aren't working that have nothing to do with your agent.

You might have gained or lost too much weight and now no one knows what to do with you. You may be traveling into a new age category and have not yet finished the journey. You might be getting stale and need to study. You might be having personal problems at home that are reflected in your work (after all, it's the life energy that fuels our talent and craft). The business might have changed, beautiful people may be in (or out).

How many projects can you list that had parts for you on which you were not seen? And were there really parts for you? You have to be right for a part not only physically and temperamentally but also on an appropriate career level as well.

Maybe you felt your agent didn't work hard enough. Maybe your expectations were out of line. Maybe you were lazy. Maybe you didn't keep his enthusiasm high enough. Maybe he was a goof-off.

Maybe the reason you want to change agents is that you are not getting as many auditions as your friends. Of course, it's hard to listen to someone else talk about his good fortune when you are home contemplating suicide.

It's possible your friend isn't being truthful and, though you and your friend may be frequently seen for the same roles, you are not exactly the same and you may be on different career tracks.

I know that it seems like going out is all that matters, but you need to cultivate some perspective before you fire your agent for that reason alone.

## Bona Fide Reasons to Leave

Maybe your agent has been dishonest with you. Obviously if there have been financial improprieties, that's a good reason to leave. There are, however, other kinds of dishonesty. I know an actor who left his agent because the agent frequently told the actor how hard he had worked to get the actor in on projects on which the actor later found he had been requested.

Maybe your agent is not out there pushing for you. How can you tell if it's just not your turn or if the agent is off playing the horses? You could drop off some pictures at the office and see if he's there and if the phone is ringing for anyone.

If you can't communicate with your agent, that is a valid reason for leaving.

✦ *Speak up. If you have a question, ask it. Doubts will build if you don't satisfy the question.*
Helen Barkan/Aimee Entertainment

✦ *The biggest problem in the actor/agent relationship is lack of communication.*
Martin Gage/The Gage Group

✦ *If your agent won't return your phone calls or have a meeting with you, you need another agent.*
John Kimble

Maybe you and your agent have different ideas regarding your potential. If this topic was not discussed up front, both of you may be feeling disappointed and misunderstood. This is a legitimate problem.

Many actors leave their agents because their careers change and they feel they can be better serviced by agents with different contacts.

✦ *Sometimes you change agents because you change. Sometimes you change agents because the agent has changed. Agents can become more or less focused, the same as actors.*
Martin Gage/The Gage Group

Perhaps your level of achievement in the business has risen. You have now, through diligent work and study and possibly a lucky break, become an actor of greater stature than your agent (very possible if fortune has just smiled on you). You feel you have outgrown your agent. And maybe you have.

*✦ Every agent has four or five horror stories about all they've done for somebody and then the person comes in and says, "I know you did a lot for me, but it wasn't enough. Someone's going to do more." Those are the ones that kill you, that keep you awake at night, that make you say, "Hey, maybe I should get out of this business."*
Jimmy Cota/The Artists Agency

*✦ I have to be honest and look at a performer's career I started and took up the road for six years and who's now making a million dollars a picture for William Morris. If I could have done that, then I would have done that. Maybe I could do it now. But, obviously, if I could have done it then, then I would have.*
Martin Gage/The Gage Group

And there are those moments when the actor's career loses momentum. One minute he's hot and the next moment he's not. He didn't necessarily do anything special to get himself un-hot. Frequently getting hot works the same way.

At a smaller agency, a downturn in your career won't necessarily make you persona non grata, but at the big agencies, it might be difficult for you to get your agent on the phone.

The larger agencies are not in the business to handle less profitable jobs, so they either drop you or their lack of interest finally tells you that you're no longer on their level. This is the moment when you might be sorry you left that small agent who worked so hard to get you started and engineered the big break for you. Will he want to see you now? He might. He might not. It depends on how you handled it when leaving.

There are different points of view, but the bottom line is that actor/agent relationships are just like any other relationship: as long as it's mutually rewarding everyone is happy, when it's not, things must change.

Some actors leave their agent on a manager's advice. Be circumspect. Maybe the change is warranted and maybe the manager is jealous of the longer term actor/agent relationship and seeks to unseat the agent.

If you have a rewarding relationship with an agent over a long period of time, why have you taken on a manager, anyway? If you are just looking for a way to leave your agent without taking responsibility, it's a pretty expensive way to avoid one uncomfortable meeting.

Maybe you want to leave your agent because the magic has gone out of your marriage just as the magic can go out of a traditional marriage if both partners don't put energy into it. Check the discussion of Actor's Responsibilities in Chapter Nine for some ideas on how to infuse some life force into the alliance. If you are both willing to save the relationship, that process will take a lot less energy and resourcefulness than to go through that just-learning-to-get-to-know-each-other period involved in any new relationship.

✦ *Stay in once place. Keep the road steady and always be focused.*
Bruce Smith/Omnipop

Maybe you want to leave your agent because the gods have smiled on you and you are suddenly a hot commodity. ICM and CAA are calling. Let's discuss that a bit.

## Be Happy for Me

An agent told me last week that a now successful client had come to his office, sat down and said, "I'm so excited. I know you'll be happy for me. I'm now so successful that Endeavor wants me."

Can you believe it? This actor wants the agent whose hard work, contacts and persistence helped him realize his dreams to be happy that the work is going to pay off for Endeavor?

Another respected independent agent had this to say.

✦ *There's no way an independent agent can defend himself about a suddenly visible, successful client leaving the agency for a corporate agency without sounding like sour grapes. We took an actress from zero to being very visible and very successful on a television show. She left because she "wanted to do more movies." In the last two months with us, we got her two movies. She's now been with the corporate agency for ten months and hasn't done a movie.*

*When she left, I said, "You are definitely screwing me no matter what you want to call it. I stood by you for five years when nobody would help you. I only hope you're re screwing me for a reason. I hope five years from now, you can look back and know why you screwed me. You traded me off for something and the question is, "Did you trade off the last person who didn't see you as a dollar sign to enter a world where they only value you as a dollar sign?*
Anonymous Agent

## Don't Wait Until It's Too Late

Just as with any other relationship you want to flourish, if something is bothering you, speak up. If there are problems, you need to talk about them. Be respectful. Don't put your agent on the defensive. If you are not going out, tell your agent that you are concerned. Do some research. Are there parts you might have legitimately been seen on? Ask him what you can do to help. Ask if he has heard any negative feedback about you or your work.

Whatever you do, don't just start interviewing other agents. You owe it to yourself and to your agent to talk before you get so angry, depressed, or resentful (pick one) that it is impossible for you to continue the relationship. If you have a conversation early on, perhaps both of you can find some way to remedy the situation. If not, at least he will have some idea of where you are coming from.

## Telling/Shopping

Before you start looking for a new agent, you must make a decision about telling your current agent you are going to leave. Most actors are hesitant not only because they are embarrassed and guilty, but also because they feel the agent might stop submitting them and the actor would be left unrepresented while he is shopping.

First of all, I doubt the agent would want to forego the commissions due on any new jobs. Second, if he wants to keep you, this is his chance to demonstrate you are making a mistake and he really is the best agent in the world, after all. And thirdly, every agent I questioned said he would never leave an actor without any representation while he was shopping.

It's taken me twenty-five years in the business and fifteen years of writing books about this process, but it has finally dawned on me that successful actors and agents are fearless actors and agents. Just as you must be willing to make specific and daring choices with material, you need to be daring in your business relationships.

Notice, I did not say reckless. To succeed you must have the courage of your convictions. If something is on your mind, you absolutely must speak up in a forthright manner.

A plus for telling your agent is that you don't have to worry about word getting back to him prematurely. Not only that, agents and/or casting directors will note your integrity. Don't date until you get divorced. There's no upside to playing both ends against the middle.

✦ *You don't know as an agent what you can do until you're out there selling that person. If someone is leaving an agent they are with, and they're saying, "I'm looking at new agents, but my current agent doesn't know so keep it quiet," it's hard to do checks, to call up casting people and say, "What do you think of so-and-so?"*
Ro Diamond/SDB Schwartz Diamond Bershad

If it is too late for a talk or you talked and it didn't help, at least leave with integrity. Even though it might be uncomfortable, get on with it. There is no need for long recriminations. No excuses. Not "My wife thinks" or "My manager thinks."

No. It should be: "I've decided that I am going to make a change. I appreciate all the work you have done for me. I will miss seeing you, but it just seems like the time to make a change. For whatever reason, it's just not working. I hope we'll see each other again."

Whatever. You don't need to be phony. If you don't appreciate what the guy has done and don't think he's done any work, just skip it. Talk about the fact that you think the relationship is not, or is no longer, mutually rewarding. Be honest and leave both of you with some dignity. You may see this person again. With some distance between you, you might even remember why you signed with him in the first place.

Don't close doors.

If you are leaving because your fortunes have risen, it is even harder. The agent will really be upset to see you and your money leave. Also, your newfound success has probably come from his efforts as well as yours. But if you are really hot and feel only CAA or ICM can handle you, leave you must.

Tell your agent you wish it were another way but the vicissitudes of the business indicate that at a certain career level, CAA and their peers have more information, clout and bargaining power, and you want to go for it.

If you handle it well and if your agent is smart, he will leave the door open. It has happened to him before and it will happen to him again. That doesn't make it hurt less, but this is business. He will probably just shake his head and tell friends you have gone crazy: "This isn't the same Mary I always knew. Success has gone to her head."

The agent has to find some way to handle it just as you would if he were firing you. It will not be easy to begin a new business relationship, but you are hot right now and the world is rosy.

## The Dumpee

If you are the one being dumped, that's depressing. Although there is no way being dumped can feel good, once you get over the pain of rejection, assessing the situation can put a whole different light on it.

There are many reasons that you may find yourself agentless. Your agent might have moved to another agency and was not allowed to bring you with him or he may have decided to retire or you may be going through a down time and not carrying your weight financially. At many agencies, each agent is responsible for his portion of the rent, phone, messengers, etc. Though the agent may love you personally, he may have to make a business decision to bet on someone else.

I recently worked with a visible actress who told me that at a down point in her career, her agent dumped her. She said that although she was crushed in the moment, ultimately it was a good thing because she had to face that representation is about business and not friendship. That bit of information freed her to make the best decision for herself further down the line, when she ended up leaving a later agent when she felt the relationship wasn't working.

When you're not working anyway and then your agent dumps you, that sucks. If you assess the situation, accept your responsibility and move forward, you're not only stronger, you're smarter.

## What Your Presentation Reveals

You've had conversations with your agent and things aren't working so now you're sending notes to prospective agents followed by your picture and resume. If you just send your old resume with your present agent's name crossed out, what does this say about you? How does it look? Not only messy, but it definitely takes you out of the "this person goes the extra mile" category.

How difficult is it to retype your resume without your former agent's name? Your note has said to the agent, I'm seeking new representation, so the agent already knows you have been signed.

There are so many notes, pictures, resumes, and balloon bouquets and the like visiting agents offices daily, that the agent and/or his assistant is screening the mail carefully.

Make sure your presentation reveals your personality and professionalism. If you're a slob, try to save that information until after the wedding.

## Wrap Up

*Questionable Reasons for Leaving*

✓ no recent work
✓ manager pressure
✓ agent disinterest

*Better Remedies than Leaving Agent*

✓ learn to communicate better with your agent
✓ take a class, study with a coach

*Speak to Agent*

✓ before things get bad
✓ before interviewing new agents

*Clear-Cut Reasons for Leaving*

✓ dishonesty
✓ lack of communication
✓ differing goals
✓ personality differences
✓ sudden career change

*When You Are Dumped*

✓ it can be painful and depressing
✓ can be a valuable learning experience

*When Querying Other Agents*

✓ the effort you make with your query shows and tells

# ☆ 11 ☆.
# Managers/TOS/Etc.

There are many avenues of thought as to the desirability of having a manager to help guide your career. Twice in my career (once in New York and once in Los Angeles), I had important managers. Not only did the service not enhance my career, but for the entire duration of each contract, I had no work at all. Since I had been working regularly before I took on the managers, you will find me a little biased about adding a manager to the budget.

Many feel that handing off their careers to a manager increases their cachet in the business. It may. It may not. Having a manager is really just having a second agent who is not regulated by the state or any of the unions, who may or may not have more contacts than your agent may or may not be inclined to work for you, and is going to cost you additional money.

If you seek a manager because you cannot get an agent, how do you think the manager is going to help you? If the agent did not see anything marketable, is the manager going to create you? Some do. That could happen. But I'd want to see some proof that the manager is credible and not just latching onto every new face in town, hoping that somehow one of them will hit whether he does any work or not.

The *Hollywood Representation Directory* currently lists about 349 theatrical agencies and over 491 theatrical managers. Hmm.

Some excellent agents, hampered by outdated agreements with the performers unions and what they deem unfair/unregulated competition from managers, are choosing to dump their agency franchises and become managers themselves. They usually end up feeling the same way about their businesses that they did when they were agents.

---

✦ *I love that agents have finally gotten to the that place where actors were: "I'd really rather direct." Now all the agents are saying, "I'd rather be a manager." I hear all of this the same way, "I'd rather be making more money for doing easier work." "I think that the guy across the street has an easier time than me. Why am I sweating it out while someone else across the street is picking money from a money tree."*

*They're all wrong. Whatever you do. It's hard work. It's an art form. You have*

*to stick with it. You have to not deviate. The more you change, the less likely you are to succeed. I'm totally shocked that somebody thinks that someone else has it much easier.*
Bruce Smith/Omnipop

Some management firms are structured almost like the old studio system. The powers that be really are powerful at places like Brillstein-Grey, Handprint, 3 Arts, and the new company being formed by top ICM film agent Ken Kamins and ICM/InterTalent guru Bill Block (Artisan Entertainment). These companies not only have all the artistic talent to acquire or create credible projects, they have the financing bases covered, too.

But, these companies, just like the conglomerate agencies, are not in the business of developing careers. They will come to you when they can use you, not vice-versa.

I think a manager that is connected and in love with you, could definitely enhance your career. I'm always quizzing fellow actors about their relationships with their agents. If they have managers, I ask if the actor feels a manager has enhanced the career.

One quasi-visible actress who had a recent break told me that she had gotten a manager and a publicist after her good fortune and that having the manager had definitely enhanced the number of movie auditions.

When I spoke to her agent to update information we discussed the business a bit and I remarked how great "Mary" was and how she constantly won our mutual auditions. We laughed a bit as he pointed out that he'd seen me on television recently, so "Mary" obviously didn't get everything. I asked him if he felt that the involvement of a manager had increased Mary's access to movie auditions. He responded, "I don't think so. But, if she thinks so, perception is everything."

I realize there might be some ego involved there, but it's much more likely that her added visibility from a hot show was responsible. The actress is not only very talented, she's extremely special. Her quality is extremely marketable. It's possible that what's pushed her career ahead is not her manager but her increased visibility.

## Research

Most agents who closed their agent doors one day and opened their managerial doors the next have credibility as far as I am concerned, but

I wonder about all those people who just woke up one day and decided to call themselves managers.

If you're going to seek a manager, do the research and make sure that as well as taste, access, stature and a small client list, the manager you're getting has all the other qualifications of a good agent.

If you just graduated from one of the Leagues and scored well in their showcases, many agents and managers may be giving you their cards. Don't let anyone rush you into signing anything. Check out all possibilities before you decide.

It's possible that a manager could get to you before you meet any agents and say, "Hey, don't bother meeting any agents, I'll take care of that for you when you are my client."

I see where they are coming from on that, because if you are going to have a manager, one of the services you might expect would be input into your agent selection. However, if you never even meet any agents, how will you make an informed decision regarding the need for a manager?

Meet with anyone who calls and listen to what they have to say. Only by gathering information and experiences can you make an informed choice.

Don't be in a hurry. You have the rest of your career in front of you and you're not magically going to pick the right person. You will need to do research and weigh all your offers. The right manager, who is connected and passionate about your career, can definitely make a difference. So could the right agent.

When Julia Roberts came to New York (already connected because of her famous brother, Eric), her manager, Bob McGowan, uncovered a part for her in the movie, *Satisfaction*. The role called for a musician, so Bob enrolled Roberts in a crash course and enticed William Morris into repping her for the job.

So, if we had McGowan for a manager and happened to look like Julia Roberts and have her charisma, who knows what could happen?

And you know what did happen? Roberts dropped McGowan and opted for William Morris and no manager, choosing to not have any more layers between herself and her work. Today, she's with ICM.

### Managers Can't Legally Procure Work

Actually, although the law is rarely enforced, managers are not legally allowed to procure work. That's the business of those people who have licenses from the state, you know, the agents?

♦ *LOS ANGELES, July 3 — Actress Jennifer Lopez has filed a petition with the California Labor Commissioner accusing her former manager of violating the state's Talent Agency Act by procuring employment on her behalf.*

*The primary charge centers on whether Medina was acting as her agent. Because Medina allegedly procured and negotiated work for her, the petition is requesting that all oral and engagement contracts she had with Handprint be voided. Those contracts saw her pay ten percent of earnings from movies and television, fifteen percent of her music, recording and publishing earnings and ten percent of her earnings from ancillary activities, including fashion and cosmetic interests.*

Chris Gardner and Peter Kiefer, Hollywood Reporter [18]

No one believes that Lopez has suddenly gotten religion and doesn't want to be in business with someone who is breaking the law. The lawsuit looks like a way to avoid paying commissions and get out of a contract but the fact remains, it's illegal for a manager to procure work for you.

And if he's not going to procure work for you, why would you be wanting a manager? There are other reasons, believe it or not.

Actress Nia Vardalos is currently involved in a similar lawsuit against her former manager.

♦ *The state court judge has refused to hear a challenge from Nia Vardalos' ex-manager to California's law barring managers from acting as talent agents. Tuesday's ruling by Los Angeles Superior Court Judith Chirlin sets the stage for the state labor commission to go ahead with a proceeding next week against Marathon Entertainment for performing as an unlicensed talent agent for Vardalos.*

*The management company sued Vardalos in January for failing to pay 15% commission from her earnings from the hit comedy feature "My Big Fat Greek Wedding," which she wrote and starred in.*

Dave McNary, Daily Variety [19]

## When It Makes Sense To Have a Manager

Managers are a definite plus for child actors who need guidance and whose families have no show business background. A manager usually places the child with an agent, monitors auditions, and sometimes accompanies the child to meetings and auditions.

If you are entering the business and need someone to help you with pictures, resumes, image, etc., managers can be helpful. However, many agents delight in starting new talent and consider this part of their service.

When you are at a conglomerate agency and it's too intimidating and time consuming to keep in touch with twenty agents, it might be advantageous to have a connected manager in your corner.

Changing agents is easier when you have a manager, because the manager does all the research, calling and rejecting of the former agent. If agent changing is the only reason you have engaged the services of a manager, have a growth experience and do it yourself.

If you have the credits to support getting a good agent, you can do that on your own. If you don't, the manager can't create them.

I have a few friends who feel the presence of a manager enhanced their careers at least momentarily. One in particular said her agents were considering dropping her, so she and the manager decided to make her more attractive to the agents by getting some jobs themselves. They read The Breakdown and the actress delivered her own submissions to the casting offices.

If the manager got a call for an appointment, the actress went in. If she got the job, they called the agent to make the deal. The agent became more enthusiastic about the actress for a while, but ultimately dropped her. The agent's earlier disinterest signaled what he had already decided: that the actress was no longer appropriate for his list. In that case, the manager, though helpful, only delayed the inevitable.

## Style/Substance

It's difficult to withstand a full court press from big time agents or managers, but remember that style is no substitute for substance.

I've never understood why an actor wouldn't want to have a personal relationship with his own agent. Unless you are an ogre with no interpersonal skills needing a buffer between you and the man is on the front line trying to get you seen, I don't see the point.

On the two unsuccessful occasions when I had a manager, the thing I liked least was that I was not supposed to talk to my agent myself.

A highly visible friend of mine recently lost a job because her manager discouraged her from speaking to the agent who might have prevailed in a negotiation in which the actress lost the job over money that would make no difference in her lifestyle. The job was in a show that became a huge hit and would have given real momentum to my friend's career. I kept saying, "Why don't you call your agent and ask what is going on?" Her reply? "I don't want to make my manager mad."

Come on! This is your career and you need to take responsibility for yourself. The more you hand off your power to someone else, the less control you have over your own destiny.

## Hidden Agendas

In addition to their goal of getting clients work, some managers use their power with their stars as an entrée to life as a producer. They hold back access to their clients if they are not given producer credit.

Network and studio brass have privately complained of what they saw as a conflict of interest that pushed their budgets higher with nothing to show for it, other than a relationship with the person with access to the star.

✦ *Many talent agents and studio executives believe that managers should focus on managing clients, not on producing their work.*

*"Of course it's extortion," said Pat McQueeney, a manager who has represented Harrison Ford for 27 years. McQueeney has always refused to put her name on any of her sole client's movies.*

*"I don't approve of it," she said. "It's double-dipping to be paid a double commission as a manager and a producer. People have said, 'Produce with us,' trying to bribe me by giving me a job I don't want, in order to secure Ford's commitment to a project. Because everybody's dream in this town is to become a producer, I feel they (managers) use their clients to benefit themselves and further their own careers."*

Claudia Eller and Brian Lowry, *Los Angeles Times*[20]

✦ *Some resent the imposition of a personal manager hired just because of his or her star access. "It's very difficult to say no [to a manager's producer credit] without offending the talent," [Shandling producer, Peter] Tolan noted, "even though in 95% of the cases, the manager brings nothing to the table."*

Lynette Rice and Scott Collins, *Hollywood Reporter*[21]

It's not just managers who withhold access. I've long heard stories from producer friends regarding strong arm tactics during Ovitz era CAA, but I was stunned to hear how even someone as distinguished, powerful and famous as Steven Spielberg could be pushed around.

✦ *Finally director Steven Spielberg, who appeared set to direct "Jurassic Park,"*
*phoned Michael Crichton to ask whether they were going to make the movie.*
*"Probably," Crichton replied, "I don't know why not."*

*Spielberg, as far as Crichton could figure out, was annoyed at Ovitz for insisting*
*that Spielberg must become a CAA client first, before the talent agent would make*
*him part of the "Jurassic Park" package that CAA would sell to a studio. As*
*Ovitz saw the world, Spielberg's signing-on as a client was a mere given. Ovitz*
*sensed that "Jurassic Park" would become a blockbuster, and he saw no reason why*
*Spielberg should hesitate to join Ovitz's agency.*

*At any rate, Crichton had begun to understand why the movie project was being*
*held up, and why no one was willing to tell him the truth about the delay. He was*
*amazed that Ovitz would allow a potential blockbuster of a movie to drift around*
*in Hollywood purgatory over such a seemingly minor issue as Steven Spielberg's*
*joining CAA.*

*Spielberg did become a CAA client, however, and Crichton confessed to "'being*
*naive that CAA was running such explicit agendas with my material."*
Robert Slater, *Ovitz* [22]

✦ *Erwin Moore [a personal manager] admitted the conflict of interest question has*
*come up many times, but never as a personal issue with me or my clients, he said.*

*When the dust has settled, people will come back to the realization that we're*
*here to serve a purpose on behalf of our clients. But the dust won't settle any time*
*soon. With managers growing more and more involved as producers, expect more*
*complications and litigation in the future.*
Lynette Rice and Scott Collins, *Hollywood Reporter* [23]

## No License Required

Even though the SAG/ATA agreements are not formally in place,
most agents still abide by the spirit of the rule which states that agents
must be franchised by the entertainment unions and the state,
displaying at least a modicum of track record, honesty and skills before
they are certified. They may only charge 10% and may only sign a new
client to a term of one year.

For managers, there is no certifying group overseeing the activity or
contracts. Commission and terms of service are totally negotiable

I know some agents in Los Angeles who became managers, realized
that they didn't have the Screen Actors Guild contract protection, and
went back to being agents again. The SAG contracts can be good for
both parties.

Don't be short-sighted. Have faith in yourself. Whether you are choosing an agent or a manager, don't just take the first person who shows some interest. Even though it may not seem that way right now, you have assets to protect: your face and your career. Many say, "Well, so what if someone wants to charge me 25%? Right now, I am making nothing, if I make money, give this person 25%."

That's fine today while you aren't making any money, but when you do work, and you have a manager that is taking 25% and Uncle Sam taking from one-third to one-half depending on your tax bracket, you will only be taking home 25% from all your work.

I don't want to give managers a bad rap, so those of you who have or end up having managers, let me know how it goes, so we can all learn. My e-mail address is Kcallan@swedenpress.com. My snail mail address is on the back of the book.

## Top Of Show/Major Role

A phrase heard more in Los Angeles than in New York, TOS/MR, refers to wages paid to guests in television episodes. Years ago, guest stars received $10,000 or more per week. In 1961, television reruns became subject to residual payments to actors. Production company management got together and decided to stop negotiating with actors playing guest leads in episodes, setting a predetermined cap for appearances on half-hour and hour shows.

SAG minimum for principal work per day is $678 on a film or a television show, a very good fee. If you are fortunate enough to work for five consecutive days, however, instead of being paid $3390 (which is five times the minimum) there is a discounted rate, $2352. The discount results in a per day fee of $474.40, or less than scale for a day's work. The discount was agreed to by SAG to encourage the hiring of actors for more days of employment.

In the recent past, SAG has addressed the discount by adding the TOS/MR designation as part of the contract, which actually just gets you back up to scale less the discount.

The TOS/MR quote is for a guaranteed number of days predicated on guest star billing. The fee difference between half-hour and hour shows is the guarantee; half-hour now guarantees five days employment at $678 per day, an hour show guarantees seven days. Days over the guarantee are paid at the same scale rate per day of $678.

There's nothing wrong in working for minimum if that your rate, but management, by attaching the TOS/MR designation, throw the phrase around as though an actor is getting some kind of preferred rate. The real money goes to high visibility actors who routinely command $15,000 for an appearance on an hour show.

There are a few shows, notably those produced by Aaron Spelling, that routinely break the top or have no top, but they also routinely hire stars whose fees are far above TOS/MR.

By and large, it has always been easier to negotiate for above-scale film and television money in Los Angeles than in New York. But even in Los Angeles, management has begun to cut supporting actors' wages in favor of the salaries of stars. Many esteemed character actors find producers stating, "This role pays scale plus 10%. Take it or leave it."

So sad.

## Packaging

A large agency representing writers, directors, producers and actors has a script written by one of its writers with a great part for one of its stars or first-billed actors. It then selects one of its directors and/or producers and calls CBS (or Paramount or whomever) and says, "Star writer has just written a terrific script for our star actress and our star director is interested. Are you?"

CBS says, "Yes," and a package is sold. Pilots, television movies, theatrical films, etc., are merchandised in this way. This phenomenon is called packaging. Nonstar actors frequently choose agencies with package potential because they feel they will end up getting jobs out of the arrangement.

In 1985, *Variety* cited an important study regarding packaging. These statistics are old, but SAG tells me nothing has changed.

✦ *The SAG report released yesterday, flies in the face of traditional Hollywood lore, which has long held that an agency putting together a packaged project will utilize as many as possible of the performers it represents.*

*The widespread belief that powerful agents routinely blackmail the studios into using their lesser known clients under threat of withholding their stars is a popular rumor with no basis in fact.*

David Robb, *Variety*[24]

The study reviewed seven packaged television series, three packaged miniseries and two packaged feature films. It found of the three hundred seventy-two roles created for these packaged projects, only twenty-seven went to actors who were represented by agents doing the packaging or slightly more than two roles per project.

Consider: if you are my client and I sell you in a packaged project, since I get a packaging fee, I get no commission for your services. Wouldn't I rather sell you for something else where I could make some money on the deal?

✦ *You maybe can put the first-billed actor, maybe the second actor, but at that point people at the studios and the networks want their creative input.*
John Kimble/William Morris Agency

The value of packaging, according to CAA's Steve Tellez, lies more importantly in the amount of access your agent is able to have with the buyers. Because the agent or someone at his company is talking to the buyers daily, there's naturally more of a feeling of comradeship.

## The Breakdown Service

The Breakdown Service is a digest of all work available to actors on a given day and is available to agents and managers only. Before the Breakdown existed, agents in Los Angeles had to drive to every studio daily, read every script, make their submissions and repeat the process at the next studio.

Finally, an enterprising chap named Gary Marsh, who was doing just that for his agent mother, called the studios and said something like, "I think I could make your life better. If you give me all your scripts, I will summarize them and make a list of the types of actors needed for the parts, the size of each role, etc., and provide that information to all the agents. This will save you the nuisance of having all those people in your offices and them the inconvenience of driving."

Thus, the much-maligned Breakdown Service was born. It costs the agents a hefty amount, but it's worth it. When agents subscribe, they must agree not to show it to actors.

Some actors get their hands on the Breakdown, anyway. A woman in Beverly Hills charges actors $20 per month for access. She hides it under a rock behind a gate. Actors drive up, lift the rock, sit in their cars, read the Breakdown and make notes. They return it to its hiding place and drive away.

Whether or not it's a good idea to have access to the Breakdown is debatable. Casting directors already don't have enough time to look at all the agents' submissions. How will they ever be able to even open all the envelopes they could get from actors much less consider them.

Whereas some actors are able to use the purloined information intelligently, others merely manage to alienate their agents. Though invaluable, the Breakdown doesn't include everything. Many roles aren't listed unless the casting director needs an unusual actor for a role.

Frequently, the script is truly not available. More times than not, the audition sheet will be filled by requests, not submissions.

Since not everything comes out in the Breakdown, it is important to assess your agent's other contacts. If your agent is not in a position to have more information than is in the Breakdown, that's still a lot of information if he uses it wisely.

The Breakdown is now not only part of the New York/Los Angeles casting scene, but it is also available via the Internet.

## Actors Access Breakdowns

Since actors can't have access to the full spectrum of Breakdowns, Gary Marsh has created a new business called Actors Access Breakdowns. As named, these are Breakdowns to which actors do have access. Casting directors will instruct AAB that certain roles are allowed full access. Both SAG and non-SAG projects are included.

You join AAB (no fee), get a username and password, and peruse the many many pages of casting notices. If you find a project with a role that you are right for, you make your own submission from pictures and resumes that you upload to the site. There is a two dollar charge per submission which Gary figures is about what it would cost to send a picture and resume via snail mail.

Many non-union and student films don't have casting directors so this is a great service for filmmakers who are not yet connected through normal channels. www.actorsaccess.com

### Your Reference Library

When I was living in New York, I was fortunate enough to get a part in what turned out to be an important film called *A Touch of Class* which shot in Spain. The night I arrived in Marbella, I found myself standing next to the wife of the writer-producer-director at a party honoring the cast.

Making conversation and truly delighted to be involved with such a lovely script (Mel Frank eventually won an Oscar for it), I said to Ann

Frank, "What a wonderful script. Is this Mel's first script?"

What did I know? I thought he was primarily a director and, as a New York actress, I was ignorant of things Hollywood. Ann was so cool. She neither walked away nor behaved in any way condescending. She just began patiently enumerating the edited version of her husband's incomparable credits.

It turned out that Mel was a famous Hollywood writer, and along with partner, Norman Panama, had written the Bing Crosby-Bob Hope *Road* pictures, plus many other classic films. I almost died of embarrassment, but Ann was all class. She patted my arm and smiled, "This will be our little secret." All the time I was apologizing for my ignorance, I was promising myself that I would never be in that position again.

If you have Internet access, it's a snap to power up www.imdb.com (Internet Movie DataBase) to check credits though I also recommend your library be stocked with books that tell you what the business is really like (*Adventures in the Screen Trade, The Season* and *Final Cut,* etc.), as well as biographies of successful people (in our business and others) that will provide role models in your quest for achievement.

Here is a list of books that will give your library a good start:

*Aaron Spelling: a Primetime Life*/Aaron Spelling
*Act Right*/Erin Gray & Mara Purl
*Adventures in the Screen Trade*/William Goldman
*AFTRA Agency Regulations*
*A Passion for Acting*/Allan Miller
*Audition*/Michael Shurtleff
*Book on Acting*/Stephen Book
*casting by ... A directory of the Casting Society of America, its members and their credits*/Breakdown Services
*Comic Insights: The Art of Stand-up Comedy*/Franklyn Ajaye
*The Complete Directory to Primetime Network TV Shows*/Tim Brooks & Earle Marsh
*The Devil's Candy*/Julie Salamon
*Equity Agency Regulations*
*The Film Encyclopedia*/Ephraim Katz
*The Filmgoer's Companion*/Leslie Halliwell
*Final Cut*/Steven Bach
*Halliwell's Film Guide*/Leslie Halliwell
*Hollywood Agents & Managers Directory*/Hollywood Creative Directory

*Hollywood Creative Directory*/Hollywood Creative Directory
*How I Made 100 Films in Hollywood and Never Lost a Dime*/Roger Corman
*How to Sell Yourself as an Actor*/K Callan
*Hype & Glory*/William Goldman
*Indecent Exposure*/David McClintock
*The Last Great Ride*/Brandon Tartikoff
*The Los Angeles Agent Book*/K Callan
*Making Movies*/Sydney Lumet
*Monster*/John Gregory Dunne & Joan Didion
*My Lives*/Roseanne
*The New York Agent Book*/K Callan
*New York Times Directory of Film*/Arno Press
*New York Times Directory of Theater*/Arno Press
*Next: An Actor's Guide to Auditioning*/Ellie Kanter & Paul Bens
*Ovitz*/Robert Slater
*Rebel Without a Crew*/Robert Rodriguez
*Reel Power*/Mark Litwak
*Ross Reports Television & Film*/Back Stage/Back Stage West Publication
*Saturday Night Live*/Doug Hall & Jeff Weingrad
*Screen Actors Guild Agency Regulations*
*Screen World*/John Willis
*The Season*/William Goldman
*Theater World*/John Willis
*TV Movies*/Leonard Maltin
*Ultimate Film Festival Survival Guide*/Chris Gore
*You'll Never Eat Lunch in This Town Again*/Julia Phillips
*Wake Me When It's Funny*/Garry Marshall
*Who's Who in the Motion Picture Industry*/Rodman Gregg
*Who's Who in American Film Now*/James Monaco
*Wired*/Bob Woodward

If you know of any books that belong on this list, let me know and I'll include them in subsequent editions. I consider books like *Wired, Indecent Exposure* and *Saturday Night Live* to be instructive and realistic about the business. They keep my values in perspective. I need reminders of how easy it is to get caught up in the glamour, publicity, money, and power of this fairytale business. I need to remember that those things leave as quickly as they come.

I mustn't forget that success doesn't fix you. It may feel better for a while, but you're always you, just with a different set of problems.

The more you read other people's journeys, the more perspective you gain.

For fun, read Tony Randall's *Which Reminds Me*. For inspiration, Carol Burnett's *One More Time*. To gain insight on how to get into and what goes on at film festivals, read Chris Gore's *The Ultimate Film Festival Guide*. Roseanne's book, *My Lives,* speaks candidly of the behind-the-scenes intrigue involved with her show. It's instructive.

## Wrap Up

*Managers*

- ✓ can provide access
- ✓ can provide guidance
- ✓ take a larger percentage than agents
- ✓ are not governed by industry standard contracts
- ✓ do your research

*The Breakdown Service*

- ✓ important tool for agents
- ✓ can be self-destructive in the hands of the wrong actor

*Reference Library*

- ✓ educational
- ✓ inspirational
- ✓ indispensable

# ⚐ 12 ⚑
# Stand-Ups/One Person Shows/Voice Work

Ray Romano, Christopher Titus, Roseanne, Drew Carey, Tim Allen, Ellen DeGeneres and Whoopi Goldberg are just a few of the successful performers and stand-up comics who crossed over into films and television. Assaulting films and television via the stand-up route has become so profitable that no less than ICM has put together a team of people who actually develop the careers of budding talents.

✦ *"For years, we've only handled established comedians because we didn't really have the infrastructure to service (unknown) people," says Steve Levine, who heads ICM's music and live performance division. "Now, we've put together a committed group here who use the resources of the whole company to build careers," he said.*
Cynthia Litttleton, *Hollywood Reporter*[25]

ICM and the rest of the agents who scout stand-ups are mostly looking for the same thing.

✦ *We've definitely steered toward a very personality oriented comic. A charismatic style comic. "The Tonight Show" might use a comic because he's a very good writer. A structural comic who writes a perfect setup and a punchline. Some of those comics wouldn't crossover into a sitcom because they might just be joke tellers.*
*We want somebody who is a very full-bodied character a la Roseanne, Tim Allen, Seinfeld. The development and casting people are looking for that. They are already walking in with a character. Some comics have stronger skills in that area.*
Bruce Smith/Omnipop

In his terrific book of interviews with other comics, Franklyn Ajaye gets Jay Leno to talk about a seven-year rule.

✦ *"I've always told comedians that if you can do this for seven years, I mean physically make it to the stage for seven years, you'll always make a living. If you've been in the business longer than seven years and you're not successful, there's probably another reason. Sex, dope, alcohol, drugs — you just couldn't physically get to the stage. Sam Kinison is sort of an example. He was funny, hilarious, but near the end he couldn't get to the stage anymore. No matter how popular you are,*

*promoters are not going to rehire you if you miss gigs."*
Franklyn Ajaye, *Comic Insights*[26]

✦ *A comedic person has to have the backing of the theatrical training, otherwise you're looking at a personality oriented project. Many stand-ups came out of theater and did stand-up as a means of survival.*
Steve Tellez/CAA

✦ *I wouldn't assume that just because you are a comedic actor that you can do stand-up. Soap opera people try to do stand-up. Most of them, because they are so pretty, have not lived that angst ridden life that comics have, so their routines become a frivolous version of comedy. The first thing you want to establish with an actor that is going into comedy is: Do they have a natural feel for it? Do they have comedic rhythm for it? There are many actors who are wonderful with comedy, but can't do stand-up. You need the stage time.*
Bruce Smith/Omnipop

✦ *A lot of comedy clubs have closed across the country, but there are still a fair amount in the northeast so it's easier to keep a comic working there as they start to develop. The more stage time they get, they better they become. We encourage them to get into acting classes, not to become actors, but just to start. We want to know what their long range goals are. In order for a comic to become popular, he needs television exposure. If you can support that with a strong act, you're going to have a good career.*
Tom Ingegno/Omnipop

✦ *I would say to really know whether you have any place in the comedy business at all, that you would have to give yourself at least two years. Less than that is not enough. The first year you'll spend just trying to get your name around, trying to get people to know who you are so they will give you some stage time. It's a long trip. Just like an actor.*
  *Don't seek representation with five minutes of material. You want to keep working. The next thing to do is to try to get work in road clubs. It's very important to get the experience. There is limited experience if you just stay in one city.*
Bruce Smith/Omnipop

The personal appearance agents that I spoke to supported what I have learned from theatrical agents and scriptwriters agents. None of them are interested in one shot representation. Many unrepresented actors (writers, directors, etc.) think that if they land a job on their own (even a development deal) and call up an agent to handle it for them, that they will be welcomed with opened arms. The agent is going to make money, right? That's not how it goes. The agent is interested in a client that has something to back it up over the long haul.

If you get a guest shot on *Everybody Loves Raymond* and call an agent with that shot as an entrée, he will probably take your call, but if you don't have a track record of credits (they don't all have to be as important as *Raymond*) then the credible agent is not going to be interested. 10% of an episode is not enough money for him to put you on his list to share all his introductions and hard work.

Stand-up and performance artist shows are a bona fide way to be entrepreneurial about the business, but there are no short-cuts to theatrical/comedic maturity. You gotta do the time.

✦ *"There are comics who try to skip whole chunks of the evolutionary charts of stand-up," says Barry Katz, a manager whose clients include Dave Chappelle, Jay Mohr and Jim Breuer. If you look and analyze successful shows, what 99% have in common is that the star of that show has been doing stand-up for at least ten years.*

*An evolved voice, a clear point of view. That's what Roseanne, Seinfeld, Ellen DeGeneres, Drew Carey and Tim Allen and all club comics who made the transition from stand-up to sitcoms have in common.*
Paul Brownfeld, *Los Angeles Times*[27]

✦ *You have to have a sense of reality, you're always chipping away at that block of ice trying to make a sculpture that could take ten years.*
Bruce Smith/Omnipop

Network execs who track the progress of stand-ups are asking themselves the same question that casting directors ask when they track the evolution of an actor: Is this someone who can be a star? Is this someone who is a supporting player? Would he appeal to middle America? Is this person balanced enough to handle the long haul? These are questions you need to realistically answer as you plan your career.

## One Person Shows

Another form of stand-up, since it's just the actor, props and an audience, is the One Person Show. Separating the vanity pieces that are just an excuse to stand up in front of people and tell *What I Did On My Summer Vacation* (using all the dialects you know) from a worthwhile evening of theater, is a piece of material that has resonance and deals with issues.

Actors like Claudia Shear (*Blown Sideways Through Life*), Julia Sweeney (*And God Said, Ha!*), Pamela Gien (*The Syringa Tree*), Paul Link (*Time Flies When You're Alive*) and Spaulding Grey (*Swimming to Cambodia*) are prime examples of material that has more than entertainment value.

Jason Alexander, Julie Harris and Ron Silver took material from the lives of famous people and/or authors and fashioned it into an illuminating evening of theater.

If you have the drive, stamina, courage and entrepreneurial ability to create an evening of theater, you will not only have a chance to act, and a vehicle for producers and casting directors to view you in, but also a source of income on the college and possibly cruise ship circuit.

## Comedian Referral Service/Rent a Comic

The Comedyzine Referral Service is a free online listing site for comedians, agents, managers and publicists all across the country. Each listing links you to their site. If you need to hire a comedian for a party, or a corporate or college function, you can select the comedian by going directly to their site (www.comedyzine.com ), or their agent's site.

If you are a comedian, agent, manager, or publicist, and wish to be listed, E-mail your URL address to: listings@comedyzine.com including your city and state. There is no charge, but you must have a web page for them to link to.

## Voice Work

One of the most exclusive clubs used to be voiceover talent who supply voices for commercials, radio and television promos, animated films and television shows and now the Internet. The club is still hard to get into, but increasingly, actors have been allowed to join.

✦ *The commercial business has changed in that it's no longer the announcers that dominate the commercials, it's the actors — the people who can 'be real.' Advertising has become much more honest in their approach, so they don't want to have charactery voices unless the particular character in the commercial calls for the character voice. If you listen to the voice stuff out there now on TV and radio, it's much more real.*

*But you have to be an excellent actor, so you can give them the range of emotions*

*they are asking for, be it comedy, understated, etc.*
Sandie Schnarr/Sandie Schnarr Talent

Although there are agents that just specialize in voice talent like Schnarr, many regular agents are getting the calls for animated television shows and films. The people you will see on those auditions will not be voiceover actors, they will be your normal competition.

If you expect to compete for more than the odd job that your regular agent will get calls for, you really should get into a workshop.

✦ *Most of the time, this happens usually by going to several voiceover workshops. When you look at it, if you've never done voiceovers, you can't in one six-week period (and that's only six classes, most of these workshops are one night a week for six weeks) compete with people who are doing this every day.*

*Using the combination of paying attention to what you see on TV, practicing what you hear on TV, and practicing what you hear on radio, you can create your own little workshop at home. You have the best teachers right there on television.*

*Bob Lloyd from VoiceCaster, told me when I first started the business to tell my actors to record the spots they see on TV, write down the copy, record themselves and listen back and forth.*

*That man who books the national Toyota spot will teach you how to read that copy. So, there's a free workshop running twenty-four hours a day. Then you do take workshops with casting directors who know what the advertisers are currently looking for.*
Sandie Scnharr/Sandie Schnarr Talent

## Voiceover Workshops

Kalmenson & Kalmenson Voiceover Casting
Cathy Kalmenson and Harvey Kalmenson
818-342-6499
www.kalmenson.com

The VoiceCaster/Bob Lloyd and Pat Lloyd
818-841-5300

Carroll Voice Casting
Carroll Day Kimble, Susan Cheico, Aleta Braxton
323-851-9966

While work as a stand-up and/or in one person shows might be a way to become more visible in the business and move your career along, the same is not true of voice work. However, if you can really get on people's lists and become a voiceover actor, you can make a lot of money.

## Wrap Up

*Standups*

✓  need 15-20 minutes of material to begin
✓  need a persona
✓  should have theatrical training
✓  gotta do the stage time

*One Person Show*

✓  needs resonance
✓  avoid vanity piece

*Voiceover Work*

✓  becoming more accessible to regular actors
✓  need to train
✓  can be lucrative

# ✑ 13 ✑
# Children In the Business

Children and parents of children who want to be involved in show business, be advised that I don't think it is a good idea. You only get one shot at being a child and being taken care of. If you blow that, you won't get another chance.

The tabloids make a lot of money running stories on the ruined lives of former child actors. I know you think you and/or your children could never have those problems. Maybe you won't. Just think seriously about what you are getting into before you take the next steps. If your child is paying your rent, the balance of power tips and there is no more family hierarchy. Remember Macaulay Culkin.

That said, my interview with stage mother/manager, now children's agent, Judy Savage pretty well shoots all my arguments full of holes.

✦ *Kids who have problems in the business came from dysfunctional families in the first place. It's not necessarily that the business goes to the children's heads, it goes to the parents' heads. I don't think the number of showbiz kids who become messed up is any greater than the general public, but you hear about them because they are so visible and they have a little more money for drugs.*
Judy Savage/Judy Savage Agency

Judy's philosophy explains why her clients and her own kids ended up not only working, but being productive grown-ups as well.

✦ *I think it's a great business and that you can pay for your braces, your caps, your car, your wedding, your house, and hopefully go on in the business or in some other aspect of life with a good start.*

*Treat it as a hobby that you are lucky enough to get paid for, it's not going to go on forever. You can count on your two hands the number of actors whose careers go on for forty or fifty years. The average career is five years for all members of Screen Actors Guild.*
Judy Savage/Judy Savage Agency

Elizabeth Taylor's life as a child actor is not one she recommends.

✦ *Looking back, I think I missed not having a childhood, not going to a regular*

*school. I had a lot of fathers and avuncular friends on the set. They were great. They used to throw me around and play baseball with me and sneak me candy and comic books. But it wasn't the same as having peers, and I think I would advise parents not to push it. It's a hard life for a child not to have a childhood. It's rough.*
Charles Champlin, *Los Angeles Times*[28]


The decision is yours, but if you do decide to pursue a career for your child or if you are a child reading this, it's easier to maintain your balance when you are a working actor, than if you are a star.

## You Don't Have to Be in New York or Los Angeles

Parents and kids write me online and via snail mail asking how they can get into the business if they don't live in New York, Chicago or Los Angeles. Judy Savage's story is a good example of how to go about it.

Summering at her folks' summer home in a lakeside Michigan summer musical area, housewife/mother/pre-med student Savage, pregnant with her third child, was the mother of a talented nine-year-old son. She was told by a New York casting director, "Sell your house. Sell your car. Take this child to New York."

Judy wasn't ready to uproot her family so drastically, but she did go back to Detroit at summer's end, got an agent and Judy's son and daughter both began working.

Judy was savvy enough to locate and read *Variety* where she saw a casting call for *Mame*. She started writing the producers, sending them pictures of her son. They kept telling her that he was too young.

Finally, her son wrote them a letter himself, sending a tape of his voice and a dollar requesting that the producers listen to his tape and use the money for postage to send the tape back if they didn't like it.

Judy received a letter by return mail saying that the producers would see her son when they came to Detroit.

After hearing him sing, the producers gave Mark a script and asked him to read a scene with the star. He had already memorized the show, so when they handed him a script, he was able to set it aside and do the entire scene with the star, touching her so deeply that she cried. He started work the next week.

Judy is a perfect example of the entrepreneurial spirit that sees no obstacle. She believes that children who are successful in the business have a true calling. Mark was lucky he had a mom who was smart enough to help him realize his dreams.

## Don't Get Professional Pictures Right Away

Since young children change so rapidly, children's agents do not expect professional pictures. Once you have an agent, he will want to advise you on your pictures, so at the beginning, a clear snapshot is all that is needed.

Mail pictures with a note giving all the vital statistics — age, weight, height, coloring and anything the child might have done involving getting up in front of people and taking direction. Professional experience is not nearly as important as the child being comfortable with people. Happy. Confident. Gregarious.

If the snapshot interests the agent, he will ask you to bring the child in for an interview. You will be invited out while the agent gets a feel for how the child is in the same kind of situation that will take place for an audition.

If you are a child reading this, let me tell you that agents are very impressed when a child makes his or her own arrangements. It means you are motivated, organized and adult about the whole thing. A children's agent told me that her role model for a child actor was a client who at thirteen had done lots of local theater, called Screen Actors Guild, got a list of agents and sent in pictures himself. He got the first job he went for: the national tour of *The Sound of Music*.

Children are paid the same daily rate as adults and will be (all things being equal) expected to behave as an adult. No sulking, tantrums or crankiness. They don't like it when adult actors do that either!

## Training

Although kids can get jobs by just being cute, outgoing, and well behaved, continuing in the business past the "darling" years demands training.

◆ *When we started, the prevailing attitude was, "Don't get them trained. Leave them natural." I was even told that about my own kids (and this was in the 1970s), but I looked around and I said, "There's something wrong with this picture, you wouldn't enter any other profession in the world without training."*

*So I started looking for an acting teacher. I had had no training and I didn't even know what I was looking for, but I found Diane Hardin's Young Actors Space and I sat there in tears the whole night long and I said, "This is what I am looking for."*

*I sent my own kids and later, all my clients. That's one of the reasons that clients that I have raised have been able to make the transition, if they wanted to. A lot of them don't want to. A lot of them go off to college and do something else.*

*Of the children that I take, if they have the passion, if they get trained, they usually get to work, even if it's only commercials.*

Judy Savage/Judy Savage Agency

## Babies

Babies are a whole other part of the business. Many children's agents don't deal with infants and babies at all unless the babies are twins or triplets. Even then, it is sometimes easier for agents to go through managers.

✦ *We rely on managers for babies because babies with a manager require less upkeep. I'll get a baby call and put it out to a manager and they'll send me a list of kids. I can just make one phone call to the manager and say, "Get these kids out." Sometimes calls come in really late and it makes it difficult.*

*With baby-moms, they are usually so new to the business that you have to do so much explaining about going on interviews and how you go, how you dress and how to get there and then they have a million questions.*

*We're not opposed to answering the questions except when we are really busy.*

Vivian Hollander/Hollander Talent Group

## Teachers for Young Actors

*Diane Hardin's Young Actors Space* is highly respected by Judy Savage and many other agents in town and all the students who ended up becoming visible actors like Chad Allen, Thomas Wilson Bryan, Kirk Cameron, Leonardo Di Caprio, Stephen Dorff, Brian Austin, Green, Mandy Ingbar, Kellie Martin, River Phoenix, Toby McGuire, Molly Ringwald, Rider Strong, Hilary Swank, Elijah Wood. For a more complete list and all the particulars on classes, check out YAS website, www.young-actors-space.com or call 818-785-7979. Weekly classes cost $40 and last three hours.

*Leah Hanes* directs Center Stage LA where classes cost from $44 to $50 depending on length of class, number of lessons, etc. Private coaching is $65 hourly. Marcie Smolin, Gayla Goehl, and Danny Weiss all teach here. Call 310-837-4536 or view the website www.centerstagela.com for complete complete information.

*Cynthia Bain* was a protégé of the late Roy London. She started her young actor classes a couple of years ago as an adjunct to the respected adult classes taught by another London protégé, Cameron Thor.

The class for serious young actors is taught much like Cameron's classes, but the scenes are for younger actors. Classes are basically scene study and script analysis, improvisation and cold reading work. Every student works in every class. Adult auditors are not welcome since Bain feels that makes her students self-conscious. For students eleven through fourteen, $280 gets you eight two-hour classes. Students fifteen and up pay $320 for eight three-hour classes. All classes are at the Laurelgrove Theater in Studio City. www.cynthiabain.com 323-654-6614.

Cynthia coaches privately at $75 per hour or for her students, $65. She's proud that several of her students have scored series.

*Barbara Daoust*'s ten-Saturday-package for ages eight to twelve and thirteen to seventeen is $300 for the two-hour classes. She coaches privately at $75 an hour. She teaches in Sherman Oaks. 818-761-8377.

Opera singer/actress *Winnie Hiller* is a mom and teaches musical theater in a swell private elementary school. She coaches kids ages ten to fifteen for film, television and school magnate auditions in both voice and acting. She charges $75 an hour. 818-781-8000.

## Photographers for Kids

Any photographer who is good can take a good picture, but photographing children requires a special talent. Here is a list of photographers who photograph kids and have been highly recommended by varying agents. You will want to make decisions based on the rapport between your child and the photographer and *don't* pay for professional pictures for your child until you have met with an agent who thinks it's worth your while. Most agents will be happy to evaluate kids from snapshots.

*Alan Weissman* is mainly a photographer for adults but does snap kids five and up, particularly working kids who are on television series. He charges $360 for two rolls of film. For that you get one 8x10 plus a proof of all the images. Additional 8x10s are $25 and a digital image ready for a website is $25 per image.

His website doesn't feature kid's photos, but you'll see his work: www.alanweissman.com. 818-766-9797.

*Carrie Cavalier* shoots kids under ten for $135. For that you get one roll plus a contact sheet, the negatives and an 8x10. Kids ten and over are $150 and up. www.cavalierphotography.com. 818-566-8290/818-840-9148.

## What Agents Look for in Young Actors

Since there are very strict labor laws in California, in addition to kids who are more interested in acting than T-ball, agents look at specific age groups for pragmatic reasons.

✦ *We always need new six-year-olds, especially six-year-olds that can play four, because it means they can work all day. We are also always looking for eighteen-year-olds who can play fifteen through seventeen. These are the perfect ages to get started. Adult agents have clients that will stay the same for ten to fifteen years, children change every six months: they grow up, they get braces, they don't want to do it, they lose teeth, they want to play T-ball, all kinds of things.*
Judy Savage/Judy Savage Agency

You have to be six to work all day and eighteen to work without a set-sitter and time set aside for schooling.

## Set Sitters

Parents should be prepared to ferry children to many auditions and, if the child books a job, to be on the set with him at all times. Not only is it a SAG rule that a parent or designated set sitter of some type be provided, but it is unwise ever to leave your child in an adult environment on his own.

Someone needs to be there to be your child's advocate. No matter what the job or how good management is about things, they are in the business to make money. Someone must be there who is not afraid of losing his job if he speaks up that the set is too hot or the kid needs a break. We all want to please and do a good job, but certain rules must be followed. The Child Actor's Hotline at SAG is 323-549-6030.

You or your designated representative should read SAG, AFTRA and Equity rules so you know when your child must be in school or resting or has a right to a break, as well as overtime and payment for fittings. SAG's Young Performers Handbook is yours for $3. www.members.aol.com/sagaftra/images/young.html 800-527-7517.

Many child actors work through managers. It's not necessary, but managers can be helpful at this stage of a career by putting a child together with an agent and making recommendations concerning dress, pictures, study and other basic details of a beginning career.

Many parents fulfill the same role and many agents expect to provide the same service without an additional charge of 15%.

There are managers in town who charge to keep a client listed until he gets a job. There are also managers who require that your child be coached for each audition by their in-house coaching staff. The coaching is free if you are booking jobs, they charge if you are not scoring. What a sweet deal for those managers. There is no risk in their investment at all since there is no investment. A working child makes a lot of money. It's a sweet deal for the manager. There is no down side. He has no investment at all in the client. He just collects money.

## Hiring the Parents

✦ *"What parents have to understand is, they are the excess baggage that comes along with the talent," says Innovative Artists' Claudia Black. "It's the parent's responsibility to make sure the child is prepared, on time and has rehearsed the scene....If agents can't get along with the parent, they won't take the kid. It's really not just about the kid being amazing," says Cunningham Escott Dipenes' Alison Newman, "It's a joint thing, fifty-fifty.*
Alexandra Lange, *New York Magazine*[29]

✦ *When I interview kids, I interview their parents, too, so I try to pick a good parent, one that has her kid's best interest at heart. Most of them are pretty philosophical about the competition. You know, there is competition everywhere. There's competition in who gets chosen in gym and Little League and dating.*
Judy Savage/Judy Savage Agency

## Wrap Up

*Children*

✓ a snapshot will do to begin with
✓ paid as adults so they must behave that way
✓ must be able to talk to anyone
✓ set sitter required
✓ it's the parents' job too
✓ get trained if you want longevity in your career
✓ be realistic about career span
✓ perspective and balance are necessary
✓ children need their peers

# ⚔ 14 ⚔
# Researching the Agents

There are various categories of agencies: big, small, conglomerate, beginning, aggressive, just getting by. Since agency/client relationships are personal, any classifications I make is subjective. I'm presenting the facts as best I can, based upon my research and personal experience both in interviewing these agents and my years in the business. You'll have to take the information and make your own decisions.

There are new agencies with terrific agents building their lists who, like you, will be the stars of tomorrow. You could become a star with the right one-agent office and you could die on the vine at CAA.

There are no guarantees, no matter whom you choose. The most important office in town might sign you even without your union card if your reel and/or resume excites them, but mostly, they want you when you are further along. Whomever you choose, if you are to have a career of longevity, you can never surrender your own vigilance in the process of your career.

## Evaluate Carefully

If you read carefully, you will be able to make a wise decision using client lists, the agents' own words, and the listing of each agency. It's unwise to write off anybody. In this business, you just don't know. One's own tastes and needs color the picture. I love my agent but you might hate him.

There are nice people who are good agents and there are nice people who are not. There are people who are not nice who are good agents and so on. Just because I may think some agent is a jerk doesn't mean he is. And even if he is, that might make him a good agent. Who knows?

If you read all the listings, you will have an overview. I've endeavored to present the facts plus whatever might have struck me about the agent: this one sold binoculars at the theater; that one was part of a sixties singing group.

Some agents have survived for years without ever really representing their clients. They wait for the phone to ring. Some agents talk a better game than they play. I believe it would be better to have no agent than to have one who is going to lie to you.

## Agent Stereotypes

We all know the stereotypes about agents: They lie, that's their job. Well, some agents lie, but most don't. Most are hard-working, professional, regular people who (like you) want to make it in show business.

Like you, they want to be respected for their work, go to the Academy Awards, and get great tables at Spago. And they, too, are willing to put up with the toughest, most heartbreaking business in the world because they are mavericks who love the adventure and can't think of a single thing that interests them more.

Many who read this book are just starting out and will be scanning the listings for people who seem to be building their lists. Many of those agents have great potential. Some don't.

## Who's Included in This Book?

I went through a real crisis about whom to include. Anybody who would talk to me? Only those agents that I could, actually in good conscience recommend? It seems inappropriate for me to try to play God about who is worthy and who is not.

On the other hand, I don't want my readers to think I would recommend everyone who is in the book. That automatically makes anyone not in the book suspect.

When I began writing these books, with the exception of the conglomerates, I only included agencies whose offices I could personally visit and interview. Today, in the interests of time and geography, there are a few that I have only met on the phone. The majority of the profiles are based on personal interviews.

Most of the time, I went to the office because that was most convenient for the agent and seeing the office refined my thinking about the agency. I didn't meet everyone in every agency or all the partners, but I did meet with a partner or an agent who was acting as a spokesman for the company. I could be wrong in my judgments, but at least they are not based on hearsay.

It's a good bet that if an agent is not included in the book, then I didn't know about them or had no access to information about them.

## Number of Clients

The number of clients listed at the end of an agency profile only refers to actor clients unless otherwise specified and, just as the box office receipts reported in *Variety* might be inflated for business reasons, so too an agency may under report the size of the list. In reality, they may have more clients than they can reasonably represent and they would just as soon not publicize that fact.

The general agent-to-client ratio you should be looking for is at least one agent for every twenty to twenty-five clients. Anything over that, it's difficult to imagine a client getting much in the way of personal attention.

## Screen Actors Guild Agency Lists

Most of the profiles in this book list a few clients from the agency's list, but some of the agents would not release any names lest they leave someone out. In those cases, they frequently give me a list and invite me to choose names. Sometimes I've gleaned names from trade ads paid for by the agency. Some information comes from trade columns devoted to information on artists and their reps.

If you are a member of SAG, you have access to any agency's client list. If you are not a member, you can consult the *Academy Players Directory* leafing through the pages to see which agents handle which actors.

The material at *APD* is not as quickly accessible as going to the union and just pulling down an agency name and checking their clients. However, seeing client pictures pared with agent names might give you a more informed idea about a particular agency.

Take the time to do the research. It's worth it.

## Less Is More

Once you feel you actually have something to interest an agent — an audition tape in your bag, a play in production and/or some swell reviews from decent venues — be discriminating in your quest for representation.

Don't blanket the town with letters. Target three agents that seem right for you and ration your money, time, and energy. It's more likely to pay off than the scattershot approach.

Agents are already inundated with reels and reviews, and while they are all looking for the next hot actor, there are only so many hours in a day. Don't waste their time or yours.

If you are just starting, don't expect CAA to come knocking at your door. Choose someone who is at your level so you can grow together.

If you have just gotten a job on your own, you will probably have some referrals already. Check them out and see who appeals to you. A job is not automatic entree. As you have probably noted throughout this book, most agents are not interested in a one shot deal and many say they are not adding to their client lists at all.

Don't despair. Agents agree that new blood is what keeps the industry going. Even if you have thirty pairs of shoes and swear you will never buy another, if you see shoes that captivate you, you will buy them. The trick is to be captivating or, more specifically, marketable.

## Body of Work

In my experience researching agents for actors, writers, and directors, I keep learning that agents are interested in a body of work. They want to see a progression of you and your product. They want to know that they are not squandering their hard won contacts on someone who doesn't have the ability to go the distance. They won't be able to buy a cottage in the south of France on their commissions from one job. Neither will you.

Like attracts like. You will ultimately get just what you want in an agent. I believe you can get a terrific agent if you make yourself a terrific client. There are no shortcuts. And today is not the last day of your life.

In her book, *My Lives*, Roseanne quotes a line from Sun Tzu's *The Art of War*, which she says everyone in Hollywood has read. It basically says: "The one who cares most, wins."

## Kevin Bacon/Referrals

As you read the agency listings, you will see that many of the agents, though they will look at query letters, are not open to being contacted by new people who have no one to recommend them.

If you don't know anyone, remember "The Kevin Bacon Game." It's the same concept as the play/movie *Six Degrees of Separation* which contends that anyone in the world can find an association with anyone else in the world through six associations; in "The Kevin Bacon Game," it only takes three degrees and in some cases, less.

It goes like this. Your mother shops at the same grocery store as

Kevin Bacon or, in my own case, I have worked with Tom Hanks who knows Kevin Bacon. Ostensibly, if I had a script I wanted to get to Kevin, I ought to be able to get it to him through Tom.

This all goes by way of saying that if you track all the odds and ends of your life, you should be able to produce somebody who knows somebody who knows somebody and come up with an authentic (however tenuous) connection to someone who can make a call for you so that you are not just querying/calling cold.

If you can't come up with a connection, you'll write the best darn letter in the world and knock some agent right on his butt. However, if you can score at "The Kevin Bacon Game" it would be best.

# ⊿ Remember ⊾

✓ Your first agent is you. You must be your own agent until you attract someone who will care and has more access than you. It's better to keep on being your own agent than to have an agent without access or passion.

✓ Make yourself read all the listings before you make a decision.

✓ Mass mailings are usually a waste of money. There is no use sending CAA or ICM a letter without entry. It's pointless to query someone you have never heard of. If you have no information about the agent, how do you know you want him? Take the long view. Look for an agent you would want to be with for years. Be selective.

✓ Don't blow your chances of being taken seriously by pursuing an agent before you are ready.

✓ Although rules were made to be broken, presuming on an agent's time by showing up at his office without an appointment or calling to speak to the agent as though you are an old friend, will ultimately backfire. Observe good manners and be sensitive to other people's space and time.

✓ Getting the right agent is not the answer to all your prayers, but it's a start!

# 15
## ⊷Agency Listings ⊶

Check addresses and names before mailing. Every effort has been made to provide accurate and current addresses and phone numbers, but agents move and computers goof, so call the office and verify information.

They won't know it's you.

# ⩗ Above the Line Agency ⩘

9200 Sunset Boulevard, #804
(just E of Doheny)
Los Angeles, CA 90069
310-859-6115

Covering this agency in this book is really a courtesy listing because Above the Line (one of the most impressive literary agencies in town) really doesn't represent actors at all. Like another top drawer literary agency, Kaplan Staller Gummer, each agency represents one lone actor left over from a previous life. They both have SAG franchises and are listed in the SAG Agency lists but neither of them is available, as it were, to date you.

So save your pictures and resumes. Unless you are an advanced scriptwriter, there's no reason to contact either of these agencies as they just toss the pictures and resumes.

**Agents**
Rima Greer
**Client List**
1

# ⚞ Abrams Artists ⚟

9200 Sunset Boulevard, 11th floor
(just E of Doheny)
Los Angeles, CA 90069
310-859-0625

A brusk, efficient man, Harry Abrams has headed or partnered a string of agencies over the years: Abrams-Rubaloff, one of the commercial forces in New York City in the late 1960s and 1970s; Abrams Harris & Goldberg, a prestigious theatrical agency in Los Angeles during the early to mid-1980s; and currently Abrams Artists both in New York and Los Angeles.

Through resourcefulness, determination, an eye for talent and the hiring of excellent theatrical agents with their own splendid client lists, Abrams has carved out an impressive agency that is respected in all areas of the business. He runs the motion picture and television department in Los Angeles.

Marni Goldman (from their agency training program), Lara Nesburn, Eric Emery, Gregg Klein and Joe Rice rep adults for film, television and theater, while Jennifer Millar, Matt Fletcher and Wendi Green run the successful Youth Division.

Names from their list are Keith David *(There's Something about Mary)*, Taylor Nichols *(The Last Days of Disco)*, Frankie Muniz *(Malcolm in the Middle)*, Hallie Kate Eisenberg *(Bicentennial Man)*, Cara DeLizia *(So Weird)*, Eric Per Sullivan *(Malcolm in the Middle)*, and Spencer Klein *(Hey Arnold)*.

**Agents**
Jennifer Millar, Wendi Green, Marni Goldman, Lara Nesburn, Joe Rice, Eric Emery, Matt Fletcher, and Gregg Klein
**Clients**
200

# ⇲ Acme Talent & Literary ⇱

4727 Wilshire Boulevard, #333
(W of Rossmore)
Los Angeles, CA 90010
323-954-2263

Lisa Lindo and Adam Lieblein founded Acme Talent & Literary in Los Angeles in 1993 to rep actors for film, television, and commercials. In 1996, they absorbed the Writers & Artists commercial department and in 1997 they opened a New York office.

Lisa left the partnership in 2002 to pursue a career as a producer-manager. Adam, a product of the UCLA film department began his career in the early 1980s producing independent feature films and segments for television magazine shows, as well as hundreds of commercials, working for star commercial directors Bob Giraldi, Mark Coppos, Rob Lieberman and others.

Adam is now the sole owner of Acme. He runs the Los Angeles office along with Gwenn Pepper who heads the television talent department. She graduated from the agency's training program. They are joined by colleagues Greg Meyer, Scott Reed, and Jackie Lewis, who helms the Youth Division.

Acme has regulars on *The Practice* (Jason Kravits), *The Sopranos, Malcolm In The Middle, Arliss, The Hughleys* and *Oz*. Comedy clients Matt Price (*Price & Bleiden*) and Jason Kravits both appeared at the Aspen Comedy Festival where Kravits won Best Sketch Comedy performer.

Acme's clients usually come to them via industry referral, but they do look at all pictures and resumes.

**Agents**
Adam Lieblein, Gwenn Pepper, Greg Meyer, Scott Reed and Jackie Lewis
**Client list**
195

# The Agency

10351 Ventura Boulevard
(at Tujunga)
Studio City, CA 91614
310-551-3000

Founded in 1984 by Jerome Zeitman, Larry Becsey, and Richard Berman, Jerome is now the sole owner of this respected agency. Jerome's career began at William Morris where he helped pioneer the concept of packaging. He produced at both Wolper Productions and Columbia Pictures before creating The Agency.

Frank Gonzales heads up the talent department. The Agency does look at pictures and resumes, but unless you have at least five co-starring credits, don't bother querying.

**Agents**
Frank Gonzales and Jerry Zeitman
**Client List**
120

# ⚓ APA/Agency for the Performing Arts ⚓

9200 Sunset Boulevard, 9th floor
(E of Doheny)
Los Angeles, CA 90069
310-273-0744

Even though APA recently closed their New York office, both the Los Angeles and Nashville branches are in tact and this smallest of the corporate agencies is still very much in business. Founded in the 1960s by ICM expatriates as a personal appearance agency, that aspect of the agency is still its strong suit.

The synergy that comes from servicing a smaller group of actors, writers, directors, producers, stand-up performers, newscasters, and concert performers also allows the kind of client nourishment one would usually only expect to get from an independent agent.

President Jim Gosnell heads up the talent division and joins colleagues Pamela Wagner, Joel Dean, Jeff Witjas, Barry McPherson, Ryan Martin, Todd Neville, and Paul Santana representing the acting clients. Nat Burgess leads personal appearance agents Troy Blakely, Josh Humistan, Jaime Kelsall, Craig Newman, Shane Shuhart, Andrew Simon, and Jason Zell.

In addition to APA's strong list of acting clients, the agency is also known as the place for comedy development and regularly holds its own showcases to introduce clients to buyers. Danny Robinson is the comedy maven along with Jackie Miller and Nick Nuciforo.

APA clients include Sam Elliott, Ronny Cox, Rutger Hauer, Morgan Fairchild, Judd Hirsh, Bai Ling, James Duval, Jamie Kennedy, Crispin Glover, George Hamilton, James Hampton, Rita Moreno and Phylicia Rashad.

### Agents
Jim Gosnell, Pamela Wagner, Joel Dean, Jeff Witjas, Barry McPherson, Ryan Martin, Todd Neville, Paul Santana, Nat Burgess, Troy Blakely, Josh Humistan, Jaime Kelsall, Craig Newman, Shane Shuhart, Andrew Simon, Jason Zell, Danny Robinson, and Jackie Miller
### Client List
250

# ◹ Agency West Entertainment ◸

5750 Wilshire Boulevard, #640N
(across from SAG/E of Fairfax/enter through courtyard)
Hollywood, CA 90036
323-857-9050

Starting in the business as a production assistant on *Hard Copy*, Holly Davis Carter's next stop was as an assistant in casting before creating Agency West in her bedroom in 1991 with just four clients.

Before the year was out, she was out of the bedroom and had moved to her first office at Hollywood and Highland.

She stayed there for five years before moving to Vine Street for another five. In 2003 she relocated to Wilshire Boulevard.

Holly is now focused on her new creation, Relevè, the only agency in town specializing in hip hop and gospel artists for theatrical representation. While Holly is busy birthing Relevè, she's handed over the reins of Agency West to Sheba Williams.

Sheba was a Communications major at California State Los Angeles with an eye toward some kind of show business career. The closest she got to it for a while was via her actor children. From that vantage point, it seemed to her that there wasn't much to being an agent.

Sheba began interning in 2002 before quickly moving up to being a sub-agent in the youth division of Agency West. She found her vision informed by the realities of the business and realized that there's much more to being a successful agent than just getting a client an audition.

Today, Sheba reps not only the youth division but the adults as well. She says the agency is multicultural with about 150 clients in both the theatrical and commercial departments.

Sheba is only interested in trained SAG actors. Although the agency's original focus was on thirty and under, Sheba is now growing the thirty and over category.

Sheba has several interns and agents-in-training that help her rep her theatrical list of about twenty to twenty-five. She's up for submitting any of her clients theatrically when she thinks they are ready. Sub-agent Nancy Chaidez will probably be franchised by the time you read this.

Housed in the same offices with DePasse Entertainment, if you are called in to meet Sheba, go early so you can find your way through the courtyard and to the north elevators to their offices.

Sheba is constantly checking out college showcases and theater across town looking for her passion — good actors. She also looks carefully at every single picture and resume that comes in.

Sheba really impressed me with her overall view of the business. Agency West continues to grow. Some of her clients are Haj, Tyrone Mitchell, Mitchal Williams (*The Lyons Den, Fighting Temptations, ER*), Jordan Mosley, and Adam Cagley.

Not content to just read the Breakdown, Agency West is constantly searching for projects for its clients, seeking to bring together a writer or director with their clients and help that package on its way.

**Agents**
Sheba Williams and Nancy Chaidez
**Clients**
20-25

# ◢ Aimee Entertainment ◣

15840 Ventura Boulevard, #215
(five blocks W of Sepulveda Boulevard)
Encino, CA 91436
818-783-9115

Yes, there really are good things in the Valley, and Helen Barkan is one of them. An agent for twenty-six years, Helen began her career at the George Hunt Agency where she first met Joyce Aimee. While Helen went on to the William Schuller Agency, Joyce opened her own agency specializing in personal appearances. The friendship turned into a partnership when the ladies decided to pool their resources, forming an office that could represent clients in both avenues of the business. Joyce still handles personal appearances and Helen is godmother to all the actors. I ran into one of Helen's clients who told me that Helen was the nicest lady she had ever met.

Clients from Helen's list include Lewis Dauber, Stan Sellers, Don Snell, Layla Galloway and Richard Davalos.

**Agent**
Helen Barkan
**Client List**
50-60

# ◢ Alvarado Rey Agency ◣

8455 Beverly Boulevard, # 406
(one block E of La Cienega)
Los Angeles, CA 90048
323-655-7978

Back in 1941, Carlos Alvarado created this agency to represent talented Latin and European actors living in Los Angeles. In 1983, Mona Lee Schilling inherited this agency from her Uncle Carlos and in September of 2000, when Mona Lee decided to retire, the first person she called was Nikkolas Rey, because she knew he would carry on the legacy of Uncle Carlos and concentrate on this increasingly important ethnic group of actors.

Rey, who began in the business as an actor, worked in a variety of positions before Mona Lee's fateful call. Originally a client of Mona Lee's, he had worked for her as an assistant before his jobs as production coordinator (Nosotros) and casting director (at Mambo casting Hispanic commercials).

Nikkolas considers his experience casting at Mambo to have been an excellent way to train to be an agent. Until Mona Lee called to say she was retiring, Nikkolas was considering becoming a casting director. The idea of following in the footsteps of Uncle Carlos and Mona Lee was too appealing to pass up, so in July of 2000, Rey became the new owner of the Alvarado Agency.

Rey feels that he not only knows the agency well, but that his activities producing and casting within the Hispanic and European acting community give him an edge in his approach to marketing his actors.

This agency is long on history as Nikkolas' colleague, Anton Calderon was also an ex-client of Mona Lee's. An actor-producer, Anton was searching for a new focus in show business when, in the fall of 2003, he reconnected with his old friend Nikkolas and accepted his offer to expand AR's Youth Division.

Clients from the agency's list of fifty or so clients are Yvette Cruise, Alma Beltran, Janice Rivera, Lucas Bentivogolio, Eddie Martin, Lucas Osta, and Danny Mora.

The Alvarado Agency reps clients theatrically and commercially, and calls in Hispanic and European actors regularly from the pictures and resumes they receive in the mail. Nikkolas believes you have to see and meet with an actor in order to know if something jumps out at you and you want to work with them.

**Agents**
Nikkolas Rey, Thomas Richards, and Anton Calderon
**Client List**
50

# ◿ Amatruda Benson & Associates ◺

9107 Wilshire Boulevard, #500
(at Doheny)
Beverly Hills, CA 90210
310-276-1851

Amatruda Benson & Associates was created by Lois Benson in 1973. Lois was widely respected as a children's agent for over twenty years. When she retired in 1995, she left the agency in the hands of Kimberly Gola.

Kimberly was a model who decided she wanted something more and began training herself for it. She began by working at a print agency and continued her education when she moved to Los Angeles and got a job as an assistant at a manager's office.

While Gola was working in management in 1993, she met and worked with Benson when they had clients in common. When Benson suggested that Gola learn the agency business by working for her in preparation for taking over the business when Benson retired, Gola accepted. The transition has been smooth and although the agency only represents children, there are a few older clients who have been here for over twenty years.

The theatrical clients at ABA are served by Joseph Le, who became an agent at this agency. Clients from his list of about 200 are Alan Morgan (*Little Rascals, The Tonight Show with Jay Leno*), Amber Bonasso (co-host of the new kid's game show *Click*) and Kristen Stewart (*The Safety of Objects*).

**Agents**
Joseph Le and Kimberly Gola
**Client List**
200

# ⚮ Amsel, Eisenstadt & Frazier ⚮

5757 Wilshire Boulevard, #510
(btwn La Brea & Fairfax)
Los Angeles, CA 90036
323-939-1188

Mike Eisenstadt always knew he wanted to do something in show business, but until he entered the fray as a casting assistant at Lorimar and took a look around, he didn't know he wanted to be an agent. Once he knew, he joined Fred Amsel Agency as a trainee. When Fred retired, Mike and his colleague John Frazier (who joined Amsel as an intern) bought the business.

Gloria Hinojosa (Capital Artists) helps them rep their adult clients while Carolyn Thompson-Goldstein (Media Artists Group) heads the Youth Department.

Clients from their list of about 100 include Danny Trejo, Janet Leigh, Mako, and Fred Willard.

Although AEF sees new clients mainly by referral or by sampling the talent in clubs and the theater, they do look at all pictures.

**Agents**
Mike Eisenstadt, Gloria Hinojosa, Carolyn Thompson-Goldstein, and John Frazier
**Client List**
100

# ⚞ Angel City Talent ⚟

4741 Laurel Canyon Boulevard #101
(just S of Riverside)
Studio City, CA 91607
818-760-9980

Mimi Meyer was a commercial agent at Jack Scagnetti Agency in 1985 when Lorri Herman hired her to help her expand the character actor department at the Judith Fontaine Agency.

Together they created a commercial department at Tom Jennings' theatrical/literary agency during the writer's strike in 1987. When the strike was over, Tom wanted out of the commercial business, so in 1990, Mimi and Lorri opened Angel City Talent. Their reputation among casting directors was so good that they managed to book a job about five minutes after opening their doors.

Angel City belongs to Mimi now. Brittany Galbreath graduated from Angel City's agent training department to join Mimi repping adults and kids for theater, film, and television.

Nick Jameson (*Gary & Mike, The Drew Carey Show*), Wayne Thomas Yorke (*Once Upon a Christmas, Any Day Now*), Sean Smith (*Time of Your Life, The Phantom of the Opera*), Rhonda Aldrich (*ER*), William Lucking (*The Rundown, Red Dragon*), Duke Stroud (*Panic*), Delanna Studi (*Dreamkeeper*), Barry Sigismondi (*Strong Medicine, CSI, The Shield, 10-8*), Lucille Soong (*Freaky Friday*), Warren Sweeney (*Skin, The Drawer Boy*), Bruce Gray (*Playmakers*), Daniele O'Loughlin (*Phil of the Future*), Ronnie Schell (*Lucky*), Honey Lauren (*The District*), George Ball (*All My Sons*), Anita Finlay (*Young and the Restless*), Laurel Green (*Miss Match*), Gwen Mihok (*ER, 8-10*), (Virginia Reece (*American Dreams*), Jill Remez (*Skin, She Spys*), and Alex Alexander (*Little Black Book, The Guardian, Dragnet*) are names from their list of about thirty-eight.

Although they look at all pictures and resumes, you really need an industry referral to be considered here.

**Agents**
Mimi Mayer and Brittany Galbreath
**Clients**
38

# ☀ The Artists Agency ☀

1180 S Beverly Drive, #400
(at Pico)
Los Angeles, CA 90035
310-277-7779

Although one of the most prestigious, elegant agencies in town, The Artists Agency remains accessible and respectful of actors at all levels. They may not sign you, but they always treat you with respect.

Originally named The Sandy Bresler Agency when Sandy left ICM in 1971 and started this agency, the present name was chosen as partners were added and subtracted. Today, the partners are Jimmy Cota, Mike Livingston, Mickey Freiberg and Dick Shepherd.

Agents who represent actors at the agency are Jimmy Cota, Bruce Tufeld (Writers & Artists), and Adele Nadel (McCartt Orek Barrett, Metropolitan).

Because this agency prizes trained actors, young people with prime theater educations (particularly the League Schools) will usually be seen though not necessarily signed.

Although they may be impressed with your background, in order to exist in an agency at this level, you are better off with a decent resume in addition to your education before you query them.

Their lists of about 125 actors includes Marion Ross, John Ashton, Ossie Davis, Ruby Dee, Joe Don Baker, Giancarlo Giannini, Billy Dee Williams, Dorian Harewood, William Allen Young, Charlie Robinson, Barbara Bain, Deborah May, and Linda Kash.

The Artists Agency also represents writers, directors and producers.

**Agents**
Jimmy Cota, Mike Livingston, Bruce Tufeld, and Adele Nadel
**Client List**
150

# ⊿ The Artists Group, Ltd. ⊾

10100 Santa Monica Boulevard, #240
(btwn Century Park East & Avenue of the Stars)
Los Angeles, CA 90067
310-552-1100

Working as a sometime secretary for his prestigious casting director brother Lynn, Hal Stalmaster was exposed to agents on a regular basis before his fifteenth birthday. Pretty soon an agent spotted him. He ended up as the lead in the Disney movie, *Johnny Tremaine*.

Though he had a decent career going, Hal says he didn't have the necessary drive to be an actor. He knew he wanted to be in the business, so after high school, college and the Army, he worked in casting and as an agent while he deciding what he really wanted to do. Hal tells me he's still deciding.

His first agent job was with his ultimate partner, Milton Grossman, who retired in 1982. Hal joined Arnold Soloway and they expanded the actor client base to include writers, directors and below-the-line.

Arnold left the agency in 1992 and Hal merged with New York agent, Robert Malcolm (PGA). Since Malcolm already had a thriving agency in New York, his addition to The Artists Group in Los Angeles meant, among other things, that this agency became bicoastal.

I met Malcolm years ago when I interviewed him at his original New York office. Dynamic and empathetic, his clients have always been crazy about him. Other agents at The Artists Group who represent actors are Rob Dee (Irv Schechter, Bauman-Hiller), Nancy Moon-Broadstreet and Mark Perara (WMA, Gersh).

Clients from their list include Jerry Orbach, Nancy Dussault, Jamie Farr, Loretta Switt, W. Earl Brown (*There's Something About Mary*), Jayne Meadows, Mickey Rooney, Charles Nelson Reilly, Harry Morgan, Dom DeLuise, Charlotte Rae, Linda Gray, Leigh-Taylor Young, Tony Lo Bianco, Theodore Bikel, and Joan Severance.

**Agents**
Robert Malcolm, Hal Stalmaster, Rob Dee, Nancy Moon-Broadstreet and Mark Perara
**Client List**
70

# ⤧ The Austin Agency ⤨

6715 Hollywood Boulevard, #204
(btwn Highland and Las Palmas)
Hollywood, CA 90028
323-959-4444

I'm so lucky that I write these books because I meet cool people that I would never otherwise know about — John Lyons being a case in point.

Arriving from Ireland on a scholarship in hotel management at Cornell in the early nineties, John quickly realized what he didn't want to do (hotel management!), but wasn't sure what he *did* want to do. Nevertheless, he moved to New York to search for his future.

Coming from a family background with serious exposure to the arts, he thought he would explore the theater. John worked part time and finally secured a job as a stage manager, "an excellent way to learn the business." He then took a three-month producing course that he feels was even more instructive.

In 1993 he created New York's Daedalus Theatre Company serving as Artistic Director. His goal to marry contemporary Irish playwrights and directors with American actors was successful from the get-go.

After seven years in New York, John moved to Los Angeles, searching for any kind of showbiz job and finally became an assistant to agent Susan Smith. Six months later, he became was an agent at the Merit Blake Agency and decided in 1999 that it was time for him to start his own agency which he named after his mother.

John says he was greener than he thought when he first started, but he is obviously a quick study since he has clients on Broadway, in series and in films. Actors from his list include Ravi Kapoor (*Crossing Jordan*), William Salyers (*Judging Amy*), Fina Toibin (*Long Days Journey into Night*), Anastasia Basil (*Terminal*), Rebecca Lowman (*Judging Amy, Will & Grace*), Francis Fallon (*Yuria and Me, Southside*), Jane Amelia Larson, Jeanie Bacharach, and Russell Milton.

The best way to get John's attention is to do good work in a play in town. He goes to see everything. John appears to be the agent every actor would want. He encourages his actors by saying, "You can't give up, because I'm not giving up."

How great is that!

**Agent**
John Lyons
**Clients**
25-30

# ✍ Badgley & Connor Agency ✍

9229 Sunset Boulevard, #311
(W of Doheny)
Los Angeles, CA 90069
310-278-9313

Erin Connor was an actress in New York who went to work for her manager, Bill Treusch, and subsequently opened his West Coast office. Once she got to Los Angeles, she was hired away by Arnold Rifkin and Nicole David (Rifkin-David, DHKPR) and ultimately by The Gersh Agency where she met partner, Jeralyn Badgley.

Jeralyn got into the business by accident. Fresh out of college, she took an apprentice publicist job at Twentieth Century Fox, which led to a job in their live tape television division. When the casting director left unexpectedly, it fell to Jeralyn and the associate producer to cast the show.

Jeralyn cast that show and others before becoming involved in production in the live tape division. Legendary agent Jack Field found her there on her last day of work on *The Midnight Special*, bought her lunch, and spirited her away to work for him. She worked at William Morris and at The Gersh Agency before joining Erin in 1985 to open an office respected for their tasty list of respected working actors. Jeralyn retired in 2001 and Erin now runs the agency alone.

Kelly Miller graduated from the agency training department at B&C and joins Erin representing clients Allan Miller, Alan Feinstein, John Pleshette, Karen Morrow, Michael Dunn, Jo De Winter, Jessica Harper, Louise Latham, and Tracey Needham.

**Agents**
Erin Connor and Kelly Miller
**Client List**
100

# ✒ Baier/Kleinman International ✒

3575 Cahuenga Boulevard, #500
(W of Barham)
Los Angeles, CA 90068
323-874-9800

Since Joel Kleinman descends from a long line of Rabbis, one might have expected him to be doing business in a synagogue, but his love of showbiz took him down a different route. High school and college acting experiences plus exposure to master studio craftspeople at a lighting job, increased his respect for theater artists and his pull toward the business. He knew his talent lay in the talker/salesman area, so he began his training with the Nora Sanders Agency.

Joel's German wife, Marget Baier, inspired his move to Germany where he worked in a series of theater/film related jobs; casting, producing, translating scripts and even acting. His growing connections in the film community led to finding European jobs for American actors and provided the background for what is now his niche as an agent — representing European actors who have come to California, and linking American actors to European jobs.

Joel returned to California in 1987 to work with Alex Brewis and Bob Cosdin before opening his own agency in 1993, and, since Marget was the architect of the international aspect of his work, Joel gave her first billing when he named his business.

Joel's list includes Levani (*Air Force One*), Peter Lucas (*Into Thin Air*), Aleksandra Kaniak (*Forbidden Games*), Clement Von Franckenstein (*Titan*), Terri Hoyos (*The Ortegas*), and Barbara Whinnery (*St. Elsewhere*).

In addition to his international business, Joel has a strong list of American actors working in both series television and films.

Although he's not really looking for new clients, Joel does look at all pictures and resumes. He works with clients of all ages for film, theater and television and also books stand-ups.

**Agent**
Joel Kleinman
**Client List**
50-60

# ⚒ Bobby Ball Talent Agency ⚒

4342 Lankershim Boulevard
(S of Moorpark)
Universal City, CA 91602
818-506-8188

When Patty Grana opened the Los Angeles office of mom Bobby Ball's thriving Phoenix agency in 1984, BBA was small and scratching. However, for years now, BBA has had thriving departments not only theatrically, but also in commercials, sports and music, as well as having one of the most prestigious dance departments in town.

Eric Stevens, who heads the Stage & Screen Division of BB, worked in public relations as soon as he graduated from high school. His first agenting job was at Camden Artists. During the actors strike of 1978, he took a break from show business and became a physician's assistant working with HIV patients. He worked both in Los Angeles and in New Orleans as both an assistant and researcher. After seven years of death and dying, Eric decided to return to show business and worked with Scott Manners at Stone Manners.

He joined BBA in 2000 as the Equity agent and gradually began to move those clients over into film and television. At this point, Eric not only reps clients Carol Lawrence (*West Side Story*), Darlene Love, (*Lethel Weapon*), Marcia Rodd (*The Four Seasons, Trapper John*), Jodi Benson (*The Little Mermaid*), Julie Budd (*The Devil and Max Devlin*), Perry Stephens (*The Lot, Norma Jean and Marilyn*), Ray Benson (*Bob and Ray*), Bruce Winant (*Carnivale, Crossing Jordon*), but also packages for his director clients (Jessica Kubbansky, Nick Degruccio, John Vaughan, Calvin Remsberg, and Rick Sparks).

*Amy's View* at the Pasadena Playhouse with Carol Lawrence was a result of that synergy. Doug Murphy was at Herb Tannen before joining BB to head up the Youth Division.

**Agents**
Eric Stevens and Doug Murphy
**Client List**
50

# ⊿ Baron Entertainment ⊿

5757 Wilshire Blvd., #659
(in the Screen Actors Guild Building/just E of Fairfax)
Los Angeles, CA 90036
323-936-7600

Rod Baron knew he wanted to be in showbiz when he grew up, he just didn't know exactly where. The northern California ex-child actor decided to major in Psychology while he was figuring that out and, upon graduation, set out for southern California to make his fortune.

He read numerous books about show business jobs and finally concluded that agenting would be the best use of all his talents.

He got a job delivering packages for commercial powerhouse, Commercials Unlimited, and within a year was an agent.

Not content to just service existing clients, Rod developed a whole new youth theatrical department for CU and by the time he left, he had five clients on series.

He opened Baron Entertainment in January 2000 during the commercial strike and managed to not only survive, but prosper. His website is amazing and gives you an idea of the kind of forward thinking that makes this agency such a force. www.baronentertainment.com.

At this point, his theatrical list is only about ten clients, but they are all doing well. Gail Monian (*American Family*), Nick Roye, J. T. Jackson, Matt Williamson, Bubba Smith, Amy Brassette (*Cedric the Entertainer*), and Mary McDonough (*The Waltons*).

Baron Entertainment handles actors, children, comedians, dancers, martial arts, etc. Though Rod is hiring a new theatrical agent, at this point he is helming the theatrical department.

**Agent**
Rod Baron
**Clients**
10

# ⊿ Bauman, Redanty & Shaul ⊾

5757 Wilshire Boulevard, #473
(SAG/AFTRA Building., E of Fairfax)
Los Angeles, CA 90036
323-857-6666

The history of this agency begins with the now deceased partners who each ran agencies on different coasts and knew each other only by telephone.

In 1975, New Yorker Richard Bauman moved west. On his first day of work, he met his new Los Angeles partner, Wally Hiller, for the first time. The partnership was successful and the agency prospered.

In 2000, two longtime New York colleagues, Mark Redanty and David Shaul, became partners. Mark handles things from New York and David helms the Los Angeles office.

David Shaul got his BFA in Theater Management in 1984 from Ithaca and his first job in New York was as an intern to prestigious casting directors Meg Simon and Fran Kumin. Even though he only spent three months there, David says it was an incredible education.

After three months, he landed his first job in an agent's office as assistant to Peter Strain at Bauman Hiller. Two and a half years later, when Strain moved to APA, David went along as a junior agent. When Strain left to form Strain Jennett, Shaul went along as the third agent.

He was at Henderson Hogan from 1993 until 1995 when he rejoined Bauman Hiller, and in 1998 when Wally died, David moved west to the Los Angeles office.

BRS has an illustrious group of clients, many of whom (like Jean Stapleton, Sada Thompson and James Earl Jones) have been with them for most of their careers. Colleagues Adam Lazarus (Peter Strain) and Colleen Schlegel (Gersh Agency, Innovative Artists) join David repping their illustrous list which includes Louise Fletcher (*Clipping Adam*), Dennis Chrisopher (*Nine Lives, Breaking Away*), Tim Carhart (*The Price of a Broken Heart*), Robert Morse (*Tru*), Michael Sarrazin, Kristin Chenoweth (*Kristin*), Paula Newson (*City of Angels*), Susan Clark (*Babe*), Renee Taylor (*The Nanny, It Had To Be You*), Stephanie Powers (*The Baby Dance*), Andrea Marcovicci, Nancy Allen, Deirdre Lovejoy, Jack Wallace, John Beasley, Chris Sarandon, Michael Nouri, Jude Ciccolella, Graham Bickel, Keith Szarabajki (*We Were Soldiers*), Chris Ellis, Parker

Stevenson, Barry Shabka Henley, Jack Coleman, Victor Williams (*King of Queens*), Robert Duncan MacNeil (*Star Trek*), Naveen Andrews, Ann Guilbert, Elizabeth Hoffman.

Clients usually come to this office by referral and work freelance only as a prelude to signing. BRS looks at all pictures and resumes.

Though Bauman died in 2003, Redanty and Shaul have elected to keep his name on the masthead maintaining that important historical link to the origins of this class agency.

**Agents**
David Shaul, Adam Lazarus and Colleen Schlegel
**Client List**
120

# ᴁ Bicoastal Talent ᴂ

3489 Cahuenga West, #A
(just W of Lankershim Boulevard)
Hollywood, CA 90068
323-512-7755

When I hear the term bicoastal, I usually think New York and Los Angeles. That just shows how provincial I am. My first thought is that an agency opened on one coast and then at some point opened the branch agency on the other coast. So much for first thoughts.

Not only did ex-actors Liz and Greta Hanley open both offices of Bicoastal simultaneously, they opened their agency during the actor's strike in 2000 and lived to talk about it. Does that tell you something about how hard these women work and how much they care?

A working actor in Chicago, Liz Hanley started her own theater company where she acted, produced, directed and was mentored by Gary Sinise and Jeff Perry of Steppenwolf. When she moved to Los Angeles in 1989, she produced, was on the board at Deaf West Theater and finally retired for a few years when she became a mother.

In 2000, her mother Greta, who had been agenting at the Diamond Agency in Orlando, decided she was ready to be her own boss and persuaded Liz to join her in her new business.

Because both Liz and Greta were actors, it stands to reason that they appreciate strong theater resumes and serious theater training. Shoshannah Stern, Greg Wagrowski, Jenny Robertson, Molly Bryant and Paul Raci are some of the fifty clients from their Los Angeles list.

Samantha Daniels joined Liz in 2001 to head up the commercial division of BTA. In addition to her background as an agent (Film Artists Agency, APA, Bobby Ball Agency), Sam trained as an actress at the North Carolina School of the Arts, studied with Uta Hagen and Sanford Meisner, worked in casting, licensed music and was a coordinator at Chelsea Studios.

**Agents**
Liz Hanley and Samantha Daniels
**Clients**
50

# ⨳ Black Talent & Literary ⨲

12034 Riverside Drive, #103
(corner of Laurel Canyon)
Valley Village, CA 91604
818-753-5424

If you want a "take charge" person as your agent, Bonnie Black is a good choice. When her mother was in the hospital and it was impossible to make a long distance call from the room, Bonnie, tired of going down the hall to the pay phone, started the business that enabled you to dial long distance from anyplace using 1+0+contact phone numbers in the state of California. She sold that business a few years ago, freeing up her energy to repair another situation that was not working.

In 1994, when her actress daughter's agent bungled an audition for a big part in a movie, Bonnie opened Black Talent with her daughter as her sole client. After six months, she had ten clients and now, she and ex-hospital administrator husband Frank have quite a list.

A mom and pop operation with 500 clients of every stripe would be the best way to describe Black Talent & Literary. Mom and pop, not just because it's a husband and wife agency, but because both Bonnie and Frank Black embrace all 500 clients as though there were related to them. Christians, they even hold Wednesday night Bible study in the office for those clients who are interested in attending.

Their list not only includes actors, writers, directors, producers and kids, they have an illusionist, a fire eater and an up close magician. They are currently in the market for a chain saw juggler.

Names from their list include Frances Black, Tom Dreesen and Johnny Dark.

**Agents**
Bonnie Black and Frank Black
**Clients**
500

# ⩘ Bloc ⩗

5225 Wilshire Boulevard, 311
(E of Fairfax)
Los Angeles, CA 90036
323-954-7730

Three childhood friends from Canada came south to create a dynamic new agency committed to representing the very best dancers and choreographers on both coasts and have quickly realized their goals.

Siblings Laney and Brendan Filuk's mother had a dance studio in Canada so it's no surprise that Laney is a dancer and that both Laney and Brendan are entrepreneurs.

Laney moved to Los Angeles to dance and act and ended up helping out her agent, Dorothy Day Otis, with the dance clients. Brendan was working at Sony music when the Filuks hit upon a new idea, an agency with a focus solely on dance.

Although their friend David Crombie had moved from Calgary to Seattle to work in technology, when Laney and Brendan suggested he join them in their Los Angeles adventure, Crombie quickly agreed. He spent a year learning the ropes of the new business before moving to Manhattan to open the New York branch of Bloc. Even though Bloc New York opened just a month after 9/11 in October 2001, the agency has prospered.

A case could be made that the name of the agency represents the names of its principals: **B**rendan, **L**aney, **C**rombie. However, the name was chosen for a more profound reason: bloc means people "coming together for a common goal" which is just what these friends have done and is the focus of their agency.

The partners worked hard to create a Bloc "brand" that represents the absolute best in dancers and choreographers. Producers and casting directors quickly responded.

You'll see Bloc dancers in all the Broadway shows, on *Saturday Night Live, Carson Daly*, and scores of commercials as well as tours for Mariah Carey, Justin Timberlake, and others.

Their choreographers include Michael Rooney (Target, Kylie Minogue, ebay), Michelle Johnston (*American Dreams*), Laurie Ann Gibson (*Honey*), Fatima Robinson (Gap, *Save the Last Dance*, Backstreet

Boys), Ricko Baird, and Marty Kudelka. More at www.blocagency.com.

A new addition to the client list is a top group of skateboarders to answer the growing advertisers demand for this specialty.

The Bloc Agency looks for three things in clients: ability to dance, the look and a good attitude.

**Agents**
Laney Filuk and Brendan Filuk
**Clients**
40

# ⚐ Bresler-Kelly & Associates ⚐

11500 West Olympic Boulevard, #352
(btwn Barrington and Sawtelle)
Los Angeles, CA 90064
310-479-5611

Sandy Bresler is a folk hero to agents. When you ask agents questions about the wisdom of hot young clients going off to CAA, agents all jump up and down and say, "What about Sandy Bresler? Jack Nicholson never went to CAA. He stayed with Sandy. Look at his career."

After talking to Sandy, however, one understands that he was never a struggling agent in the strict since of the word. He may have been broke, but he always had stature. He started with The William Morris Agency as a secretary (refusing the mailroom route) and quickly became an agent. When he left WMA, he spent about a year assisting his father, producer Jerry Bresler. He then went to CMA (ICM's predecessor) and when that agency cut back, he opened his own office and sort of struggled. True, he did have to use the other half of his lawyer's office for space, but he still had Jack Nicholson, who was already Jack Nicholson.

It wasn't long before some CMA buddies joined him (Bresler, Wolff, Cota and Livingston, The Artists Agency). In 1984, twelve years after he opened the original office, Sandy left TAA with associate (now partner) John Kelly and formed Sandy Bresler & Associates.

Kelly became a partner in 1990. Bresler-Kelly & Associates recently downsized their list and now represent a select list of fifteen established clients like Nicholson and Yeardly Smith (*As Good as it Gets, The Simpsons*), Judith Ivey, Harry Dean Stanton and Leslie Nielsen.

In addition to being a successful agent, Bresler is also generous with his time, speaking to young actors at free agency seminars sponsored by The Screen Actors Guild.

**Agents**
Sandy Bresler and John Kelly
**Client List**
15

# ⨮ Don Buchwald & Associates ⨴

6500 Wilshire Boulevard, #2200
(at San Vicente)
Los Angeles, CA 90048
323-655-7400

Don Buchwald had his own exclusive New York theatrical agency before joining forces with Harry Abrams at commercial powerhouse Abrams-Rubaloff in 1969. Eight years later, Don returned to agency ownership when he opened a powerful theatrical/commercial agency of his own.

Tim Angle's career began in New York with J. Michael Bloom, followed by stints at Triad, William Morris and Robert Abrams before subsequently joining DBA as president of the Pacific Division repping actors, writers, producers and directors for theater, film and television.

Tim's colleagues are Neil Bagg (Susan Smith & Associates), Bobby Moses (Paradigm), Mark Scroggs, Peter Young (Gersh), Tracy Christian (Peter Strain Associates), Michael Greenwald, and Julia Buchwald. Damon Frank heads the Personal Appearance division.

Their list of visible clients is stunning and includes George Takei (*Star Trek*), Ron Perlman (*Beauty and the Beast*), Terry Farrell (*Becker*), Howard Stern, Louis Zorick (*Mad About You*), Sherri Saum (*Beggars & Choosers*), Lesley Boone (*Ed*), Christine Estabrook (*Nikki Cox Show*), Scott Lowell (*Queer as Folk*), Lisa Banes (*Son of the Beach*), Robert Bogue (*Blackheart*) Harry Van Gorkum (*Fearing Mind*), William Converse-Roberts (*Any Day Now*), Robert Floyd (*Sliders*), Annabelle Gurwitch (*Dinner & a Movie*), Scott Bruce (*Popular*), Rosalind Chau (*Deep Space 9*), Erik Passoja (*Thank You, Good Night, After Sex*), Suzanne Westenhoefer (*A Family Affair*), Rachel Boston (*American Dreams*), Charlotte D'Amboise (*Chicago*), Cheryl Ladd (*Her Best Friend's Husband*), Amy Locane (*Mystery Woman, Bad Karma*), Stacy Galina (*Hidden Hills, Children of the Corn*), Ludivine Sagnier (*Swimming Pool*), Mr. T, Hulk Hogan, Al Santos (*Gross Point*), Daniel J. Travanti, Jay Thomas, Delane Matthews, Louise Fletcher, Sabrina Lloyd, Ally Sheedy, Robert Picardo, and Ahmet and Dweezil Zappa.

This agency does look at pictures and resumes, but is not interested in seeing unsolicited audition tapes. Send picture and resume and if they are interested they will request a tape.

**Agents**

Tim Angle, Bobby Moses, Julia Buchwald, Mark Scroggs, Michael Greenwald, Peter Young, Neil Bagg and Tracy Christian

**Client List**

130 (Los Angeles)

# ⊿ Buchwald Talent Group ⊵

6500 Wilshire Boulevard, #2210
(at San Vicente)
Los Angeles, CA 90048
323-951-4539

In 1998, as Don Buchwald & Associates contemplated the future of
the business and the increasingly important role that kids and young
adults were playing in the scheme of things, they decided their young
clients needed their own company, so DBA enlisted the efforts of one
of their senior agents, Philip Leader, moved him down the hall to brand
new offices with a brand new name and invited him to create BTG to
represent kids and young adults for film, television and theater.

Although the Indiana native intended to work with abused kids,
when his folks nixed the idea of an acting career, an extended visit with
relatives in New Mexico pulled him into show business. They
introduced him to commercial producers at Don Niera Productions
who invited Philip to work with them in Los Angeles. His experience
at DNP enriched his understanding of the business and whetted his
appetite for more. When Leader saw an ad for an opening in the
mailroom at Don Buchwald & Associates, he jumped on it. After three
months, he was assistant to Cynthia Land and three-and-a-half years
later, he was an agent.

Leader's colleague, Patrick Welborn joined BTG in 2003.

BTG's client list is impressive. Some from their list include: Jake
Thomas (*The Cell*), Sean Marquette (*Titus*), Miko Hughes (*Clock stoppers,
Magic Rock*), Samm LeVine (*Freaks and Geeks*), Shari Perry (*Any Day
Now*), Jeremy Suarez (*Brother Bear, Treasure Planet*), Daniel Smith (*Me and
Mr. Smith, Jersey Girl*), and Shane Sweet (*Married with Children*).

The age range at BTG is from five to twenty-five with the largest
group being boys in the thirteen to eighteen age category. Although
most of their clients come via industry referral, Phillip and Patrick do
look at all the snapshots and pictures that come in, so if you have a
resume and/or a great face, they might just respond to your letter —
if you are a motivated kid.

I was surprised to learn that Phillip and Patrick have several clients
who don't live in Los Angeles and who audition via tape (mom and
camcorder). If a producer is interested, of course, you'll need to be in

Los Angeles, but what a convenience to know that you don't have to pack up your entire family and move to Los Angeles, just because "Mary" has an audition.

**Agents**
Philip Leader and Phillip Welborn
**Clients**
150

# ⚱ CAA ⚱
# Creative Artists Agency

9830 Wilshire Boulevard
(at little Santa Monica)
Beverly Hills CA 90212
310-288-4545

The rise of CAA is a real Frank Capra story.

✦ *When these dynamic men left William Morris to start the agency, they didn't have any clients. They didn't have any financing. They didn't have any offices. In fact, between the five of them, they only had one car...They couldn't afford to hire a receptionist. So each of their wives filled in one day a week.*
Charles Schreger, *Los Angeles Times*[30]

The founding fathers are gone, but president Richard Lovett, co-chairs Lee Gabler and Rick Nicita, and senior vice-president Michael Rosenfeld have kept the agency's status in tact, although William Morris, UTA and ICM are nipping ferociously at their heels.

CAA has never regained the power and prestige of the Mike Ovitz days, but is still listed #1 in *Variety* by the guys who run the studios.

✦ *When it comes to representing and packaging talent and filmmakers, CAA still remains the leader.*

*With an array of star talent that few can match, CAA takes the survey's only A grade. Actually, an A-, but when you can identify clients by first name only -- names like the Two Toms, Gwyneth, Sandra, Keanu and Nicolas — you're talking about the predominant packaging force.*

*"Without a doubt," said one producer, "CAA is the best organized, (has) the best synergy. It is a very warm and fuzzy place if you're a client. But it's a cold and distant one if you're not. You're either in the club or you're not."*

*Others echoed those concerns, decrying CAA's ranks as A-list obsessed agents who "are no good unless you're a big fish or a client. Their favor bank works in one direction, and their arrogance has caught up with them."*
Claude Brodesser, *Variety*[31]

According to the *Los Angeles Times* in 1999, CAA had 125 agents and about 1,200 clients. That's about one agent for every ten clients. I doubt that time considerations break down that way, so if you're not Tom Hanks or Meryl Streep, you might not get as much attention as they, but still, having CAA say your name would be worth a lot.

Clients include the cream of theater, film, television and music talent: Julia Roberts, Hilary Swank, Gwyneth Paltrow, Helen Hunt, Renee Zellweger, Sandra Bullock, Cameron Diaz, Nicole Kidman, Julianne Moore, Kate Hudson, Tom Hanks, Bonnie Hunt, Gary Sinise, Robert Redford, Al Pacino, Robert Downey, Jr., Gene Hackman, Michael J. Fox, Robert Redford, Julia Louis-Dreyfus, Paul Newman, Tom Cruise, Sally Field, Gene Hackman, Kim Basinger, Barbra Streisand, Chevy Chase, Robert De Niro, Glenn Close, Madonna, Meryl Streep, Whoopi Goldberg, Michael Douglas, Sylvester Stallone, Demi Moore, and many many others.

Ever on the cutting edge, CAA has a new media department with eight agents dedicated to the Internet and technology clients. In 2003 they finally opened a New York office headed by ex-William Morris theater heavyweight, George Lane. CAA also maintains a Nashville office representing their impressive music clients.

Agents Kevin Huvane, Rick Nicita and David O'Connor were listed on *Premiere Magazine's* power list at #46. Lawrence Kasdan's *Mumford* deal (brokered by David O'Connor) reportedly included a fee cut in exchange for complete casting autonomy, so all those stories about CAA clients never hearing of offers deemed less than by their agents, seem to be a thing of the past.

*Variety* editor Peter Bart wrote a love letter to CAA.

✦ *This week... I reviewed the latest developments at CAA. Having vowed never to open a New York office, CAA hired an accomplished theatrical agent, George Lane, away from William Morris, proclaiming its intention to become a force on Broadway. At the same time, it signed a few other top players in music and TV and was enmeshed in a series of high-profile movie deals.*

*It also acquired a market research company and was expanding its relationships with major advertisers who were eager to forge links with CAA's roster of celebrities.*

*Clients of the agency gladly volunteer their analyses of the CAA work ethic. You feel the whole place is behind you, says one director who asked not to be quoted. You don't feel you're represented by a lone agent, while the guy in the next office is trying to get your job for someone else.*

Peter Bart, *Variety*[32]

By and large, lists of agents at the big agencies are guarded like Fort Knox, so other than the partners and the tech agents, my agent listings are tentative and based on the trades.

### Agents
Richard Lovett, Lee Gabler, Rick Nicita, Michael Rosenfeld, Kevin Huvane, David O'Connor, Rick Kurtzman, David Tenzer, Adam Krentzman, Glenn Bickel, Sonya Rosenfield, Rand Holston, Steve Tellez, Joe Rosenberg and many others

### Client List
Very large

# ◿ Conan Carroll ◸

6117 Rhodes Avenue
(btwn Laurel Canyon & Whitsett/N of Oxnard)
North Hollywood, CA 91606
818-760-4738

Pennsylvania native Conan Carroll went to New York to be a star, but soon found out that, though persistent and businesslike, he was "talent-free," so he went to work on Wall Street. When he missed the business, he did a mass mailing to find an agency that would let him start at the bottom and learn to be an agent. J. Michael Bloom was the only taker, so Conan's agenting journey began when he answered phones in their commercial department.

He became an agent with Pat House at The Actor's Group in New York before coming west on spec, landing a job as casting director Kathleen Letteries' secretary, and subsequently becoming manager of casting at NBC for a year.

His Los Angeles agenting journey includes Michael Slessinger, The Artist's Group, Irv Schechter and a one-year partnership with Kathleen Schultz before he started this agency in January of 2002.

Fran Tolstonog likes the number thirteen. She was at both Henderson Hogan and then Bauman Hiller for thirteen years and Conan hopes she'll be with him for at least that long.

The third theatrical agent is Alexander Castellano who was a manager before joining Conan.

Fran, Alexander, and Conan rep a list of about one hundred that includes Leslie-Anne Down, Erin Gray, Peggy McCay, Eileen Ryan, and Lawrence Hilton Jacobs.

Like most agents, Conan prefers referrals but does check out all pictures and resumes.

Conan Carroll also has a literary department headed by Steven Roche and a commercial department headed by Stella Archer.

**Agents**
Conan Carroll, Fran Tolstonog, and Alexander Castellano
**Clients**
100

# ⚞ Ray Cavaleri ⚟

178 S Victory Boulevard, #205
(134 W to Victory & E almost to Olive)
Burbank, CA 91502
818-955-9300

An actor at thirteen, Ray Cavaleri worked steadily for four years until the business slowed down for him. Just as well, he had just decided that he "really wanted to direct" and headed to college.

His BA in English and MA in Directing from California State Northridge began a whirlwind of activity teaching/producing/directing at various schools and theaters. One year, he directed twenty-five fully staged musicals and a comedy. Somehow his wife and children didn't divorce him although I can't imagine they knew what he looked like.

The theater program was cut back at his high school and Ray returned to show business where hopefully he would have more time for real life. His first thought was to be a casting director, but since his resumes landed on CD desks on the first day of the actor's strike, he was in the wrong place at the wrong time. He opted to be an agent instead and landed his first job at Career Artists International.

By 1972, he was ready to start his own business repping actors, young adults, kids, comedians, martial artists, writers, directors, producers, sports personalities, stunts performers and musical artists.

Ray's list includes Don "The Dragon" Wilson, Richard Norton, Sophia Crawford, and Shedrack Anderson III (*Just Deal*). Although he's become the man to call for martial artists, Ray's also known as a rich source of character actors and beautiful people.

Cinthia Becks heads the Children's and Young Adults department.

Cavaleri looks at all pictures, resumes and tapes and will look at home produced videos. He's happy to see young actors and will help you get your SAG card if you are younger than eighteen. If you're over twenty, you should be in the union to query this office.

**Agents**
Ray Cavaleri and Cinthia Becks
**Client List**
150

# ⚜ Charles Talent ⚜

11950 Ventura Boulevard #3
(at Radford)
Studio City, CA 91604
818-761-2224

Bert Charles was a child actor in San Diego and studied Business at the UC San Diego with no thought of being in the business. A chance job as an intern at an agent's office convinced him that agenting was the perfect place to combine his acting background and his business brain. After spending five years at prominent San Diego talent agency, Shamon Freijtas, he felt ready for Los Angeles and opened Charles Talent in 1996. He started with a few of his San Diego clients, but quickly filled in his list with "good talented people that I like."

Boston native James Kelley attended NYU, worked in the music business, and was a gentleman farmer in Connecticut before he pulled up stakes to fulfill his dream to be in the movie business. His first stop in the William Morris mailroom was "a graduate course in how the business works." His stint in the Motion Picture Department there instilled in him respect for trained theater actors.

James worked at Alive and Island Alive developing films in the five to seven million dollar range. When those studios closed, he worked at a manager for a while but his William Morris days had left their mark; he wanted to be an agent.

When a mutual friend introduced James to Bert, he joined the company. Charles Talent has about ninety theatrical clients and 200 commercial clients. Their actors are all classically trained with impressive Broadway and regional credits. Liann Pattison (*Cider House Rules*), Loanne Bishop (*General Hospital*), Michael Childers (*Six Feet Under*), Subash Kundammal (*Alias*), Ben Dodge (*Ricky Blitt Pilot*), Harry Carey, Jr. (*Last Stand at Saber River*), and Stefan Umstead (*The Ice Cream Man*) are a few names from their list.

**Agents**
Bert Charles and James Kelley
**Clients**
90

# ☜ Tory Christopher Agency ☞

7920 Selma Avenue, #12
(just W of Fairfax)
Hollywood, CA 90046
323-436-0891

Stagestruck San Antonio native Tory Christopher was involved in music and dance classes from his earliest memory and at thirteen ran away from home to "be a star" in Hollywood. Although he told his mom he was leaving, she didn't quite believe it until she received his phone call from the then-seedy Hollywood Roosevelt Hotel room he had managed to finance from money made mowing lawns.

Although it makes a good story now, Tory says it wasn't a happy experience and he doesn't really know what he was thinking of. He returned to San Antonio a few days after and finished school. He found that although still a challenge, life as a seventeen-year-old in Hollywood, was a lot better than at thirteen.

That was in 1978 and Tory had $300 and no place to live. A friend offered a couch for a few days and suggested that first Tory needed a job. His first showbiz job was as a tour guide at Universal Studios.

As he began his acting career, the 1980 actors' strike intervened and Tory ended up traveling the world for four years as a professional roller skater. A book about Hollywood agents, *The Dealmakers*, crossed his path then and made him think an agenting career might interest him some day.

But that day was yet to come. When Tory's skating days were over, he went to broadcast school and spent time in radio in Oklahoma, then in Texas as a newscaster, a program director, and helicopter traffic reporter.

In 1989, he returned to Los Angeles to pursue acting again. He worked as a bartender, became a regular stand-up at the Comedy Store, a recurring extra on *Star Trek: Deep Space 9*, *Frasier* and *Cheers,* and had a recurring Under Five role on *Days of Our Lives.*

He wrote and directed short films and worked as a stand-in and production assistant at Paramount before the long buried idea of being an agent asserted itself.

By this time, he certainly had a background of experience in just about everything related to the business. In July of 1997, he opened his own agency. Since he had been working in stand-up, he not only had an affinity for comedy, but a whole list of stand-up friends whose work he wanted to represent. When he examined that group for prospective clients, he came up with thirty that he felt had potential.

His idea for establishing a comedy niche didn't quite work out. Though the producers he knew from his work took his calls, they didn't know Tory as an agent and weren't ready to shop with him. His first successes came in nighttime drama and then in commercials when Tory realized he could exploit his skating background to provide hockey players for beer and soda commercials.

People began calling Tory for "extreme sports" personnel. Just as it's faster and easier for an actor to develop a commercial resume, talent agencies face the same challenge. The success of his commercial department has supported the birth and evolution of the theatrical department.

Although Tory represents actors, children, comedians, legit, models, sports, stunts, teen, variety, young adults and new media, the focus of the agency is now geared basically toward teenagers other than those clients who have been with Tory since the beginning.

The theatrical list of about forty-five includes Nathan Funk, Matthew Christopher, Lacie Harmon, Linda Porter, Ernie Sanchez, Austin Olah (*Sidewalkers*), Liam Kyle Sullivan (*The Convent*), and David Grammer.

The successful commercial department at this agency serves as a farm team for the theatrical list with clients being submitted for theater, film and television as their experience and resumes grow. It's headed by Gregg Robbler.

Tory is always looking for new young talent to add to his teen list, and he doesn't expect young actors to have their union card yet. Older actors need a referral to get Tory's eye.

**Agent**
Tory Christopher
**Client List**
45

# ◿ Cinema Talent Agency ◺

## 2609 Wyoming Ave, #A
(near Burbank Boulevard & Buena Vista)
## Burbank, CA 91505
## 818-845-3816

During Angeleno Nona Harbison's eighteen-year-stay in Australia running a nursing home, she managed to find movie and television jobs for extras. When she returned to this country, she spent a year with an agent/manager friend who "showed her the ropes" so that by 1993, she was ready to open her own agency.

She filled her client list by scouting young talent at showcases and ran the agency alone until her son Taylor Jacobs joined her.

Names from their theatrical list of about fifty include Stephen Blackehart, Mariah Shirley (*Titus*), and Daniel Southworth (*Burning Kingdom*).

Although Nona and Taylor do check out the pictures and resumes that come in, if you want to get their attention, you need a referral. Since the agency is small, they feel they can only do a good job representing two or three clients in each category and, if that category is filled, no matter how terrific you are, they are dedicated to the clients they already have.

**Agents**
Nona Harbison and Taylor Jacobs
**Clients**
50

# ✎ W. Randolph Clark Company ✎

13415 Ventura Boulevard, #13
(near Dixie Canyon & Fulton)
Sherman Oaks, CA 91423
818-385-0583

He doesn't really have an accent, but my Texas ears were hearing something familiar during my interview with Randy Clark. I wasn't all that surprised to find out the Randy and I not only come from the same neck of the woods, but that we went to the same Texas college.

This soft-spoken gentleman started out in production at Casa Mañana in Fort Worth. He left the Lone Star State for a month-long stint as a stage manager in San Diego and never returned.

By the time he got to Los Angeles and began pursuing an agenting career, his mentors were legendary agents Robert Littman and Alex Brewis.

He opened his own agency in 1980 and until December 1986 he handled only technical people (editors, scene designers, costumers, etc.) When Randy decided to expand his agency to include actors, he decided to specialize in kids and teenagers.

Ever ready to establish a new niche, Randy has started a new Senior Division highlighting older actors, so he now has clients at both ends of the age spectrum.

As the mother of two working actor sons, Arlene Tsurutani had a great perspective on what kids go through in the business and that's what prompted Randy to invite her to come work for him in 1988. By 1990, she was a franchised agent and now helps Randy rep an eclectic group of clients.

Randy chooses young clients who are outgoing and easy to talk with and says he is meticulous about checking showcases and teachers. He looks at all pictures and resumes.

**Agents**
Randy Clark and Arlene Tsurutani
**Client List**
80

# ⚞ Coast to Coast Talent Group ⚟

3350 Barham Boulevard
(at Lake Hollywood)
Los Angeles, CA 90068
213-845-9200

Back in 1989 when the former owners of Coast to Coast were looking to sell their agency, Elyah Doryon was just graduating as a Political Science major. Though he knew nothing about show business when he started, he learned on the job. His drive and intelligence coupled with taste and ingenuity have paid off to raise Coast to Coast far above what it was when he bought it.

His brother Jeremiah Doryon joined the agency as soon as he got out of college and today runs the business side of things.

Buffalo native Kevin Turner (Paradigm, APA, Epstein Wykoff) runs the theatrical division of Coast to Coast. Meredith Fine and Dana Edrick represent the important children and young adults at this agency. There is also a division that represents sports personalities.

Adult clients include Judith Scarpone (*Twilight of the Golds*), Ric Young (*Alias*), Jihmi Kennedy (*Glory*), and T'Keyah Crystal Keymah (*In Living Color*). In addition to Oscar nominee Haley Joel Osment, the Youth Division clients include Scotty Leavenworth, Kevin Christy, Kente Scott, Marina Malota, Jake Richardson and Ernest Thomas.

Coast to Coast is not actively seeking new clients, but they do look at pictures and canvass local theater productions. When they call people in, their interest is based on the look, the resume, and the age group (usually the eighteen to thirty year old age range).

Elyah thinks actors who make it are persistent, continually train themselves, and work at keeping themselves visible in the marketplace.

This office doesn't just send in pictures and wait for the phone to ring, they are out calling on casting directors. I was impressed.

**Agents**
Elyah Doryon, Kevin Turner, Meredith Fine and Dana Edrick
**Client List**
60 adults/50 children

# ⚐ Contemporary Artists ⚐

610 Santa Monica Boulevard, #202
(at 6th Street)
Santa Monica, CA 90401
310-395-1800

After the demise of MCA in 1963, Ron Leif left and opened this office. Known at one time as Contemporary Korman, this agency reps writers, directors and producers.

My only contact with this agency for the past few years has been with its answering machine. I couldn't tell you for sure that anyone is even there. For that reason, I suspect that Ron has pretty much retired and is now servicing only long time clients.

Clients from their list have included Diane Hull, Su Hyatt, Joe Costanza, Louis Nye, Al Rossi and Gloria DeHaven.

**Agents**
Ron Leif
**Client List**
49

# ✍ The Coppage Company ✎

5411 Camellia Avenue
(btwn Chandler and Burbank)
North Hollywood, CA 91601
818-980-8806

It's easy to see how Judy Coppage, the personification of charisma, became a vice-president of production and development at Hanna Barbera Studios before anyone even knew what that meant. And it's easy to see how she was one of the first women to break through into the executive area in show business.

One of those fortunate people who knew from the get-go that she was destined for Hollywood, she left home in Seattle for UCLA, earned two degrees, and hit the ground running. An executive at Paramount as well as HB, it didn't take long for Judy to see that as a woman in corporate showbiz there were plenty of limitations. She realized that she could parlay her entrepreneurial skills and her love of artists into a much more satisfying life on her own. Judy started her own business in 1984 representing writers and expanded her focus to include actors in 2003.

Judy's list of acting clients is select — only eight. Among them are Mayim Bialik (*Blossom, Beaches*), John Lehr (*They Shoot Divas, Don't They?*), and the Vogt twins, Peter (*Tracy Morgan Show*) and Paul (*Mad TV*).

When Judy believes in you, she is fearless in her efforts. Committed to the clients she already has, Judy only accepts industry referrals.

**Agents**
Judy Coppage
**Client List**
24

# Coralie Jr. Theatrical Agency

4789 Vineland Avenue, #100
(btwn Magnolia & Moorpark)
North Hollywood, CA 91602
818-766-9501

Coralie Jr. (yep, folks, that's her real name) has been repping horses, orangutans and actors for over twenty years. She booked the monkeys for *Every Which Way But Loose*, the drunken horse in the Lee Marvin classic *Cat Ballou*, and one of the leads (Angelo Rossito) in *Mad Max: Beyond the Thunderdome*. Boy, talk about one-stop shopping.

Coralie first worked as an actress was when she was two days old. By the time she worked in the old *Our Gang* comedies, she was a veteran. Coralie says she's "not like any other agency."

That's surely true for Coralie Jr. books commercials, variety acts, musicians, writers, animals, lookalikes and about 150 actors who just act (as opposed to those who also juggle). And now she says she also books writers and musicians..

Coralie's associates are Stuart Edward, Gary Dean, and Brent Swan (Shapiro Lichtman) who also heads up the new literary department.

**Agents**
Coralie Jr., Stuart Edward, Gary Dean, and Brent Swan
**Client List**
150

# ⩔ Defining Artists Agency ⩔

4342 Lankershim Boulevard
(S of Moorpark)
Universal City, CA 91602
818-506-8188

Once employees at Bobby Ball Agency (with whom they currently share an office), Kim Dorr and Kurt Patino have now opened their own agency repping actors for theater, film and television.

Kim's theater degree from the University of Denver led to work as an actress at the Denver Centre and the National Theater Conservatory, but she traded her career for a life as a wife and mother in 1984.

When her husband's career moved the family to Los Angeles, Kim worked as an assistant in preproduction at the Arthur Company where her organizational abilities and theater background quickly propelled her into the job of casting. After 8½ years, The Arthur Company called it quits, so in 1993, Dorr joined Bobby Ball.

Originally hired to rep commercial actors, Dorr created a theatrical department which thrived immediately.

Dorr's partner, film school grad and independent filmmaker, Kurt Patino, originally headed the kid's theatrical department at BBA and though DAA does rep a few select young clients, the emphasis here is on adults.

Kim won't let me name any clients, so you'll have to consult the SAG agent listings for that information.

**Agents**
Kim Dorr and Kurt Patino
**Clients**
50

# ⬂ Diverse Talent Group ⬃

1875 Century Park East, Suite 2250
(S of little Santa Monica)
Los Angeles, CA 90067
310 201-6565

Diverse Talent Group was created in March 2000 when CSA & Associates (Christopher Nassif) and Premiere Artists Agency (Susan Sussman, Michael Packenham and Carolyn Kessler) merged. Packenham and Kessler departed, leaving Nassif and Sussman as the principals.

LeLand LeBarre and Tom Harrison defected from Henderson Hogan to create a new talent department of about 120 working actors like Kristy Swanson (*Buffy*), Will Friedle (*The Random Years*), Bryan Krause (*Charmed*), James Patrick Stuart (*Andy Richter Controls the Universe*), Yaphet Kotto (*Homicide*), and Katee Sackhoff (*Max Bickford*).

Le Barre trained at UTA and Harrison was at Epstein Wykoff before their stints at Henderson Hogan. Adrienne Spitzer and Stephen Rice round out the agent roster repping a list of about 120 clients.

Diverse reps actors, young adults, teens, children, comedians, scriptwriters, producers, songwriters, sports personalities and models. They also have strong commercial and below-the-line departments.

Submissions are usually only considered by referral.

**Agents**
Leland LaBarre, Tom Harrison, Suzanne Bennett, and Nicole Cataldo
**Client List**
120

# ⚞ Ellis Talent Group ⚟

4705 Laurel Canyon Boulevard, #300
(btwn Moorpark & Riverside)
Valley Village, CA 91607
818-980-8072

Pam Ellis started her showbiz career as a development executive at Metro Production Corporation and, although successful, she felt her interests lay elsewhere. At Twentieth Century Artists, she worked as a receptionist before mentor Diane Davis franchised her as an agent and she found her true calling. After 3½ years with Diane, she moved to The Booh Schut Agency.

Pam spoke in glowing terms of both Booh and Diane who, Pam says, gave her a wonderful grounding in the business preparing her for anything that might come along. She worked briefly with Dick Lovell before joining Rogers Entertainment as Director of Creative Affairs. Pam worked with comedian Edward Jackman and his wife, Karen Taussig at Jackman Taussig before opening her own agency in 1993.

Gabrielle Allabashi (Gold Marshak) and Jeremy Jones who became a franchised agent at ETG join Pam in repping clients Michael Des Barres, Scott Lawrence, Judith Scott, Carey Eidel, Cynthia Steele and Pat Cranshaw.

Although ETA does look at pictures and resumes, they rarely call anyone in from mailings.

**Agents**
Pam Ellis-Evenas, Gabrielle Allabashi, and Jeremy Jones
**Client List**
50

# ⋈ Endeavor ⋈

9701 Wilshire Boulevard, 10th floor
(at Roxbury)
Beverly Hills, CA 90212
310-248-2000/310-248-2020

Writer-director powerhouse Endeavor burst on the scene in 1995 when key ICM agents David Greenblatt, Tom Strickler, Rick Rosen and Ariel Emanuel defected to set up shop. Adam Venit (CAA) and David Lonner (ICM, CAA) ultimately created a talent department which now includes new partners Patrick Whitesell and Brian Swardstrom (Banner Entertainment).

Mentioned in the same sentence with CAA, ICM, William Morris and UTA, Endeavor continues to acquire a star actor list rivaling their collection of star writers and directors. Patrick Whitesell was co-head of the motion picture talent department at CAA before he defected, bringing along clients Drew Barrymore, Ben Affleck and Matt Damon.

In September 2003, Endeavor had some defections of its own when Lonner and Steve Rabineau jumped ship to William Morris taking many of their clients with them.

Children's agent Iris Burton recently formalized a co-representation arrangement for her young clients, opting to share her take in exchange for exposing her young clients to Endeavor's TV packaging deals.

Whitesell's clients join Adam Sandler, Omar Epps, Dustin Hoffman, Marcia Gay Harden, Vincent D'Onofrio, James Caan, Adam Kaufman, William Fichtner, Cristen Coppen, Jeremy Piven, Christopher Walken, William Lee Scott, Diane Lane, Amy Smart, Michael T. Weiss, Jayne Hamil, Jack Noseworthy, and Carlos Oscar on Endeavor's growing list.

### Agents
Adam Venit, Patrick Whitesell, Brian Swardstrom, Bonnie Bernstein, Jeb Brandon, Leanne Coronel, Sean Elliott, Cory Gahr, Craig Gartner, Scott Melrose, Jaime Misher, Shelly Morales, Tito, Olowu, Stephanie Ritz, Elyse Scherz, Greg Siegal, Lee Stollman, and Kevin Volchok
### Client List
Large

# ◺ Epstein/Wyckoff/Corsa/Ross & Associates ◿

280 S. Beverly Drive, Suite 400
(S of Wilshire Boulevard)
Beverly Hills, CA 90212
310-278-7222

Craig Wyckoff was a working actor when he decided that agenting appealed to him more than acting. At that point, he joined the Los Angeles based William Felber Agency and developed their television and film department.

In 1981, he joined with theatrical lawyer Mark Freeman and opened the Freeman-Wyckoff Agency and, by 1983, he had bought out his partner and was sole owner of The Wyckoff Agency. Over time, Craig has had various alliances: Littman, Freifeld, Marshak and Wyckoff and Marshak/Wyckoff, but since 1991, he has been partnered with New York agent Gary Epstein.

Gary is responsible for getting his musician neighbor Larry Corsa into the business. When he told Larry he was opening his own agency and suggested representing actors as an alternative to playing with bands, Larry decided to give agenting a try.

In 1991, when Gary decided to open a West Coast office for Phoenix, he sent Larry to Los Angeles. When Epstein and Wyckoff decided to merge shortly after, Larry was part of the package.

In January of 1999, Larry, who now heads both the Commercial Department and the Children's Department, became a partner along with Randi Ross, another Phoenix veteran who continues to work with Gary in New York.

The agents at EWCR who represent actors theatrically include Bret Carducci, who became franchised here after assisting at Gersh; Renee Panichelli, who relocated from EWCR's New York office; Craig; and Larry. Alex Solowitz (*Together*) and E. J. De Lapeña (*Run, Ronnie, Run*) are two from their list of about 150.

**Agents**
Craig Wyckoff, Larry Corsa, Bret Carducci, and Renee Panichelli
**Client List**
150

# ⚞ The Barry Freed Company ⚟

468 N Camden Drive, #201
(Sharper Image Building/corner of little Santa Monica)
Los Angeles, CA 90210
310-860-5627

In 1984, after fourteen years of handling theater, film and television at ICM, Barry Freed decided to start his own agency. In 1991, he sold that agency and immediately started another. In addition to the strong list of working actors that Barry always attracts, Barry now represents martial artists, below-the-line, comedians, young adults, and scriptwriters for film only, no television.

Clients from his list of about fifty are Ron Moody (*Oliver*), Lionel Mark Smith (*State and Main*), Don Knotts, Jennifer Rhoades, Barry Van Dyke, James Curley, Ari Barak, Bari Hochwald, Don Reilly, Charley Rossman, Josh Roman, Roy Stuart, Rutledge Taylor, Tessa Shaw, Richard Winter, and Judy Cain. Barry faithfully checks all pictures and resumes, but as with most agencies, it's always best to have a referral.

**Agent**
Barry Freed
**Client List**
40

# ⊰ The Gage Group ⊱

14724 Ventura Boulevard, Suite 505
(btwn Van Nuys & Kester)
Sherman Oaks, CA 91403
818-905-3800

One of the most effective and respected agencies in town is owned by Martin Gage. Originally an actor, Martin was hit by a cab returning from his third callback for the role of Baby John in *West Side Story*. Whether Martin took this as a comment on his acting, I don't know, but when I met him, he was an agent with Fifi Oscard and for a while, they were partners.

Of the many attributes I admire about Martin, those at the top of the list include his honesty as a human being and his fearlessness. If you note his comments throughout the book, you'll see what I'm talking about.

Gerry Koch was a scholarship acting student at Southern Illinois University who became interested in the technical side of the business and got an MFA in directing at the University of Minnesota. After several years as a director, artistic director and running his own theater in the Midwest, Gerry went to New York where he worked in props on Broadway and built scenery with famed set designer Santo Loquasto.

An old college chum was running The Gage Group in New York and persuaded Gerry to give agenting a try. He quickly graduated from the front desk to bookkeeper to agent.

Actor Pete Kaiser's day job as a bookkeeper at The Gage Group/New York quickly became more interesting than pursuing an acting career so when a full-time job opened up, he switched sides of the desk and quickly became franchised. He relocated to the Los Angeles office in 2002.

Oklahoma native Kitty McMillan was an actress-dancer before she married one actor and gave birth to another. When her husband died, she cast for a while before joining Henderson Hogan as an assistant. Though she was planning to retire, Martin hired her, has turned her into an agent and says that she can never ever leave him. I think her clients feel the same way.

Though Mark Fadness' degree from the University of Wisconsin was in theater and he aimed to be a director, he didn't do much toward it when he moved to San Francisco or even when he moved to Los Angeles in 1984. He'd worked in a series of "stupid jobs" before moving to Los Angeles, but once here, when a friend pointed out an opening at The Gage Group, Mark started his showbiz career at a bookkeeper.

He's now head of the commercial department at GG, works on a few film and television projects, and still makes sure the rest of the Group gets paid.

I'm proud to say that I am one of the lucky members of the Group. Other members are Julio Oscar Mechoso, Shirley Knight, Gerry Katzman, Carlos LaCamara, Marianne Muellerleli, Ian Ogilvy, Ellen Travolta, Barbara Tarbuck, Eddie Jones, Michael Learned, Ben Murphy, Caitlin Hopkins, Linda Hart, Tom Virtue, Joe Campanella, Gretchen Wyler, Paul Benedict, Biff McGuire, Michael Moriarty, Leslie Uggams, June Squibb, Holmes Osborne, Ernie Sabella, Harriet Harrris, and Lucy Lee Flippen.

Most clients come to this agency via referral.

**Agents**
Martin Gage, Gerry Koch, Pete Kaiser, Kitty McMillan, and Mark Fadness
**Client List**
170

# ⚏ The Geddes Agency ⚏

8430 Santa Monica Boulevard, #200
(just E of La Cienega)
Los Angeles, CA 90069
323-848-2700

Ann Geddes founded her agency in Chicago in 1967 representing and nurturing a talented group of actors for the busy Chicago marketplace. In 1983, Ann left her Chicago office in the capable hands of associates and moved to Los Angeles to open a West Coast office.

Since Ann and many of her clients moved to LA together, they bonded closely with Ann monitoring not only her clients' auditions but their actor-energy, being ever sensitive to signs as to when it was time for them to renew themselves by doing a play or returning to class.

Richard Lewis (Henderson Hogan) entered the business formally via the mailroom at Contemporary Korman, but since he had an actress-mother and a writer-producer father, he feels as though he has been in the business since birth. Although he sampled being a manager briefly and took a year or so off from the business after a period of burnout, his heart belongs to agenting.

He now joins Ann repping clients Chelcie Ross (*A Simple Plan, Basic Instinct*), Ron Dean (*The Fugitive, The Client*), Elise Mirto, Maree Cheatam, Tanjie Ambros, Dakin Matthews, Natalija Nogulich, John Aniston, Masi Oka, Morroco Omari, Emy Coligado, and Rodney A. Grant (*Wild, Wild West*).

Ann is particularly talented in dealing with the developmental period of an actor's career and many of her insights are featured elsewhere in this book. Although the agency looks at all pictures and resumes, their client list is quite selective. The Chicago office continues to represent talent for that city as well as groom clients and agents for the Los Angeles office.

**Agents**
Ann Geddes and Richard Lewis
**Client List**
100

# ⊿ Laya Gelff Agency ⊾

16133 Ventura Boulevard, Suite 700
(W of the San Diego Freeway)
Encino, CA 91436
818-996-3100

Laya Gelff worked as an associate producer for NBC news before her ten-year sojourn as Executive Director of the Emmys. Her entrance into the agency business in 1985 came courtesy of her husband, actor Ed Metzger.

Laya had already begun to augment his representation by making phone calls for him and handling certain details, when it occurred to her that she could get a franchise with SAG, AFTRA and AEA and make calls for other actors, too, and actually start a business.

Laya is concentrating more on writers than actors these days, but keeps her franchises active for actors who catches her eye. Right now, that's about ten.

She does look at all pictures and resumes.

**Agent**
Laya Gelff
**Client List**
10

# ⤝ The Gersh Agency ⤟

232 N Canon Drive
(just S of Santa Monica)
Beverly Hills, CA 90210
310-274-6611

There was a time when agents weren't even allowed past the studio gates and Phil Gersh can tell you about that because he was there. Phil opened his agency in 1970 and acquired a New York branch in 1984.

The Gersh Agency represents actors, directors, writers, producers, below-the-line personnel, authors, commercial and voiceover talent.

Agents who represent actors at the agency are Bob Gersh, Leslie Siebert, Lorrie Bartlett, Chuck James, Kenneth Kaplan (Kenneth Kaplan Agency, APA, Innovative), Paul Rosicker, Mark Schumacher, Megan Silverman, Larry Taube, Bert Norensberg, Aaron Yarosh, Doug Edley, Matthew Blake, and Warren Zavala.

Rick Greenstein heads up the comedy/PA department. The client list shared by The Gersh Agency on both coasts is outstanding. Some of their impressive clients are Calista Flockhart, Fran Drescher, David Schwimmer, Jane Krakowski, Barry Bostwick, Roma Downey, Patsy Kensit, Lea Thompson, Dan Butler, Jeffrey DeMunn, Victor Garber, Dan Hedaya, Eriq LaSalle, Christopher Lloyd, Esai Morales, Robert Prosky, Michael Rooker, John Glover, Dan Futterman, Brian Benben, Harry Hamlin, Noah Taylor, Megan Mullally, Bruce Davison, Miguel Ferrer, Catherine Hicks, Julie Delpy, Richard Lewis, Holland Taylor, Debra Messing, Audra McDonald, Cynthia Nixon, Kristin Davis and Kyle Secor.

## Agents
Lorrie Bartlett, Bob Gersh, Chuck James, Kenneth Kaplan, Kami Puttnam, Paul Rosicker, Mark Schumacher, Leslie Siebert, Megan Silverman, Larry Taube, Bert Norensberg, Aaron Yarosh, Doug Edley, Matthew Blake, Warren Zavala
## Client List
220

# ✍ Grant Savic Kopaloff & Associates ✍

6399 Wilshire Boulevard, #414
(at La Jolla)
Los Angeles, CA 90048
323-782-1854

Susan Grant (The Artists Group), Don Kopaloff (Donburry Management, Ltd., IFA, CMA, ICM, The Kopaloff Company) and Arnold Soloway (WMA, Lester Salkow, Kumen-Olenick, Susan Smith Agency, The Artists Group) created this agency in 1997. Arnold left to start his own management company, and now Ivana Savic, who became an agent at this company, joins the masthead as partner.

Kopaloff heads up the lit department here and Ivana helms the below-the-line department. Larry Metzger (Contemporary Korman, Vickie Light) runs the theatrical department at this agency. He didn't want to name any clients, so you'll either have to check the *Academy Players Directory,* or if you are a SAG member, check the client listings.

Metzger, who started as an actor and trombone player, began agenting at Contemporary Korman in 1978 and worked there for eleven years before joining Vicki Light's agency. Larry burned out a little after Vicki died and spent five years working in a communications company before he felt the call to come back to the business. He returned to Contemporary (Korman) Artists where he worked until he joined GSK in 1999.

GSK represents actors, writers, novelists, playwrights, directors, editors, personnel for new media and directors of photography.

New clients come to SGK mainly through industry referral but they do look at all pictures and resumes.

Their website, www.gsktalent.com, is under construction.

**Agents**
Larry Metzger
**Client List**
17

# ⚹ GVA ⚹

9229 Sunset Blvd. #320
(at Doheny)
Los Angeles, CA 90069
310-278-1310

Originally an executive with Warner Bros. Music, principal Geneva Bray created GVA in 1996 naming it after the airport code for her favorite city and namesake. In a time when many agencies are closing their doors, Bray has just added a fourth agent, so obviously, her music exec talents translated into the theatrical side of the business very well.

Bray is not the only one with a musical link as her colleague, film school grad Tony Martinez, spent some time producing videos for groups like The Black Crowes and Run DMC. Prior to that, Tony was a freelance cameraman who shot things as diverse as live surgery in Birmingham, Alabama to documenting factory conditions in the Dominican Republic.

When he decided he was ready to move from his native East Coast to California, he came with no plan in mind. Agent friends thought he would be a natural in the agency business and set him up for an interview with prestigious STE where he quickly landed a job as an assistant.

In a few months, STE merged with Paradigm and Tony moved along with the rest of his team. Within two years, he was ready to be an agent and joined Epstein/Wyckoff before joining GVA six years later. Adrienne Spitzer (Diverse) and Gwen Pepper (Acme, Michael Green) joins Geneva and Tony repping Tony Todd (*The Rock, Candyman*), J. Kenneth Campbell (*Collateral Damage, Ulee's Gold*) and their other clients.

**Agents**
Geneva Bray, Tony Martinez, and Adrienne Spitzer
**Clients**
100

# ◿ Buzz Halliday & Associates ◹

8899 Beverly Boulevard, #715
(the old ICM building, W of La Cienega)
Los Angeles, CA 90048
310-275-6028

Buzz Halliday started out in the business as a child actor, was a teen television star in Schenectady and has a nice list of Broadway credits ranging from *Idiot's Delight* in 1957 to *Put It In Writing* in 1963. Buzz left the business for a while to raise a family and when she returned to acting, her agent was so shorthanded that Buzz juggled her career as an actress with a part time gig as her agent's assistant wearing sunglasses when she dropped off pictures, resumes and submissions at casting directors' offices.

The sunglasses hid her identity, but not her view of what actors were actually up against and which casting executives did their jobs. When Buzz finally became a full time agent, her experiences during those years left her better informed than most actors and/or agents.

When Buzz decided to leave her agent as an employee and as an actor, she was recommended to agent Dulcina Eisen, who was looking for someone to start a musical theater department. Dulcina was a conscientious mentor, allowing Buzz to listen in on the progress of every conversation, negotiation and deal.

Buzz moved to California in the early 1990s, spending a year producing concerts and building contacts in the business. Those contacts paid off for her next job as an agent, where she was responsible for the entire agency. Three years later, Buzz elected to leave, opening her own agency in 1994.

With her select client list, Buzz has managed to double her volume of business each year. Although she won't allow me to name clients, she did tell me that among her list of mostly actors, she has an Emmy award winning composer, a musical conductor, the first woman host of a game show, and a director-choreographer. She says she always has clients touring with shows and working as guest stars in television.

Buzz is an agent who works for her clients. She not only doesn't wait for the phone to ring, she calls on people. How many people can say that about their agents? Buzz and associate Gail Honeystein (who trained with Buzz) are accessible to their clients and make the time to sit and discuss careers. They check out all pictures and resumes and see every project any of their clients are involved in. Since Buzz knows the New York casting directors, she feels comfortable covering her clients for both coasts.

**Agents**
Buzz Halliday and Gail Honeystein
**Client List**
Always under 35

# ⊿ The Beverly Hecht Agency ⊿

12001 Ventura Place, #320
(just W of CBS/Radford)
Studio City, CA 91604
818-505-1192

Teresa Valente Dahlquist always wanted to be an agent, so when she heard that children's agent Beverly Hecht was looking for someone to buy the successful agency she created in 1973, it was thrilling to sell her own business (unrelated to entertainment), take over Beverly's, and begin making dreams come true for herself and others. In 1994, Teresa stepped into a new career that fit her like a glove.

Her keen eye uncovered an eleven-year-old client who got the first two jobs he went up for, one of them carrying a major movie.

Teresa impressed me with her spare list. She and associate Mary Dangerfield (Stars/San Francisco) represent a list of about four clients commercially and ten theatrically. Teresa says she can't give the kind of service a client deserves if the list is bigger. Her children's list ranges from age five to twenty-one although in the *Hollywood Representatives Directory* she says she reps clients from six to one hundred and six.

BHA reps adults commercially only, but if a client knows about a part, she will submit and negotiate. She will also tell you to get a theatrical agent because she knows she hasn't the time to service that part of your career.

Teresa is keeping her list purposefully small, but she still looks at all pictures and resumes since children are constantly changing.

**Agent**
Teresa Valente Dahlquist
**Client list**
10

# ⩗ Hervey/Grimes Talent Agency ⩗

10561 Missouri, #2
(btwn Santa Monica & Olympic)
Los Angeles, CA 90064
310-475-2010

Pam Grimes and Marsha Hervey's showbiz background came courtesy of their actor-children. Waiting for their kids, these two entrepreneurial moms realized that while they were, in essence, managing their children, they had absorbed lots of valuable show business savvy and could capitalize on that information.

They started out as managers of adults, but after a while decided they would prefer the protection of a Screen Actors Guild contract when they signed their clients, so they became agents.

The age range of their clients is from birth to age ninty-four, evenly split between adults and kids. Hervey and Grimes' list of about 150 is comprised of clients for theatrical, or commercials, or both.

Clients from their list include Jamie Renee Smith (*Ask Harriet, Dante's Peak*), Camryn Grimes (*The Young and the Restless*), and Henry Darrow (*Zorro*).

Pam and Marsha look at all pictures and resumes.

**Agents**
Pam Grimes and Marsha Hervey
**Client list**
150

# ⟑ Daniel Hoff Agency ⟑

1800 N Highland #300
(at Franklin across from the Church)
Los Angeles, CA 90028
323-962-6643

Angeleno, Daniel Hoff majored in communications at Pepperdine University planning to manage bands. Preparation for that career included jobs at booking agencies, in Artists Relations, and talent scouting, spending time in clubs living the music business life. In 1998, he rebelled agaist the lifestyle and began coordinating music video shoots with Propaganda Productions

His next job at a talent management company reading the Breakdowns fueled a fantasy to become a talent agent repping his actor friends. In 1992, weighing the pros and cons of joining a large agency and working his way into the system, Daniel opted to start his own company with two clients, two headshots and the Breakdowns.

Within three months, Daniel was so successful he was able to expand from his home office with two clients into an impressive office repping clients for film, television, comedy, music videos, musical theater and print. Daniel now focuses on the commercial department.

Theatrical department head, Nancy Abt, knew from the time she was fifteen that she wanted to be an agent. She got her first job right out of college at David & Lee in Chicago where she spun off her own separate division called Third Coast Artists. She moved to Los Angeles in 1998 working briefly at ICM before joining Daniel that same year.

Her list of about forty-five includes Sy Richardson, Frank Novak, Josh Jacobson, Patricia Place, Alicia Loren and Lynette Dupree (*Bring in 'Da Noise, Bring in 'Da Funk*), Renn Woods (*Hair, Roots, Jumpin' Jack Flash*), Franklin Dennis Jones, Chris Robinson (*General Hospital*), Sandra McCoy (*Living the Lie*), Kate Linder (*The Young and the Restless*), Mary Jo Catlett, Napiera Danielle (*As the World Turns*), and David Jennings (*Brooklyn, Once Upon a Mattress*).

Debra Manners joined DHA in 2000 to create the Youth Division She started her agenting career with her brother Scott at Stone Manners and agented for thirteen years before switching to a casting career (Sheila Manning, Henderson Zuckerman, Michael Mann, Dorothy Coster). Debra cast on *Nash Bridges, Marshall Law,* and *Passions,* and produced a show with Patrick Duffy and William Shatner.

Names from her youth list (ages four to seventeen) include Shane Hunger (*Sleepover*) and Eddie Hassell. Debra also has a developmental department for clients eighteen and under.

Although Nancy and Debra check pictures and resumes religiously, they say that in order to get their attention, you do need an industry referral.

Shane Cormier came to DHA from Interscope Records to create the new hugely successful Voiceover department.

**Agents**
Danny Hoff, Nancy Abt, Debra Manners and Shane Cormier
**Client List**
45

# ⚞ Hollander Talent Group ⚟

14011 Ventura Boulevard, #202
(btwn Woodman & Hazeltine)
Sherman Oaks, CA 91423
818-382-9800

I first met Vivian Hollander years ago when I was fortunate to work with her son, David. At that point, Vivian was just David's mom, shepherding him around sets. Vivian became an activist for kids, working with the Screen Actors Guild to modernize child labor laws allowing older children to work longer hours than toddlers.

Since her presence on the set gave her an intimate view of what it takes for a child to make it in show business, she began to think about becoming an agent.

In 1982, she joined her son's agent, Estelle Hertzberg, at Twentieth Century Artists where Estelle had started the children's division. For almost fifteen years, Estelle and Vivian worked together nourishing the careers of their young clients.

By 1996, Vivian decided she was ready to start her own agency and asked Estelle to come with her. They opened with 90% of her list from Twentieth in tact. Estelle has left to become a manager and Stefane Wetherholt, who started her showbiz career as an assistant here, is now Vivian's associate.

The client list ranges in age from infants to early twenties and then jumps to clients who are over sixty-five, which is good news to older actors who sometimes have problems finding representation.

Although a client list of 300 is large at an agency of this size, since there is no delineation between theatrical and commercial clients and because children change constantly, the numbers don't seem excessive.

The agency tracks school productions, small theaters and looks at all snapshots and pictures that come in, keeping abreast of new young actors. One of their hottest new clients, Andrew Cisneros, was discovered in a high school production and got the first job he went on, a significant role in a new movie.

Other clients from Estelle and Vivian's list include Brooke Bridges (*Touched by An Angel*), Penny Bae Bridges (*True Crime*), Breck Bruns (*General Hospital*), Natalie Marston (*Magnolia*), Jamie Snow (*The Amanda Show*), Aaron Meeks (*Soul Food*), Charlie Stewart (*Life with Bonnie*), Hailey

Johnson (*Daddy Day Care*), Jillian Clare (*Days of Our Lives*), Jordan Warkol (*Songs in Ordinary Time*), Connor Carmody (*The Bold and the Beautiful*), Chelsea Tavares (*Unfabulous, The Lion King*), and Paul Langdon (*Strong Medicine*).

Infants and toddlers up to age three-and-a-half are not seen since they change so quickly, but their pictures are kept, filed and tracked, so if you have a child in this category, it still doesn't hurt to send a snapshot with the child's statistics and a contact number written on the back.

The agency holds a special Super Saturday several times a year calling in 60-100 children whose picture and/or background interests them or who have been recommended to them. This agency also represents clients for print and voiceovers.

**Agents**
Vivian Hollander and Stefane Wetherholt
**Client List**
300

# ⚓ The House of Representatives ⚓

400 S Beverly Drive, #101
(at Olympic Boulevard)
Beverly Hills, Ca 90210
310-772-0772

Pam Braverman and Artists Agency alums Ginger Lawrence and Denny Sevier managed to open this agency just two weeks after the 1994 earthquake. If they could do that, I believe this group is focused enough to do anything.

The fact that they had already been in business with each other in one way or another must have helped. Pam and Ginger owned an entertainment personnel agency in 1983 until Pam decided to concentrate on her family instead of the agency. Ginger took her contacts to The Artists Agency where she met Denny.

Ginger told me when they opened that their chief aim was to represent good actors. With clients like Jack Riley, Harris Yulin, Ray Wise, Nan Martin, Frederic Forrest, Stuart Whitman, Millie Slavin, Michael Fairman, and Robert Hooks, I think they've got that covered.

Ginger says The House of Reps responds to every picture it gets. An agency that treats actors as well as they treat casting directors seems pretty cool to me.

**Agents**
Ginger Lawrence, Pam Braverman, and Denny Sevier
**Clients List**
60

# ⩘ Howard Talent West ⩗

10657 Riverside Drive
(btwn Lankershim & Cahuenga)
Toluca Lake, CA 91602
818-766-5300

Entrepreneur Bonnie Howard is just the sort of person you would like to have working for you: organized, intelligent and seemingly fearless. In 1986, when she burned out as a travel agent and closed her business, she decided to take a year and research show business to see where she might fit in.

She took film related courses at UCLA and USC, studying film research, script supervision and acting. She then got a job prompting at a theater and worked as an extra.

Her prompting job ultimately led Bonnie to start her own agency when an actor in the show suggested that Bonnie might make a good agent. She started two businesses: Howard Talent West and The Extra Connection, a call-in service for extras.

She started both businesses in 1987, just fourteen months after she started her research into show business and, by 1991, HTW was so successful she had to close The Extra Connection for lack of time.

Today, HTW represents about 150 actors for film, television and commercials. Some clients are signed across the board and some are signed either theatrically or commercially only.

Bonnie says her clients range in age from under a year to eighty-five. John Walmsley (*The Waltons*), Tony Becker (*China Beach*), Jodee Thelan, Joe Estevez, Cheryl Bricker, Judy Kerr, Marla Frees, and Gina St. John are all clients from her list. Bonnie is one of those rare agents who is seeking good female character actors, so ladies, take heed.

Bonnie looks at all pictures and resumes.

**Agent**
Bonnie Howard
**Client List**
150

# ⚞ ICM ⚟
# International Creative Management

8899 Beverly Boulevard
(just W of Robertson)
Los Angeles, CA 90048
310-550-4000

Just like actors, talent agencies have good years and bad years. ICM's stars (both astrological and theatrical) are currently in flux.

✦ *Julia Roberts, the first actress to earn $20 million a picture, has severed ties with her talent agency, International Creative Management, where she'd been a client since 1991.*

*No reason was publicly offered for the move, nor was it clear whether Roberts would sign on elsewhere. Since her longtime agent, Elaine Goldsmith-Thomas, left to become a partner in Revolution Studios in October 2000, the Oscar-winning actress ("Erin Brockovich") had been represented by ICM Chairman Jeff Berg.*

*The move is a major blow to ICM, particularly since Cameron Diaz followed her agent, Nick Styne, to Creative Artists Agency last year.*

*The agency still represents a chunk of Hollywood talent, however, including Denzel Washington, Mel Gibson, Michelle Pfeiffer and Richard Gere.*
Elaine Dutka, *Los Angeles Times*[33]

The powerful Jeff Berg leads the agency through showbiz's changing tides. ICM will surely survive with clients Chris Rock, Cher, Judy Davis, Marg Helgenberger, Helen Mirren, Maggie Smith, Brad Garrett, John Mahoney, Kim Cattrall, Cheryl Hines, Stockard Channing, Lena Olin, Gena Rowlands, Kathy Bates, Paul Newman, Sam Waterston, Dennis Miller, Jay Leno, Peter MacNicol, Vanessa Redgrave, Ellen DeGeneres, Henry Winkler, Marlee Matlin, Woody Allen, Garry Marshall, Mel Gibson, Eddie Murphy, Jodie Foster, James Woods, Henry Winkler, John Larroquette, Christian Slater, Downtown Julie Brown, and many many others.

*Variety* queried studio execs for a feature in October 2001 as to which were the top agencies:

If you are hot and deciding which of the star agencies to choose, go to the *Variety* archives online at www.variety.com or to the Motion Picture Academy Library and look up the article.

Formed when Ashley-Famous and CMA merged in 1971, this agency has many, many clients and many, many agents. The most famous are powerful Sam Cohn who heads the New York office and Los Angeles' charismatic Ed Limato. Limato was profiled in a *Vanity Fair* article, "The Famous Eddie L.", in January 1990. The article is worth researching if you are considering ICM. Limato is co-president of ICM along with Nancy Josephson.

Agencies large and small tend to be secretive about the size of their client lists so it's rare to find anything published about this subject but the *Los Angeles Times* reported in 1999 that ICM had 125 agents and 3,400 clients. That number is probably comparable to any of the other big star agencies. That breaks down to about twenty-seven clients per agent, if the clients were divided equally, which is very unlikely. In any event, ICM continues as one of the great conglomerate agencies.

I was fascinated to learn that there is a programming department at ICM. A high profile ICM client who was heading his own series, told me that his agency was instrumental in getting the protected timeslot that allowed his series to stay on the air well past five years. There must be similar divisions at William Morris and CAA, though I have never heard of them. If you are an actor with the heat to front your own series, this would be something to consider.

No matter which agent is responsible for you, it's clear that ICM would be an astute choice for anyone with the credits and/or heat to compete with their stable of luminous clients.

### Agents
Toni Howard, Chris Andrews, Leigh Brillstein, Jack Gilardi, Martha Luttrell, Risa Shapiro, Joe Funicello, Andy Cohen, Brian Mann, and others
### Client List
Very large

# IFA Talent Agency

8730 Sunset Boulevard, #490
(E of Doheny)
Los Angeles, CA 90069
310-659-5522

Illene Feldman began her agency career at Herb Tobias in 1981. She then spent four years with Triad before a long stint at United Talent Agency. In 1995, she left UTA to start a smaller more personal agency taking along several UTA agents and clients.

In addition to Illene, agents representing actors at IFA are David Lillard (UTA), Wendy Murphey (UTA), Joe Vance and Christy Hall.

Actors from IFA's illustrious list include Marshall Bell (*Northfork*), Peter Fonda, Troy Garity (*Soldier's Girl*), Ryan Gosling (*The United States of Leland*), Chris Penn (*Masked & Anonymous*), Tim Roth (*Whatever We Do*), Juliet Stevenson (*Bend it Like Beckham*), Mare Winningham (*The Maldonado Miracle*), Benicio Del Toro, Bridget Fonda, Joey Lauren Adams, Noah Wylie, Pete Postlethwaite, Tracey Ullman, Phillip Rhys (*24*), and Brian Cox.

Ilene was extremely gracious when she declined to be interviewed saying that she's not interested in personal publicity.

As a result, my information is from the trades.

**Agents**
Illene Feldman, David Lillard, Wendy Murphey, Joe Vance, and Christy Hall
**Client List**
40

# ⩗ Innovative Artists ⩗

1505 Tenth Street
(near Lincoln/Colorado)
Santa Monica, CA 90401
310-656-0400

It was 1982 when Gersh alums Scott Harris and the late Howard Goldberg opened the West Coast office of Robert Abrams (Abrams Harris & Goldberg). When Abrams exited, it became Harris & Goldberg, then, after Howard passed away, the present name was chosen.

In addition to Scott, agents who rep actors at IA are Steve Lemanna (Ambrosia Mortimer; Epstein, Wyckoff, Lemanna), Marnie Sparer, Michael Packenham (Diverse Talent Agency), Louise S. Ward, Meredith Wechter, Adena Chawke, Craig Shapiro, Thomas Cushing, Nevin Dolcefino (Gersh) and David Rose.

During the first quarter of 2000, IA added an Independent Film Division headed by Scott that reps films for domestic and international distribution as well as literary properties and remake rights for foreign films, sort of a producer's rep within a standing agency.

Denver native Jeff Morrone created Innovative's Young Talent department in 1995. Since his departure to become a manager, Amy Abell (Gersh) and Abby Bluestone rep Innovative's youngest clients.

Clients include Edie Falco (*The Sopranos*), John Amos (*John Q*), Bryce Dallas Howard (*The Woods*), Kate Nelligan (*Cider House Rules*), Frances Fisher (*Unforgiven*), Patti LuPone (*Summer of Sam*), Jason Biggs (*American Wedding*), Alicia Silverstone (*Scooby-Doo 2*), Traci Lords (*First Wave*), Alyson Hannigan (*American Wedding*), Katherine Bell (*JAG*), Illeana Douglas (*Missing Brendan*), Kelly Hu (*X-Men 2*), Lorraine Bracco (*The Sopranos*), Jill Clayburgh (*Leap of Faith*), Doris Roberts (*Everybody Loves Raymond*), Peter Boyle (*Everybody Loves Raymond*), Elliot Gould (*Ocean's Eleven*), Gary Busey (*Quigley*), Jeremy Sisto (*Six Feet Under*), and Andrew McCarthy (*Kingdom Hospital*).

Innovative represents actors, directors, below-the-line personnel, producers, writers and young adults.

**Agents**
Scott Harris, Steve Lemanna, Marnie Sparer, Adena Chawke, Craig Shapiro, Thomas Cushing, Nevin Dolcefino, David Ledderman, David Herd, Steve Muller, Michael Packenham, Louise S. Ward, Meredith Wechter, Amy Abell, Abby Bluestone, and David Rose
**Client List**
400 +

# ⩘ Innovative at Ford Models ⩗

8826 Burton Way
(btwn Robertson and Doheny)
Beverly Hills, CA 90211
310-276-4440

Innovative at Ford Models specializes in beautiful creatures for film and television. I don't know whether the beauties here are even more beautiful than the beauties in the Beauty division at the regular Innovative office or just what the distinction is, but I@FM exists to further the film and television careers of the prestigious Ford models.

Kim Byrd and Emily Golan are the lucky agents who spend the day with beauty all around them.

They are currently not accepting any pictures or resumes, but it doesn't hurt to check for the moment when their current crop "age" out of their system.

**Agents**
Kim Byrd and Emily Golan
**Clients**
A large and lovely list

# ⚴ Kaplan-Stahler-Gumer Agency ⚰

8383 Wilshire Boulevard, #923
(at San Vincente)
Beverly Hills, CA 90211
323-653-4483

I only include this agency to save you postage. Read on.

Mitchell Kaplan and Elliott Stahler are prestigious literary agents running their own respected literary agency, but it was not always thus.

There was a day when Mitch and Elliott were just esteemed theatrical agents at Progressive Artists. However, as they made the decision to turn in their actor clients for writers, one of the actors refused to let go.

That's why Kaplan and Stahler retained their theatrical franchise and service an exclusive theatrical list of one.

The lucky actor with his own private agent is Earl Boen. You'll see the agency on lists of franchised agents, but neither they nor Earl are anxious to increase the size of the list.

Partner Bob Gumer who joined Kaplan and Stahler from ICM a few years ago, is also not interested in adding actors to his list.

**Agents**
Mitch Kaplan, Elliott Stahler and Bob Gumer
**Client List**
1

# ⊿ Kazarian/Spencer & Associates ⊾

11365 Ventura Boulevard, #100/Box 7403
(one block W of Tujunga)
Studio City, CA 91604
818-769-9111

Since Cindy Kazarian and Pamm Spencer were my commercial agents years ago at WHJ (Wormser Heldfond Joseph), the precursor to this amazing agency, I thought KSA was still simply a commercial powerhouse. I had managed to miss the evolution of KSA.

Cindy and Pamm's initial contribution to WHJ was to support Julie McDonald's pioneering concept: a Dance Department. Until then, dancers didn't have agents, but just as Cindy, Pamm and Julie stepped into that void, the dance business began to explode with music videos, MTV, and films like *Dirty Dancing*.

In 1988, when WHJ owners Sandy Joseph and Brian Rix decided to become managers, they offered "the kids," the chance to "buy the store" and Cindy and Pamm never looked back.

Today there are four separate, autonomous departments: Young People, Equity, Character, and Hip, Edgy & Beautiful.

Bonnie Ventis and Jody Alexander came to KSA from Herb Tannen Agency to create a department for *Young People*. A theater major at Cal State Long Beach, Bonnie Ventis was a stage manager in Long Beach before relocation to Los Angeles necessitated a new job. A friend mentioned Tannen. That's where she met Jody Alexander.

Jody knew her major in Drama at Cal State Northridge was just a first step so, during finals, she interviewed for a receptionist job at Goldin Dennis Karg. Soon she was assisting the three partners and, within a couple of years, she was an agent. Sheila Manning stole her away to cast commercials for five years before Jody returned to agenting at Tannen joining Bonnie in creating an outstanding Young People's department.

Thinking a kid's department had great potential, Cindy and Pamm searched for two hot kid agents who could create a kid's powerhouse for KSA. Bonnie and Jody managed to deliver, quickly launching the careers of Elijah Wood and Jonathan Taylor Thomas.

Colleague Philip Marcus joins Bonnie and Jody repping clients Ethan Damps (*American Dreams*), Austin Majors (*NYPD Blue*), Olivia

Hack (*Gilmore Girls*), Julian Rodriguez (*24*), Kimberly Williams (*Joan of Arcadia*), Madison McReynolds (*CSI*), Willy Goldstein (*Oliver Bean*), Shayna Fox and Joseph Ashton (voices on *Rocket Power*), and Lindsay Haun and Marcus Toj, the movie surfer hosts on the Disney Channel.

Victoria Morris heads up the *Equity Department*. Not to be confused with departments that book for film and television, Victoria books strictly for Broadway and regional theater. Victoria started at KSA as a dance client, but kept finding Equity jobs and marrying them to clients until she began defining herself not only as an agent, but as head of her own brand new department as the Dance Department morphed into the Equity Department. Nancy LeMenager (*Never Gonna Dance*) and Riva Rice (*Chicago*) are two of her clients.

Managing to retire from an earlier life with ATT at the tender age of thirty-two, Riley Day finally tired of travel and was receptive to a part time job in the dance department at WHJ. Now Riley is KSA's general manager and also the head of the *Character Department*, one the most interesting aspects of KSA.

Realizing that no agencies were helping artists with disabilities, Riley became a champion for disabled actors. As the department grew, Riley's assistant, Leslie Stokoe, became his colleague and the two of them began to focus on another overlooked group, actors over fifty.

Clients from the Character list are Liz Sheridan (*Seinfeld*), Steve Paymer (*Scream Queen*), James Kelly, and Mitch Longley (*Las Vegas*).

Mara Santino and Ryan Daly are the team repping those lucky folk with the "WB look", you know, *Hip Edgy & Beautiful*.

Mara came from Pittsburgh to Los Angeles to be an actress. She quickly realized her fortunes lay elsewhere and since she didn't know where, she took a receptionist job at KSA to look around. In a few weeks she became an assistant, and three years later, an agent. Her partner in crime, Ryan Daly (Strong Morrone) arrived in late 2003. Their list includes AJ Lamas (*American Family*), Cris Judd (*I'm a Celebrity, Get Me Out of Here*), Ryan Starr (*American Idol*), Matt Cedeno and J. Kenneth Johnson (*Days of Our Lives*), Rochelle Aytes and Faune Chambers(*The White Chicks*), Maximillan Alexander (*All My Children, Take Me Out*), and Jack Krizmanich (*Passions*).

KSA also reps athletes, stuntmen, models, game shows and celebrities. They also have a vibrant New York office. www.ksa.com

**Agents**
Cindy Kazarian, Riley Day, Leslie Stokoe, Victoria Morris, Mara Santino, Ryan Daly, Bonnie Ventis, Jody Alexander, and Philip Marcus
**Clients**
Very large

# ⟆ The Eric Klass Agency ⟆

139 S. Beverly Drive, #331
(south of Wilshire Boulevard )
Beverly Hills, CA 90212
310-274-9169

Eric Klass began his career working with one of the class acts in agenting, Peter Witt. When Witt retired to produce, Eric and fellow Witt agent, Mike Belson decided to open their own office. They partnered for twenty-five years before Mike decided agenting wasn't fun anymore and retired to golf and an occasional acting job.

Eric still loves the business and his clients and is one of the four people in Los Angeles who really doesn't want to be an actor, so he's pressing on alone. He has shortened his list in order to give the kind of hands-on attention his clients expect.

Clients from his list of about twenty include Joanna Last, Mariclare Costello, Peter Haskell, Dianne Kay, Kenneth Mars, Grant Goodeve, Robert Donner, James Gleason, Joseph Hacker, and David Greenlee.

Eric continues to be that cool guy who cares about his clients so much that he makes me choose who to list because he doesn't want to leave anyone out.

This office returns phone calls and treats actors like human beings. From Klass, you get class. What else could you ask?

**Agents**
Eric Klass
**Client List**
16

# ⊠ Paul Kohner, Inc. ⊠

9300 Wilshire Boulevard, #555
(at Rexford)
Beverly Hills, CA 90212
310-550-1060

When this agency was founded by Paul Kohner sixty-two years ago, it was the first U.S. stop for European directors, writers and actors and represented the likes of William Wyler, Billy Wilder and Ingmar Bergman. In fact, Bergman is still a client.

Kohner vets Pearl Wexler and Gary Salt bought the agency from Paul in 1987, a year before he died, and retained not only Kohner's name, but the old world graciousness that was so much his hallmark.

I'm sad to report that Gary died in 1999. He remains one of the nicest and most articulate agents I ever interviewed.

In the recent past, new agents have been added to the theatrical roster, Samantha Crisp and Amanda Glazer from William Morris, and Sheree Cohen, who was formerly a manager.

They join department head Pearl Wexler in representing their list of about 120 clients that include Jerry Stiller, Dwayne Martin, Gordon Clapp, Richard Roundtree, Barry Pepper and Tracee Ross.

You may send pictures and resumes, but you'll really need someone to recommend you to this agency.

**Agents**
Pearl Wexler, Samantha Crisp, Amanda Glazer, and Sheree Cohen
**Client List**
120

# ⤳ McCabe-Justice ⤶
### formerly Henderson Hogen McCabe

8285 Sunset Boulevard, #1
(corner of Sweetzer)
Los Angeles, CA 90046
323-650-3738

Pretty soon, I'm going to have to stop referencing the Henderson-Hogan history of this agency since there's really no trace of the original business. Maggie died in 1994 and Jerry Hogan and Bryan McCabe elected to go their own separate ways in early 2002. Not only that, Bryan moved from the sunny Beverly Hills office into new digs on Sunset Boulevard and I think there's only one client left from the old list.

Whew!

Bostonian Bryan McCabe was a stage manager on the East Coast hoping to become an assistant director when he moved west. Without connections or enough money to just hang until something happened, he answered an ad in the *Hollywood Reporter* to become an assistant to Maggie Henderson. Though Bryan expected Henderson Hogan to be a momentary job, he must have liked it since he never left. And now he owns the place. Not bad.

Bryan's new partner, Todd Justice, was a manager before he joined the agency program, working for Bryan Mann at ICM. He joined Bryan McCabe in 2001 and became a partner in 2003.

The Los Angeles client list at HH numbers less than a hundred. Names from the list include John Kapelos, Paul Gleason, Bonnie Root, John Rubenstein, and Juliet Landau.

### Agents
Bryan McCabe and Todd Justice
### Client List
less than 100

# ⚐ Media Artists Group, Inc. ⚐

6300 Wilshire Boulevard, #1470
(at Crescent Heights)
Los Angeles, CA 90048
323-658-5050

A man brimming with ideas and passion, ex-actor Raphael Berko became an agent's assistant in order to submit himself for auditions. When the *Hollywood Reporter* wrote a story about his double life, the jig was up. SAG told him he had to choose between being an actor or an agent. Twenty-nine-year-old Raphael bought The Caroline Leonetti Agency, changed the name and started booking his clients.

At one time, the agency had many clients of many different stripes, but today, MAG has reformatted itself as a boutique agency with fewer than sixty clients.

Azeem Chiba and Hadi Halawana (Michael Green Agency) join Rapheal and Kyle Lawrence repping their confidential list of actors.

MAG sees new people only by referral.

**Agents**
Raphael Berko, Azeem Chiba, Hadi Halawana, and Kyle Lawrence
**Client List**
less than 60

# ◢ Meridian Artists ◣

9229 Sunset Boulevard, #310
(W of Doheny)
Los Angeles, CA 90069
310-246-2600

An actor in New York who began his agenting career working for Sanford Leigh, J. Michael Bloom quickly established himself as a driving commercial force in his own right with his first agency, J. Michael Bloom, in the early 1970s. It wasn't long before he took some of his commercial earnings and hired impressive theatrical agents to help him build an amazing New York and, later Los Angeles theatrical list with clients Alec Baldwin, Freddie Hoskins, and Uta Hagen.

In 1997, Michael sold his various businesses and his name to a large conglomerate that promptly went bankrupt. Those who didn't know the inside story, thought Michael was involved, but luckily, it was only his name He was long gone before troubles began.

In April of 1999, without legal recourse to his own name, Michael created Meridian Artists and began again. Michael and colleague Marc L. Bass (APA) rep a select group of clients. Cedric Yarborough (*Central Comedy*), Tony Amendola, and Jordan Baker (*The Out-of-Towners*) are a few names from their list.

**Agents**
J. Michael Bloom and Marc L. Bass
**Client List**
50

# ⚐ Metropolitan Talent Agency ⚐

4526 Wilshire Boulevard
(at Rossmore)
Los Angeles, CA 90010
323-857-4500

An actor and a writer in an earlier life, Chris Barrett spent only eight months working as an agent for J. Michael Bloom before opening McCartt Oreck Barrett. That was in 1983 and MOB, as it was called, was known as one of the places to shop for interesting actors, some of whom still grace Chris' client list.

By 1989, Chris was ready to add other creative elements to his agency, so he left MOB and formed Metropolitan, where he still represents a distinguished list of writers, producers, showrunners, directors, actors and comedians.

Chris's business mind is always teaming. *The Wall Street Journal* found his creative compensation idea noteworthy.

◆ *For each commission dollar coming in from a deal, 30% is scored for the agent who originally brought in the client, no matter how long ago. The next 30% goes to the employee currently representing that talent. The final 40% goes to whoever has landed the deal in question. The same employee frequently performs all these functions, but many deals link two, three or more agents.*
Thomas Petzinger, Jr., *The Wall Street Journal*[35]

Cloris Leachman, Austin Pendleton, and Jane Seymour are three of Metropolitan's long-time clients who are repped by Chris and colleagues Karen Foreman (CAA), Dan Baron, Gabrielle Krengel, Bob Alcorn, Karen Goldberg, and Melisa Spamer.

Metropolitan also represents directors, writers, and producers This is an agency that you will need a referral to gain entrée.

**Agents**
Chris Barrett, Karen Foreman, and Melisa Spamer
**Client List**
85

# ⚒ H. David Moss & Associates ⚒

733 N. Seward Street, Penthouse
(N of Melrose/E of Highland)
Hollywood, CA 90038
213-465-1234

Growing up in a Beverly Hills showbiz family, David Moss might easily have followed his brother Bud into the agency business at the beginning of his career, but much to the chagrin of his family, David trained to become a bullfighter and moved to Spain where he fought successfully for four years before injuries cut his career short.

Although he worked for a while as an actor, in 1967 Moss ultimately took his bullfighter nerves of steel into the agenting arena apprenticing with Sid Gold at the old Gold Fields Agency (precursor to Jack Fields to Gores Fields to Paradigm) before opening his own agency in 1969.

An invitation to return to the ring for an exhibition of senior bullfighters brought David back to the ring in 2000. Although his friends and family thought he was crazy, Moss trained, bought new equipment and journeyed to Mexico where he drew the biggest bull of the day, was tossed and gored, but rose unharmed to become the most popular bullfighter of the day.

A documentary film crew heard he was picking up his cape again and chronicled his journey, so you might end up seeing David onscreen sometime soon. In the meantime, he returns to a more familiar arena, agenting his list of clients that includes Antonio Fargas (*Starsky & Hutch*), Walter Koenig (*Star Trek*), Jeremy Kemp, Barbara Luna, Georg Stanford Brown, Karen Kondazian, Paul Karr, Gary Conway, and Paul Kent.

David represents actors, comedians, directors, martial artists, newscasters, sports personalities and teenagers at his offices above The HBO Comedy Space/Melrose Theater.

Agent
H. David Moss
Client List
40

# ᴁ Omnipop ᴂ

10700 Ventura Boulevard
(one block W of Lankershim)
Studio City, CA 91604
818-980-9267

Though I couldn't have imagined Long Island as a spawning ground for an influential showbiz agency, Omnipop has managed to thrive and then some. Tom Ingegno (pronounced "engine-yo"), Ralph Asquino and Bruce Smith started this agency on Long Island in 1983 and they prospered from the beginning. An eclectic lot, the Omni partners were all stand-up performers, musicians or managers who booked themselves and their friends on college circuits and later clubs. As they graduated to bigger, more diverse venues and clients, starting an agency was a logical progression.

Omnipop consciously chooses staff who share this background. Their taste and savvy led them to create their own niche representing stand-up comics for personal appearances, television, film and commercials.

In their one concession to tradition, Bruce Smith moved to Los Angeles to open a West Coast office in 1990.

Omni used to book stand-up performers exclusively, but has now expanded to include very well trained comedic and legit actors. Though constantly evolving, the bottom line at Omni is still talented, interesting people who have something to offer.

Although the Los Angeles office is only interested if you have already spent at lE a year in the business and are playing a decent venue, the E Coast office see themselves as the farm team, developing the stars of tomorrow, so they're a little more approachable. Still, you really should have twenty to thirty minutes worth of material before you query this agency as a stand-up.

Clients routinely work *The Tonight Show, The Late Show with David Letterman, E! Entertainment, Late Night with Conan O'Brien,* clubs, film, theater and some, like Christopher Titus (*Titus*), Nadya Ginsburg (*Hype*), Bill Dwyer (*Battlebots*), Susan Yeagley (*Off Limits*), Andy Kindler (*Everybody Loves Raymond*), Teresa Strasser (*Lovers Lounge*), and Christopher Moynihan (*Gary & Mike*), either have their own series or are series regulars.

Omnipop's website is filled with information and pictures of all their clients and the agency. If you want to know more about these guys, check out www.omnipop.com..

There are some helpful insights from Bruce and Tom about career progression for stand-ups elsewhere in the book.

Contact this office before you send an audition tape. The best way to access these folk is via a phone call or letter stating who you are and what you've done. If they find you and/or your background interesting, they will either ask to see a tape or come see you work.

Agents in the Los Angeles office who represent talent are Bruce Smith, Tom Markwalter and Jamie Ducat, who joined Omnipop in 2000 (JID Management).

**Agents**
Bruce Smith, Tom Markwalter and Jamie Ducat.
**Client List**
55 both coasts

# ⇘ Origin Talent ⇙

4705 Laurel Canyon Blvd.
(across from Gelson's at Riverside)
Studio City, CA 91607
818-487-1800

Marc Chancer and Annie Schwartz are impressive. They opened Origin Talent just before pilot season in 1999 and managed to generate six hundred auditions for their twenty clients during that period. That translates into thirty auditions for each actor and this was during a season where teens were the only people casting directors wanted to see, and they didn't have a single teen on their list!

Brooklyn born Marc Chancer started in the business as an actor, but let casting director Joel Therm talk him out of it when Joel suggested that Marc (who, trust me, is a hunk) was not good-looking enough to be in this business.

Not just an actor, but an avid fan with a knowledge of actors and careers, Marc impressed J. Michael Bloom enough that after only six months as his assistant, he became the Equity Theater agent at Michael's office.

Marc left Bloom in 1987 to help Judy Scheon start her agency in her garage with two telephones and an assistant. He worked for Judy for twelve years and that's where he met Annie.

Annie Schwartz started her showbiz career at seventeen, working as an assistant for legendary agent (now manager) Mike Greenfield. Since this was before the Breakdown Service, Mike was out reading scripts all day and selling clients while Annie ran the office.

Her education at Mike's prepared her for her next job as an assistant working for Jenny Delany at Triad, where she became a franchised agent and first met Judy Schoen.

Annie left the business for eight years to raise her three children. When she decided to re-enter the business in 1997, she reconnected with Schoen, who hired her.

Three years later, when she left Schoen, Marc felt it was time for them to start an agency together. Their idea of working with a smaller group of clients they were passionate about, has united them and been the impetus for their successful agency.

Clients from their list include Patrick Bristow (*Ellen*), Eric Lutes

(*Caroline in the City*), J.P. Manoux (*Phil of the Future*), Kevin McCarthy, Jack Mcgee (*Rescue Me*), Kathleen Noone (*Passions*), Jane Elliot (*General Hospital*) Michelle Phillips, Marcia Wallace, Kym Whitley (*Beauty Shop the Movie*), Michael Bofshever, Robert Clendenin (*Good Morning Miami*), and Jay Pickett (*Port Charles*).

Annie and Marc have a studio at their offices and put clients on tape and help them package themselves for certain jobs. They absolutely won't take "no" for an answer when they believe in someone.

Though Origin wants to keep their list at its present size, they do look at pictures and resumes and accept referrals from industry professionals.

### Agents
Marc Chancer and Annie Schwartz
### Clients
50

# ⚞ Osbrink Agency ⚟

4343 Lankershim Boulevard, #100
(one block S of Moorpark)
Universal City, CA 91602
818-760-2488

Another stage-mom whose on-site education led to a career as an agent, Nancy Osbrink started her agenting career working part-time for her son's agent, Susan Crowe. When Nancy realized she was making a life choice, she spent two years at UCLA taking every entertainment law and showbiz related course available, so when she opened her own one woman/one room agency in 1983, she was ready.

That humble beginning has led to one of the most successful agencies repping babies through young adults (age thirty is the cut off) in the city. While waiting to meet Nancy, I was struck by the energy in the office and the relationship between the young clients and all the office personnel as they arrived. Lots of hugs and laughs. The Osbrink Agency looks to be a place where they really understand and like kids.

Nancy reps clients from fifteen days old up to sixteen years. Partner Scott Wine (whose clients are sixteen to thirty) and Sarah Shyn (CAA) are adamant that they only represent clients who are self-motivated.

They are quick to ride herd on young clients that they think might be getting carried away by the make-believe world and insist on a cooling off period between big projects to ground the kids again.

Clients include Jake Lloyd (*Star Wars: The Phantom Menace*), Raven-Symone (*Dr. Dolittle II*), and Lindsay Felton (*Caitlin's Way*).

Although the Osbrink Agency canvasses headshots and resumes that come in unsolicited, most clients come via referral from the industry, clients and/or friends.

**Agents**
Cindy Osbrink, Scott Wine, and Sarah Shyn
**Clients**
200

# ⊿ Pakula/King & Associates ⊿

9229 Sunset Boulevard, #315
(W of Doheny)
Los Angeles, CA 90069
310-281-4868

Nina Pakula taught film, acting and directing for twelve years at Christopher Columbus High School in the Bronx, directing plays and bonding with her students in the way that only a gifted teacher can do. When the world changed and students began showing up stoned for class, Pakula decided to leave while she still had good memories. Her actor husband was feeling the call of California, so they decided to embark on an adventure and see what the W might hold for them.

Pakula met with casting directors, producers and others in the business, searching for a place to put her showbiz skills that wouldn't take as long as developing a career in directing. The consensus was that she would make a good agent, so she pounded the pavement calling on agents much as an actor does looking for work.

The thirteenth agency, Century Artists, was looking for an assistant. Since she was the same age as the agents and had a masters degree plus thirty credits and had been a teacher, it took some work convincing them that she really really wanted to be their assistant.

After six months, she was doing everything except closing the deal. They treated her well, but didn't need another agent, so she left to join Vicki Light at The Light Company, where she helped build that office for six and a half years.

Her next stop was another exercise in agency building when she joined Harry Abrams just as he was opening a new West Coast office. It was there she met her now partner, lawyer Joel King, who had sublimated his ego to work as her assistant and learn the business.

Abrams' vision for a William Morris type agency was not Nina's so after a time she prevailed upon Joel (by then an agent at Michael Slessinger) to join her in creating an agency where family is really more the climate than the corporate reality of a William Morris.

The agency opened on October 24, 1994 and from the first moment, PKA was successful. They already had relationships with the casting community who not only called them for jobs, but recommended talent for their list.

They list about seventy-five working actors like Hattie Winston (*Becker*) Alex Desert (*Becker*), Kimberlin Brown (*Bold and the Beautiful*), Mitch Pileggi (*The X-Files*), Beverly Garland and Jon Cypher.

Nina and Joel feel actors endure more hardships than the average person and seek to provide a supportive atmosphere with hands-on managerial attention.

Nina says they are particularly attentive to their actors who are on series. Knowing that series work, though lucrative, can leave you high and dry when it's over, PKA works diligently to make sure the resume doesn't just list one job for five years.

Although they have found clients from a picture and resume, that is a rare occurrence. Their clients usually come to them from referrals. Hilary Steinberg is the third agent on their roster and graduated from the agency training program at Pakula/King..

**Agents**
Nina Pakula, Joel King and Hilary Steinberg
**Client list**
75

# ⩚ Paradigm ⩚

10100 Santa Monica Boulevard, 25th floor
(at Century Park East)
Los Angeles, CA 90067
310-277-4400

In 1993, Gores Fields and STE merged with each other as well as with two prominent literary agencies, Robinson, Weintraub & Gross and Shorr, Stille & Associates, to form a new prestigious and powerful mini-conglomerate.

Partners at Paradigm are Sam Gores (David Shapira, SGA, Gores Fields), Clifford Stevens, and ex-William Morris executive Robert Stein, who serves as head of the motion picture department.

Though Paradigm has continued to grow since the merger, they have managed to retain their intimate family style representation while reaping the informational rewards of their expanded coverage.

The background of the theatrical partners is distinguished. The late Jack Fields long ago cornered the market on important character actors and represented them with style and class with help from associate Judith Moss (Richard Dickens Agency).

Clients from their illustrious list of actors include Allison Janney, Billy Baldwin, Billy Zane, Randy Quaid, Mark Harmon, Danny Aiello, Antonio Sabato, Jr., Charles Durning, Penny Fuller, Barbara Babcock, Andy Garcia, Laurence Fishburne, Philip Seymour Hoffman, Chris Cooper, Campbell Scott, and Elizabeth Pena.

Agents who represent actors at Paradigm in Los Angeles are Sam Gores, Robert Stein, Arthur Toretzky (ATM), Joel Rudnick, Judith Moss, Alisa Adler, Sandi Dudek (ICM), Jim Hess (Irv Schechter), Michael Lazo (Writers & Artists), Monica Barkett, Jonathan Blueman, Sara Ramaker, Susie Tobin, Katie Mason, Ollie Mossie, Adel Nur, and Paradigm trained Kari Whittlesey-Esterin and Andrew Ruf. In order to access this agency, you need entrée.

Paradigm is moving in the first quarter of 2004, so verify the address if you're sending material. The new address will be 360 N. Crescent, N Building, Beverly Hills, CA 90210.

**Agents**
Robert Stein, Sam Gores, Arthur Toretzky, Joel Rudnick, Judith Moss, Alisa Adler, Monica Barkett, Sandi Dudek, Jim Hess, Michael Lazo, Kari Whittlesay-Esterin, Michael Lazo, Kate Mason, Adel Nur, Jonathan Blueman, Andrew Ruf, and Jonathan Silverman
**Client List**
200+

# ⨼ Players Talent ⨽

13033 Ventura Boulevard, #N
(btwn Fulton & Coldwater)
Studio City, CA 91604
818-528-7444

Los Angeles native Joe Kolkowitz was originally a professional tennis player and coach of famous athletes. His friendship with the director of the O.J. Simpson "running through airport commercials" led to his starting the first agency representing athletes for commercials, television and movies. That was in 1983 and the name of the agency was Sportscasting.

In 1997, he changed the name to Players Talent. Primarily interested in athletes of every kind, those who catch Joe's eye will be physically unusual, very young, very big and/or very attractive. He represents a few broadcasters, comedians and Hispanics. Though he wouldn't name any of his sixty clients, he did say he has some exceptional child athletes and a national champion tapdancer.

Although Joe says he looks at all pictures and resumes, he doesn't look at tapes unless he is already interested.

**Agent**
Joe Kolkowitz
**Clients**
60

# ⊿ Progressive Artists Agency ⊾

400 S. Beverly Drive, #216
(S of Olympic)
Beverly Hills, CA 90212
310-553-8561

Bernie Carneol was a casting director before he joined classy old-line Kumen-Olenick in 1975. When K-O retired, Bernie was the logical successor. Bernie's flair and originality are reflected in his client list. An eye for the talented and off-beat has resulted in an impressive track record in finding and developing important stars. Belle Zwerdling is his associate.

PAA handles actors, comedians, directors, musical artists, and producers and they also package.

Clients from their list include Lu Leonard, Katey Sagal, and Ruth Kobart. This boutique agency is warm, supportive and well-connected.

**Agents**
Bernie Carneol and Belle Zwerdling
**Client List**
49

# ⚖ Relevè ⚖

5750 Wilshire Boulevard, #640
(The Spelling Building/at Fairfax)
Hollywood, CA 90036
323-857-9040

Starting in the business as a production assistant on *Hard Copy*, Holly Davis Carter's next stop was in casting. She created Agency West in 1999 and, in 2003, she birthed its spin-off, Relevè, the only agency in town specializing in crossover music talent. Holly's mission is to move her hip hop and gospel clients to the theatrical side of the business.

Hip Hop artists, Usher, Master P, and Little Romeo are her major crossover clients.

If you want to attract Holly, you need to be established in one area, preferably music since that's her speciality. She says her clients are usually recommended or someone she goes after.

Holly pretty much convinces me she can do anything.

**Agents**
Holly Davis Carter
**Clients**
15

# ⚞ The Savage Agency, Ltd. ⚟

6212 Banner Avenue
(E of Vine/N of Santa Monica Boulevard)
Los Angeles, CA 90038
323-461-8316

Judy Savage started out to be a doctor, but life with her children turned out to be more interesting, so she followed a path cut by her son. Judy's son had asthma and couldn't play sports, so she got him involved in singing and dancing which for some reason didn't make him wheeze. Turns out, he could sing four octaves, so when at nine years of age, he was cast in the touring company of *Mame*, Judy took her other two toddlers and went on the road with him for a year!

Her kids all starred in theater, film and television and still became productive grown-ups (a composer, a film editor and a news anchor). So much for my theory that kids in the business are robbed of their childhoods and end up as unhappy adults.

For fifteen years, Judy managed her children as they grew up in the business. In 1978, she opened her own agency. She says the first ten years were rocky, but the last ten have been amazing.

Judy says one of the best decisions she ever made was hiring Helen Garrett, whose career runs the gamut from being a child actor, mother of a child actor and agent to child actors at her own agency.

Helen joins Judy and Pilar Cleere repping clients Rider Strong (*Party of Five*) and Larisa Oleynik (*3rd Rock from the Sun*).

Judy's clients cover both ends of the spectrum. Her young 'uns are from age three to twenty-six, and the adults are sixty plus. Judy says she can successfully represent clients long after they are children, but that at a certain age, they leave home and make their lives as adult actors with adult agents. Sort of like leaving home in real life.

Ever one to grow with the times, Judy has expanded her Voiceover Department and formed a company that produces reality shows.

**Agents**
Judy Savage, Helen Garrett, and Pilar Cleere
**Client List**
200

# ⊿ Scagnetti Talent & Literary Agency ⊾

5118 Vineland Avenue, #102
(btwn Magnolia & Camarillo)
North Hollywood, CA 91601
818-762-3871

Jack Scagnetti was a newspaper man, a magazine editor and a public relations man before he started his own writing career as a biographer to the stars. Scagnetti has written fifteen star biographies, among them Valentino, Laurel & Hardy and Clark Gable. As the author of the definitive Gable biography, Jack appears on A&E three times a year to moderate Gable's Biography.

Jack opened his own agency in 1975 to represent writers and actors and now represents scriptwriters, authors and actors for theater, film, television and commercials. Jack says his theatrical list sports about 250 names. Clark Gable's son, John Clark Gable, is on his list as well as John Grinage, who was in *Rebel Without a Cause* with James Dean and was a regular on *Night Stalker.*

Jack runs the business alone with help from several able assistants and does everything by mail. He's not interested in people dropping by his office. He calls in two new actors a day, four days a week from the 100 pictures and resumes a week he receives.

His need right now is for actors in the eighteen to twenty-five age range. In order to make his list, you must be at least eighteen years of age, not just look it.

**Agent**
Jack Scagnetti
**Client List**
250

# ◢ The Irv Schechter Company ◣

9300 Wilshire Boulevard, #400
(at Rexford)
Beverly Hills, CA 90212
310-278-8070

The Irv Schechter Company's muscle has always been its literary department. Irv still maintains his list of important directors and scriptwriters, but the agency overall has scaled back.

The talent department is run by daughter Mieke (Mee-ka) Schechter. Mieke earned her MA in broadcast journalism and interned with broadcast journalist agent Ken Linder before joining her father's agency.

**Agents**
Mieke Schechter
**Client List**
50

# ⌁ Schiowitz/Clay/Ankrum/Ross Inc. ⌁

1680 N. Vine Avenue, #614
(at Hollywood Boulevard)
Los Angeles, CA 90028
323-463-7300

Originally a producer/general manager (*Nuts, Sister Mary Ignatius, Pump Boys & Dinettes, Uncommon Women & Others, Cloud 9*), Josh Schiowitz took his contacts, Rolodex and his marketing and organizational skills, and opened his agency (Schiowitz Clay & Rose) in 1987.

Clay & Rose departed along the way and in 2003, Josh entered a new era partnering up with two agents from Twentieth Century Artists, David Ankrum and Jae Ross. Although they all represent the list of actors, David also heads the literary department and Jae handles the choreographers, stage directors and all Equity contracts.

Because they have such a strong musical comedy list, their clients are constantly on Broadway. SCR recently opened its New York office which is run by Laurie Walton.

Actors from their list include Elmarie Wendell (*The West Wing, 3rd Rock from the Sun*), Kathryn Joosten (The *West Wing*), Dion Basco (*City Guys*), Natalie Desselle-Reid (*Eve*), Ted Lange, Susan Egan (for theater only) and Philip Anthony-Rodriquez (*Jake 20*).

Charles says they review all pictures and resumes, but admits they rarely call anyone in from a mailing. Their list is a combination of referrals and heavy theater credits. Josh says, if they specialize in anything, it is in really good actors.

**Agents**
Josh Schiowitz, David Ankrum, and Jae Rees
**Client List**
70

# ◢ Schnarr Talent ◣

8500 Melrose Avenue, #212
(just west of La Cienega)
West Hollywood, CA 90069
310-360-7680

From Saginaw, Michigan, Sandie Schnarr didn't know anything about the business when she went to work as a receptionist at Sutton, Barth & Venarrie in 1980. All she knew was that she had gone as far as she could go in her previous job and she wanted a future.

She certainly got one! As a receptionist and later, agent, Sandie interacted with all the clients and quickly decided that the voice/animation clients who were so supportive of one another, were the ones that she wanted to spend time with.

After four years at SB&V, Sandy quit to ponder her next move. That decision was taken from her when she found out that she had cancer. She won her year-long battle with the disease and, between chemo and surgery and all the attendant challenges, she decided that when she got well, she was going to start her own business.

She began haunting voiceover workshops and seeing who was up-and-coming and also got many referrals from casting directors and even other agents who spied voices on the rise.

She opened her office in January of 1985 and is the only agency in town to only represent voice talent. Her list of about 150 works constantly. Sandie says she rarely takes on new voices and really only listens to tapes of voices that are industry referrals.

She says that if you hope to get voice work, you need to have a tape that makes it sound as though you have done several national commercials and that, if you can't afford a voiceover workshop, you can create your own by transcribing the copy of commercials and taping yourself doing them.

**Agent**
Sandie Schnarr, Victoria Joyce, Artt Butler, and Melissa Grillo
**Clients**
150

# ◁ Judy Schoen & Associates ▷

606 N. Larchmont Boulevard, #309
(south of Melrose/between Vine & Gower)
Los Angeles, CA 90004
323-962-1950

In 1988, Atlanta native Judy Schoen created this agency. A working actress in New York in 1969, she worked as a production stage manager before WMA lured her into the business of agenting.

Judy died in 1999 after a brief illness and the agency is now owned by Schoen vet Michelle Mazurki (Bresler Wolfe, Cota & Livingston, Artists Agency, J. Michael Bloom, The Gamble Office).

Michelle had been with Judy for twelve years, handling administrative duties and the logical step was for Judy to step in to keep Schoen's rich legacy going.

Jinny Raymond (Writers & Artists), Joy Keller (Artists Agency, David Shapira, The Gage Group), and John Williams (promoted from within) join Michelle repping clients Joe Morton, Joe Regalbuto, Elizabeth Berridge, Deborah Mooney, Jessica White and Anita Gillette.

**Agents**
Michelle Mazurki, Jinny Raymond, Joy Keller and John Williams
**Client List**
100

# ◿ Kathleen Schultz Associates ◺

6442 Coldwater Canyon, #206
(just N of Victory Boulevard)
Valley Glen, CA 91606
818-760-3100

After graduating from UCLA with a minor in Theater Arts,
Kathleen Schultz thought she would use her training to become an
actress, but ended up having twins instead. Although she worked nights
to help with family finances, it wasn't until a casting director at Quinn
Martin (her mother) heard there was a job as a secretary at Dade/Rosen
that Schultz entered show business.

By the time Mike Rosen left to start a literary agency almost twenty
years later, Kathleen was not only an agent, but Ernie Dade's partner.

When Ernie retired in 2000, Kathleen continued on her own except
for a brief moment in partnership with Conan Carroll. Back on her
own, she's in the same offices she shared with Ernie with some of the
same clients.

Ellen Geer, Patrick Gorman, Dwayne Hickman, and Candy Azzara
are from Kathleen's list of under a hundred.

Kathleen's list is all working actors. She's started some high profile
actors and is interested in developing young talent again and adding a
few more ethnic faces of all ages.

**Agents**
Kathleen Schultz
**Client List**
less than 100

# ◿ Screen Artists Agency ◺

4526 Sherman Oaks Avenue
(just W of Sepulveda/S of Ventura Boulevard)
Sherman Oaks, CA 91403
818-789-4896

As mom to three child actors, the wife of a television producer Jack Burditt (*Watching Ellie, Frazier, Mad About You*), the daughter-in-law of novelist-producer Joyce Burditt (*The Father Dowling Mysteries*) and writer-producer George Burditt (*Three's Company, Silver Spoons*), Cyndee Burditt thought it was time she got into the business officially, not just as an advisor to her family.

So in 2001, she got a job working for Patrick Hart, the original owner of Screen Artists Agency. Her plan to work for Patrick for a long time learning the business was short-circuited when six months into her training, Patrick decided to retire.

Cyndee took a leap, bought the company, and moved it from its North Hollywood home to new digs in Sherman Oaks.

Although Cyndee says she wouldn't have minded a little more prep time, she's doing very well. She is maybe the only agency in town with both theatrical and commercial client lists where the number of theatrical clients (137) outweighs the commercial clients(87).

Clients from her list include Kacie Borrowman (*Passions*), Victoria Reiniger-Prescott (*CSI*), Bryton McClure (who was little Richie on *Family Matters*) and fourteen-year-old C. J. Johnson (*Dickie Roberts, Star Search*). Though her background is with kids, only about a dozen of her clients are under eighteen.

Although Cyndee says that it's rare to bring someone in from a "transom submission," three of her most successful clients came to her in the mail.

**Agent**
Cyndee Burditt
**Clients**
137

# ◿ SDB Partners, Inc. ◣

1801 Avenue of the Stars, #902
(S of little Santa Monica)
Los Angeles, CA 90067
310-785-0060

Ro Diamond, Susie Schwartz and Louis Bershad set up their new offices in such a hurry that they laughingly say that SDB stands for Still Doing Business. Although these three formidable agents parted company abruptly with old boss, Bob Walker of Century Artists, Ltd. to start their own agency in 1994, they managed to hit the ground running.

Ro's background includes her first agenting job with Lionel Larner in New York and a few years with Phil Gersh in Los Angeles before working at Century Artists. Straightforward and professional, she comes off as a shrewd businesswoman and as a gracious woman of taste. Susie, Louis and Ro have been together since 1976. Steven Jang, who began his agenting career at this office, joins Ro, Susie and Louis representing their list of heavy hitter working actors.

Clients from their list include Bruno Campos (*Jessie*), Jenny O'Hara (*Mystic River*), Cassidy Rae, Thomas Wilson Brown, James Cromwell (*Babe*), Julie Cobb, Mitchell Ryan, Alexa Vega, Kaley Cuoco, Rae Allen, and Luis Avalos.

SDB is respectful of actors who work at their craft in the theater and always have clients working Equity jobs both in Los Angeles and New York.

**Agents**
Ro Diamond, Susie Schwartz, Louis Bershad and Steven Jang
**Client List**
60

# ◢ David Shapira & Associates, Inc. ◣

15821 Ventura Boulevard, #235
(W of Haskell)
Encino, CA 91436
818-906-0322

David Shapira's life was changed by an agent's pinstriped suit. En route to life as a lawyer, he encountered the celebrated agent, Jerry Steiner. Shapira thought Jerry looked so elegant in his pinstriped suit that the would-be barrister (apparently not aware that even the Yankees wear pinstripes) decided to be an agent.

Shapira quit school at seventeen to work in the mailroom at General Artists Corporation where a friendship with Rod Serling helped him switch mailrooms (Ashley-Famous) with a hefty raise to $75 a week.

This was years ago and the rest, as they say, is history. It took only seven months in the mailroom before David, figuring this was going to take too long, lied about his age (you had to be 21 to make deals) and became an agent.

David has, at various times, worked with Marty Baum, Meyer Mishkin and Max Arnox (who cast *Gone with the Wind*). In 1974, David opened his first office (Goldstein/Shapira).

In addition to actors, David Shapira & Associates packages and reps scriptwriters, book authors, directors, producers and voiceover artists.

Agents who represent actors at this agency are David, Doug Warner, Donna Gaba, Harold Augenstein, Donna Gaba, Marc Kamler, Matt Shapira, Susan Simons

Clients at this agency include Lorenzo Lamas, Suzanne Somers, Ryan O'Neal, Krista Allen, Kristi Swanson, and Linda Evans.

Shapira maintains a very select client list of actors and writers. Not for beginners.

**Agents**
David Shapira, Doug Warner, Donna Gaba, Marc Kamler, Matt Shapira, and Susan Simons
**Client List**
70

# ⊿ Jerome Siegel Associates, Inc. ⊾

1680 N Vine Street, #613
(at Hollywood )
Hollywood, CA 90028
323-669-2836

Literary agent Jerome Siegel has been an agent for thirty-five years and always represented a few actors, but in 2000, he hired David Sacks to preside over a formal theatrical division.

David Sacks was an actor, director and producer in northern California for sixteen years before moving to Los Angeles.

His first agenting experience was with Mark Levin and the Husson Agency in 1970 before he joined Atkins and Associates.

David joined Jerome in 2000 and has a select list of actors who work pretty regularly. Liz Torres (*Gilmore Girls, American Family*), Jesse Ramirez (*Constantine*), and Gary Bullock (*Racing Stripes*) are three from his list.

Instrumental in the early careers of Nick Nolte and Richard Moll, David continues to have a discerning eye, particularly for character people.

Although he does check the pictures and resumes that come in, David's clients come mostly from referrals or are uncovered from his constant theater going.

**Agent**
David Sacks
**Clients**
12

# ⚹ Michael Slessinger Agency ⚹

8730 Sunset Boulevard, #270
(W of La Cienega)
Los Angeles, CA 90069
310-657-7113

Originally named The Actors Group, when Michael started his agency there was much confusion because many agencies have some version of that name. Michael finally just named the agency after himself, saving us all the trouble of figuring out which one was his. When Michael created his agency in New York in 1980, it was known chiefly as a source for beautiful actors. Today MSA is known as a rich reservoir of good characters as well.

A working actor friend of mine swears by Michael. Though his career had been going along fairly well, he felt he was not making any real progress until he went to Michael.

In 1984, Michael came west to open his Los Angeles office with a list of respected actors he had developed in New York. As time passed, Michael's business became more and more Los Angeles based, so he closed his New York office.

Billy Miller began his career at this agency and joins Michael in repping his list of about seventy-five clients.

Actors from their list include Kathy Kinney (*The Drew Carey Show*), Wayne Tippit, Sheryl Lee Ralph, Leigh McCloskey, Billy Wirth, Caroline Kava and Janet Hubert.

The age range of the client list of seventy-five goes from seventeen to seventy. MSA looks at all pictures and resumes.

**Agents**
Michael Slessinger and Billy Miller
**Client List**
75

# ⊿ SMS Talent, Inc. ⊾

formerly Silver Massetti & Szatmary Agency/West, Ltd

8730 Sunset Boulevard, #480
(W of La Cienega)
Los Angeles, CA 90069
310-289-0909

In October 1989, respected New York agent Monty Silver tapped former associate Robbie Kass (Woo Kass, Abrams Artists) and his then colleague, Donna Massetti, to open the West Coast presence of his revered New York agency.

Kass has since become a manager, while partner, Donna, began her agenting career with Monty in New York. Marilyn Szatmary, who cast for producer Manny Azenburg in New York before becoming an agent (The Gage Group, J. Michael Bloom, APA, Robert Abrams), joined this agency as a partner in 1996.

Greg Mehlman (J. Michael Bloom) and Charles Silver (Monty's nephew) complete the agency roster at SMS representing clients David Hyde-Pierce (*Frazier*), Charles Kimbrough (*Murphy Brown*), Paul Guilfoyle, Jeffrey Jones (*Dr. Dolittle, Stuart Little*), and Michael Gross. This office is committed to actors with a strong theatrical resume.

**Agents**
Donna Massetti, Marilyn Szatmary, Greg Mehlman, and Charles Silver
**Client List**
120

# ⚞ Scott Stander Associates, Inc. ⚟

13701 Riverside Drive, #201
(at Woodman/Downey Savings Building)
Sherman Oaks, CA 91423
818-905-7000

Talk about your showbiz family — Scott Stander was a child actor; sister Jacqueline was a professional musician at eleven and attended the Berkley College of Music at fourteen; dad was a doctor who played the trumpet, managed musical talent, and ran a record company; and mom was a singer before she traded that career for motherhood.

Their neighbors were the Bee Gees, Jimmy Buffett, and the Eagles, so it was only natural that this brother-sister team continued their paths into other areas of the business.

Jacqueline moved to Los Angeles in 1983 to continue her music career and ultimately became a manager and then an agent. Scott arrived ten years later. His career running theaters at home in Florida brought him together with former Miss America, Lee Merriweather, who was impressed by Scott and suggested he move to Los Angeles and become an agent.

He followed her advice, working in another agency for five years before opening SAA in 1998 when Lee became his client. Jacqueline joined him soon after and this brother-sister team continues to run their "baby William Morris" repping and booking celebrities.

In addition to representing their stable of celebrities for personal appearances and national tours, they also book tours for clients' one person shows. Adrienne Barbeau, Joe Bologna, Renee Taylor, Red Buttons, Ann Miller, Gary Burghoff, Arlene Dahl, Ann Jillian, and Hal Linden are names from their list.

Current tours they have booked are Frank Gorshin's Tony-nominated show, *Say Goodnight, Gracie*; Renee Taylor and Joe Bologna in their various shows; and *Debbie Reynolds in Concert*. www.scottstander.com

**Agent**
Scott Stander and Jacqueline Stander
**Clients**
200

# ⩗ Stone Manners ⩘

8436 W Third Street, #740
(E of La Cienega)
Los Angeles, CA 90048
323-655-1313

The offspring of a famous British agent, Tim Stone came to Los Angeles and established UK Management, providing services for British actors in this country. Although he used his British list as a base, Tim's list quickly became more eclectic. Tim moved to New York in 2003 to open Stone Manners' New York office.

Although he was the son of a stand-up comic and a June Taylor dancer, partner Scott Manners, the eldest of five children, managed to escape the lure of show business until he was cast in a college play at Irvine. A talented golfer with a major in business who considered being a golf pro, Scott became as passionate about acting as he was about golf.

He began to study with Jeff Corey who introduced him to truths which not only helped his acting, but led him to agenting as a profession. His clients benefit from the passion, drive, empathy and intelligence that Corey helped focus.

Scott's first agency job was for Fred Amsel, where he worked as a gofer for only two months before Fred tossed him into the deep water of agenting. Scott then worked with Rickey Barr at Richard Dickens Agency before landing at Stone Masser in 1983. By April 1986, the name was changed to Stone Manners Masser and, by August of that year, the name reflected the partnership as it exists today.

Stone Manners reps actors, directors, producers, scriptwriters, young adults and teens. Colleagues Holly Shelton and Glenn Salners (Lichtman Salners) and Mark Perara (The Artists Group) join Tim repping the acting clients in this growing agency.

**Agents**
Scott Manners, Holly Shelton, Glenn Salner, and Mark Perara
**Client List**
They won't say

# ⚐ Peter Strain & Associates ⚐

5724 W Third Street, #302
(W of La Brea)
Los Angeles, CA 90036
323-525-3391

Peter Strain didn't always know he wanted to be an agent, but he always knew that he wanted to be in show business. He studied directing at St. John's University and took directing classes at Circle-in-the-Square.

Peter says his only credential when he began his agenting career with Fifi Oscard in New York was enthusiasm. That trait obviously served him well, for his next stop was a high class commercial agency, Jacobson-Wilder, before joining and ultimately becoming partner at Bauman & Hiller.

He spent time with APA before opening an agency with Renee Jennett (Strain & Jennett Associates, Inc.) in 1988. By 1990, Jennett had moved on to Don Buchwald & Associates, and Strain was on his own. In 1995, he left his New York office in the hands of his associates and moved west to open a Los Angeles presence for his agency.

Strain's director-eye informs his preference for offbeat actors who are not dead on. He loves clients who are normally considered hard to cast, feeling he has been able to use more of his own creativity when he gets them appointments.

Harold Augenstein (David Shapira) and Karen Spencer (MTA) join Peter representing their list of about ninety that include Joe Mantegna, Rene Auberjonois and Georgia Engel.

**Agents**
Peter Strain, Harold Augenstein, and Karen Spencer
**Client List**
90

# ⊲ Mitchell K. Stubbs & Associates ⊳

8675 W Washington Boulevard, #203
(on the Helms Bakery campus at Hutchenson)
Culver City, CA 90232
310-838-1200

Mitchell Stubbs left Atlanta for Los Angeles to be an actor in 1984. After studying for two years and checking out the landscape, he decided that he really didn't have the passion for acting needed to sustain a career, so he left the business and worked at a Fortune 500 company.

Though he was making lots of money, Mitch was miserable being away from the business. He quit his job on a Friday ready for any job in the business and on Monday a friend recommended Mitch for an assistant job with Susan Smith Associates. He interviewed on Wednesday and by the next Monday, he was working for Smith.

Only a year and a half later in 1991, Mitchell was an agent. He stayed with Susan until November 1995. The third time proved to be the charm for J. Michael Bloom, who had already asked Mitch twice to join him. Five weeks later, Mitch was running Michael's Los Angeles office. Michael and Mitch had an amazing run booking so many pilots one year that the trades took notice of it.

Michael sold the business in April 1998 and by August when his contract was up, Mitch opened his own agency. He left Bloom on Friday and with the help of his colleagues, they managed to open for business the following Monday.

They outgrew that space and in 2003 moved to Culver City where Mitchell and old friend and colleague from the Susan Smith Agency, Judy Page, rep a distinguished list of clients.

It's clear that Stubbs runs not only a successful agency, but a warm family group of agents and clients as well. Mitch and his company represent an impressive list of about seventy to seventy-five clients like David Ogden Stiers, Ken Howard, Penny Johnson Jerald (*24*), CCH Pounder, Andrea Parker, Michael Winters (*Gilmore Girls*), Ron Glass, Kiersten Warren, and Jerry Hardin.

Even though they are a Los Angeles agency, they managed to put veteran clients Jerry Hardin and Michael Winters into their first Broadway shows.

MKS does look at all pictures and resumes, but if you really want to do business with them, you'll need a referral from an industry source.

MKS recently opened a commercial department headed by Carrie Johnson.

**Agents**

Mitchell K. Stubbs, Diane Perez, Meghan Schumacher and Ray Moheet

**Agent List**

70-75

# ⚡ TalentWorks ⚡
### formerly HWA Representatives and/or Gold/Liedtke Agency

3500 W. Olive Street, #1400
(at Riverside Drive)
Burbank, CA 91505
818-972-4310

TalentWorks is the agency created when Harry Gold and Bonnie Liedtke (Gold/Liedtke Agency) merged their agency with Patty Woo (HWA Representatives). Allies for years, the new partners finally made it official in December 2003.

Originally an actor, Harry Gold went through the agency training system at the Robert Light Agency and at Herb Tannen before opening Harry Gold in 1981. He partnered with Darryl Marshak (Gold/Marshak) and, in 1992, Bonnie Liedtke (Gold/Marshak/Liedtke) became their partner. Bonnie created the dynamic children/young adults division at TalentWorks.

Harvard valedictorian Patty Woo was a struggling actress when she worked as a pollster and later as a financial analyst for the Harris Poll before her first taste of agenting as an assistant at New York's Monty Silver Agency .

She left Monty to partner with Robby Kass (Kass Woo) for ten years before her partnership with ex-casting director Barbara Harter (Harter Woo) laid the groundwork for HWA.

The Manhattan office of TalentWorks is in the capable hands of Diana Doussant (APA) and Jay Kane.

The list of Los Angeles clients is impressive with Leah Remini, Danny Nucci, Farrah Fawcett, Wallace Shawn, William Shatner, John Benjamin Hickey (*It's All Relative*), and youth list clients Martin Spanjers (*8 Simple Rules for Dating My Teenage Daughter*), Griffin Frazen (*Malcolm in the Middle*), and Chad Michael Murray (*Freaky Friday, One Tree Hill*) being just a few.

The theatrical division is serviced by the partners along with Suzanne Wohl (William Morris) and Ryan Glasgow (Gold/Liedtke). Bonnie heads the youth department along with Brandy Gold.

Actors regularly leave larger offices to work with TalentWorks and find their careers much improved.

**Agents**
Harry Gold, Patty Woo, Bonnie Liedtke, Suzanne Wohl, Ryan Glasgow, and Brandy Gold
**Client List**
300

# ⚞ Twentieth Century Artists ⚟

15760 Ventura Boulevard, #700
(one block W of Haskell)
North Hollywood, CA 91436
818-325-3832

Dynamic Diane Davis has been running her own agency for over twenty-five years. Her late husband created Twentieth Century Artists, and Diane, who had been a talent agent at Mary Ellen White, joined the agency about a year after it opened.

Other agents who represent actors at this agency are David Ankrum and Shane Preston, whose agenting career began here.

Twentieth Century Artists represents both adults and teens.

Actors from her list of about fifty include Robert Ginty, Clarence Gilyard (*Walker, Texas Ranger*), Conrad Janis, Bill Lucking, Ryan McDonald, Robert Mandan, Majel Barrett, Robert O'Reilly, Dirk Benedict and Dennis Howard.

The feedback on Diane from clients has always been that she and her agency are effective, vital and strong. Agents who have trained at Twentieth Century and have gone on to open their own offices all speak glowingly of their mentor. If actors and even other agents all think this woman is aces, how could you lose?

**Agent**
Diane Davis
**Client List**
50

# ⚖ UTA ⚖
# United Talent Agency

9560 Wilshire Boulevard, #500
(at Rodeo Drive)
Beverly Hills, CA 90212
310-273-6700

In 1983, three agents with vision, James Berkus (IFA), Robert Stein and Gary Cosay (WMA), created Leading Artists and spoke of it as an intimate William Morris. In 1986, their future partners, former William Morris agent Marty Bauer, and entertainment lawyer Peter Benedek created the literary powerhouse, Bauer Benedek.

The two agencies merged in 1991 and, when they acquired two more partners, Jeremy Zimmer (ICM) and Martin Hurwitz (New World Entertainment), United Talent was born.

When InterTalent disbanded and Triad was acquired by William Morris at about the same time, some high profile clients and agents were left in the wake and were quickly scooped up by the company.

Partner Berkus was listed as #80 on *Premiere Magazine*'s 1999 list of Hollywood's Most Powerful. Berkus in particular seems to understand that the future of the film business is with the bright new filmmakers.

◆ *Financiers are realizing that there's no such thing as a foolproof package, and they're increasingly turning toward filmmakers with fresh ideas even if they're not easily told in three sentences.*

*When major stars like Bruce Willis and Tom Cruise are making movies with M. Night Shyamalan and Paul Thomas Anderson...you know we're not in Kansas anymore.*
Claudia Eller, *Los Angeles Times*[36]

The main strength here is writers, producers and directors, but the daily addition of actor clients like Jim Carrey, Harrison Ford, Kevin Costner, Madonna, Claire Danes, Paul Reiser, Mark Wahlberg, Vince Vaughn, Janeane Garofalo, Mandy Patinkin, Garry Shandling, David Strathairn, Michael Ian Black, Ruben Blades, Julie Bowen, Drew Carey, Anthony Edwards, Carmen Electra, Calista Flockhart, Joanna Gleason, Lauren Ambrose, Kathy Baker, Alan Ball, Helena Bonham Carter, David Chase, Don Cheadle, Rachel Griffiths, Patricia Heaton, Matt

LeBlanc, Bernie Mac, Joe Pantoliano, William Petersen, Tony Shalhoub, Jonathan Pryce, Kelsey Grammar, Janet Jackson, Eriq La Salle, Jane Leeves, Ben Stiller, Joely Richardso n, Mimi Rogers and Kevin Murphy instantly tell you the level at which UTA operates.

Partner John Lesher, who graduated from Harvard with a major in East Asian languages, started his showbiz life as Bauer's secretary when it was still Bauer Benedek. He co-manages the motion picture department with Dan Aloni and board member Jeremy Zimmer. Agents repping acting talent include Allison Band, Howard Cohen, J.J. Harris, David Schiff, Nick Stevens, David DeCamillo, Jason Haymen, Adam Isaacs and others.

With their string of top director clients like Barry Levinson (*Liberty Heights*), Paul Thomas Anderson (*Magnolia*), David O. Russell *(Three Kings)*, Wes Anderson *(Rushmore)*, Kimberly Peirce *(Boys Don't Cry)* and Ben Stiller (*Reality Bites*), James Gray (*Little Odessa, The Yards*), Boaz Yakim *(Fresh)*, Tom Shadyac *(Patch Adams)*, Frank Darabont (*The Green Mile, Shawshank Redemption*), Jessie Nelson (*Corrina, Corrina*), Tom Cherones (*Seinfeld*), Gregory Hoblit *(Hart's War)*, Beeban Kidron (*Used People)*, Jonathan Lawton (*Kirina*), Greg Mottola (*The Daytrippers*), Ben Ross (*The Young Partner's Handbook, RKO 281*), the Coen Brothers (*O Brother, Where Art Thou*), Curtis Hanson (*LA Confidential)* and Frank Pierson (*Citizen Cohn*), it's easy to see why, when Harrison Ford wanted to gain first exposure to the new young filmmakers, he chose UTA.

Every day it seems I read of yet another top level actor, director or scriptwriter signing with UTA.

**Agents**
James Berkus, David Schiff, Gary Cosay, Allison Band, Howard Cohen, Jason Heymen, Adam Isaacs and many many others
**Client List**
Growing daily

# ⚒ William Morris Agency ⚒

151 El Camino Drive
(S of Wilshire Boulevard)
Beverly Hills, CA 90211
310-274-7451

Mr. William Morris (yep, there really was one) started this agency in 1898. The IBM of the Big Three, William Morris continually reinvents itself. At one point in history the unchallenged #1, today William Morris, like other star agencies, continues to fluctuate based upon the current client base.

In 1999, ICM co-chief Jim Wiatt defected to William Morris to serve as president and co-CEO of what people began to refer to as the new William Morris.

+ *[Wiatt] oversees an agency that has 235 agents and claims about 4,000 clients worldwide in offices in Beverly Hills, New York, London and Nashville.*
Claudia Eller and James Bates, *Los Angeles Times*[37]

Wiatt brought with him such clients as Eddie Murphy, Sylvester Stallone, William Friedkin, Nora Ephron, Renny Harlin, Richard Donner, Neil Simon, Tim Allen, Lauren Shuler Donner, Lorne Michaels and two of ICM's most prized agents, David Wirtschafter and senior literary agent Amy Ferris.

Along with wanting to continue his professional relationship with Wiatt, Wirtschafter (who joins as an Executive VP and a member of the board) was drawn to the new William Morris management structure. The new William Morris seeks to establish a business where all parties report to each other, bypassing a more elite hierarchy.

Establishing the new William Morris has not been pain-free. The decision to consolidate the talent portion of the motion picture department in Los Angeles hit the New York office hard as many dyed-in-the-wool New Yorkers had no intention of relocating to Los Angeles.

What remains after the many changes, is a sleeker, more powerful, less bureaucratic agency that reps not only actors, writers, directors and producers, but athletes, newscasters, political figures and almost any other being of notoriety. If having the most agents means you have the most power, William Morris wins hands down. On a list of agents I looked at, William Morris had 222 as compared to 95-125 for both

ICM and CAA.

In any event, the number of agents is staggering. I'm not going to attempt to list all the names as the list is way too long and supposedly confidential. The *Hollywood Creative Directory* somehow manage to penetrate the iron curtain, so for a detailed up-to-the-minute list of names, check it out. The *HCD* tracks the names of conglomerate agents effectively.

William Morris may or may not be #1 as of this writing, but perennially, at Oscar time, when the big agencies take out ads to congratulate their nominees, William Morris has the longest most impressive client list.

Robert Duvall, Billy Bob Thornton, Willem Dafoe, Forest Whitaker, Daniel Day-Lewis, Christopher Walken, Emma Thompson, Matthew Modine, Lili Taylor, Ashley Judd, Cary Brokaw, Robert Altman, John Rubinstein, John Travolta, Bruce Willis, Julianne Moore, Tim Burton, Clint Eastwood, Stephen Frears, Diane Keaton, John Malkovich, Alec Baldwin, Danny Aiello, Charlie Sheen, Dean Stockwell, Bill Cosby, Sean Hayes, Ray Romano, Alfre Woodard, and Candice Bergen are just a few more of William Morris's amazing list.

#### Agents
Aaron Kaplan, Greg Lipstone, John Fogelman, Reno Ronson, Robert Stein, Todd Feldman, Amy Ferris, Steve Dontanville, Nicole David, John Burnham, Cassian Elwes, Julie Colbert, John Fogelman, Rachel Shapiro, Sara Bottfeld, Alan Gasmer, David Lubliner, Hylda Quelly and many many others

#### Client List
More and more every day

# ⋈ Writers & Artists ⋈

8383 Wilshire Boulevard, #550
(btwn San Vincente & Gale Streets)
Beverly Hills, CA 90211
323-866-0900

In 1971 when Joan Scott created her agency (Joan Scott Agency), she hadn't thought to include writers, when she did, she changed the name to reflect that. Retired now, Joan handed the agency over to Marti Blumenthal, William Craver, and David Brownstein.

Although the talent agent/client list is impressive, the literary department may be even more important. W&A recently hired away two important UTA literary agents, Steven Small and Ryan Martin, in their move to establish themselves as an alternative to the large conglomerate agencies for both writers and actors.

W&A's list of illustrious agents and clients continues to grow. Agents representing actors are Steven Small, Cynthia Booth, Chris Schmidt (Bauman and Hiller), Norman Aladjem, Sarah Clossey (TV production), Todd Eisner, Jason Priluck, Dina Shapiro. David Brownstein was in business affairs at Walt Disney before he joined W&A.

Representative acting clients include William H. Macy (*State and Main, Fargo*), Tom Amandes (*The Long Kiss Goodnight, The Pursuit of Happiness*), Lolita Davidovich, Vincent Berry (*Free Willy III*), Scott Cohen (*The Last Laugh*), Alexandra Lee (*Party of Five*), Greg Germann (*Ally McBeal*), Dean Cain (*Lois & Clark*), Michael Chiklis (*The Commish, Wired*), Majandra Delfino (*Roswell*) and Peter Falk.

Writers & Artists closed its New York talent department and continues as a rich source of writers, directors, composers, lyricists, screenwriters and television writers.

**Agents**
Chris Schmidt, Norman Aladjem, Sarah Clossey, David Brownstein, Todd Eisner, Steven Small, Cynthia Booth, Jason Priluck, and Dina Shapiro
**Client List**
300

# ⟋ Zanuck, Passon and Pace, Inc. ⟍

4717 Van Nuys Boulevard, Atrium, #102
(at E 101 Van Nuys offramp)
Sherman Oaks, CA 91403
818-783-4890

Michael Zanuck was a keyboard player and drummer in his home town of Columbus, Ohio when he slid into booking lounge acts and promoting musical groups and talents like Michael Bolton. In 1994, he thought he'd replicate the experience in Los Angeles, except that he would rep actors.

His first jobs were at The Bigley Agency and at Honey Sanders. Just two years later, he was in partnership with financial genius Gary Passon and Pittsburgh musician Jerry Pace.

So, in 1996, Zanuck, Passon and Pace, Inc. opened their offices in Sherman Oaks and, by 2001, in the middle of pilot season, it seemed time to open a New York office. Things are obviously going very well.

Michael and Jerry represent a list of almost 200 actors that sports seven actors on series and a stable of stalwarts like Gary Sandy (*WKRP in Cincinnati*), Fabian, Teresa Saldana, Basil Hoffman, James Hampton, Russ Tamblyn, all the grownup kids from *Leave It To Beaver* (Jerry Mathers, Tony Dow, Frank Bank, Ken Osmond), and Harrison Young, (the older Tom Hanks in *Saving Private Ryan*), among others.

In addition to repping actors, children, comedians, new media, sports personalities and young adults, Michael managed to put four songs in the movie *Paulie*. Barry Rick handles the commercial clients.

Michael says he absolutely does call people in from pictures and resumes although an industry reference is always best.

Their commercial department did such a good job with kids and young adults that Jerry is currently building a theatrical list for children/young adults. If you're between six and nineteen, here is an agency that's ripe for a query.

**Agents**
Michael Zanuck and Jerry Pace
**Client List**
175+

# ⚓ 15 ⚓
# Glossary

*99-Seat Theater Plan* — The Los Angeles version of the Showcase. Originally called Waiver. Producers give actors a minimal expense reimbursement per performance. It's not much, but it adds up; at least you're not working for free.

Producers must also conform to Equity guidelines regarding rehearsal conditions, number of performances, complimentary tickets for industry, etc. If you participate in this plan, be sure to stop by Equity and get a copy of your rights.

*Academy Players Directory* — Catalogue of actors published annually for the Los Angeles market. Shows one or two pictures per actor and lists credits and representation. If you work freelance, you can list your name and service. Some list union affiliation. Casting directors, producers and whomever else routinely keeps track of actors use the book as a reference guide. Every actor who is ready to book should either be in this directory or its New York counterpart, *Players Guide.*

*Actors' Equity Membership Requirements* — Rules for membership for the union covering actors for work in the theater state you must have a verifiable Equity Contract in order to join, or have been a member in good standing for at least one year in AFTRA or SAG.

Initiation fee is currently $1000 as of 4/1/03, payable prior to election to membership. Basic dues are $118 annually as of 11/03 Additionally, there are working dues: 2% of gross weekly earnings from employment is deducted from your check just like your income tax.

*Actors' Equity Minimum* — There are eighteen basic contracts ranging from the low end of the Small Production Contract to the higher Production Contract covering Broadway houses, Jones Beach, tours, etc. Highest is the Business Theater Agreement, for industrial shows produced by large corporations. All monies are discussed online at "contracts" at www.actorsequity.org.

*Actor Unions* — There are three: Actors' Equity Association (Equity) is the union that covers actors' employment in the theater. The American Federation of Television and Radio Artists ( AFTRA) covers television and radio actors, broadcasters and recording artists. Screen Actors Guild (SAG) covers actors employed in theatrical motion pictures and filmed television product. The unions continue discussions about the potential of joining together under one overall labor organization.

*AFTRA Membership Requirements* — anyone expecting to work in the news and entertainment industries can join. AFTRA's initiation fee is $1300 as of 11/1/03. Minimum dues for the first six-month dues period are $60. After joining, a member's dues are based on his or her earnings in AFTRA's jurisdictions during the prior year. Dues are billed each May and November. For information on contracts log onto www.aftra.org.

*AFTRA Minimum* — Check AFTRA's web page for rates.

*AFTRA Nighttime Rates* — Check AFTRA's web page for rates.

*Atmosphere* — another term for Background Performers, a.k.a. Extras.

*Audition Tape* — Also known as a Composite Cassette Tape. A videotape usually no longer than six minutes, showcasing either one performance or a montage of scenes of an actor's work. Agents and casting directors prefer tapes of professional appearances (film or television), but some will look at a tape produced for audition purposes only. Usually on VHS, will probably be on DVD soon.

*Background Performers* — a.k.a. Atmosphere and/or Extras

*Breakdown Service* — Started in 1971 by Gary Marsh, the Service condenses scripts and lists parts available in films, television and theater. Expensive and available to agents and managers only.

*Clear* — The unions require that the agent check with a freelance actor (clearing) before submitting him on a particular project.

*Composite Cassette Tape* — See Audition Tape.

*Equity-Waiver Productions* — See Showcases.

*Freelance* — Term used to describe the relationship between an actor and agent or agents who submit the actor for work without an exclusive contract. New York agents frequently will work on this basis, Los Angeles agents rarely consent to this arrangement.

*Going Out* — Auditions or meetings with directors and/or casting directors. These are usually set up by your agent but have also been set up by very persistent and courageous actors.

*Going to Network* — Final process in landing a pilot/series. After the audition process has narrowed the list of choices, actors who have already signed option deals have another callback for network executives, usually at the network. Sometimes this process can include an extra callback for the heads of whatever studio is involved.

*Industry Referral* — If you are looking for an agent, the best possible way to access one is if someone with some credibility in the business will call and make a phone call for you. This could be a casting director, writer, producer or the agent's mother, just so it's someone whose opinion the agent respects. If someone says, just use my name, forget it, they need to offer to make a phone call for you.

*The Leagues* — A now defunct formal collective of prestigious theater schools that offer conservatory training for the actor. The schools still exist, but there is no longer an association. As far as agents are concerned, this is the very best background an actor can have, other than having your father own a studio. Schools in this collective are American Conservatory Theater in San Francisco, CA; American Repertory Theater, Harvard University in Cambridge, MA; Boston University in Boston, MA; Carnegie Mellon in Pittsburgh, PA; Catholic University in Washington, DC; The Juilliard School in New York City, NY; New York University in New York City, NY; North Carolina School of the Arts in Winston-Salem, NC; Southern Methodist University in Dallas, TX; The University of California at San Diego in La Jolla, CA; and the Yale School of Drama in New Haven, CT. Addresses are listed in Chapter Three.

*Letter of Termination* — A legal document dissolving the contract between actor and agent. Send a copy of the letter to your agent via registered mail, return receipt requested, plus a copy to the Screen Actors Guild and all other unions involved. Retain a copy for your files.

*Major Role/Top of Show* — See Top of Show

*Open Call* — refers to auditions or meetings held by casting directors that are not restricted by agents. No individual appointments are given. Usually the call is made in an advertisement in one of the trade newspapers, by flyers or in a news story in the popular press. As you can imagine, the number of people that show up is enormous. You will have to wait a long time. Although management's eyes tend to glaze over and see nothing after a certain number of hours, actors do sometimes get jobs this way.

*Overexposed* — Term used by nervous buyers (producers, casting directors, networks, etc.) indicating an actor has become too recognizable for their tastes. Frequently he just got off another show and everyone remembers him as a particular character and the buyer doesn't want the public thinking of that instead of his project. A thin line exists between not being recognizable and being overexposed.

*Packaging* — This practice involves a talent agency approaching a buyer with a writer, a star, usually a star director and possibly a producer already attached to it. May include any number of other writers, actors, producers, etc.

*Paid Auditions* — There's no formal name for the practice of rounding up twenty actors and charging them for the privilege of meeting a casting director, agent, producer, etc. There are agents, casting directors and actors who feel the practice is unethical. It does give some actors who would otherwise not be seen an opportunity to meet and be seen by casting directors. I feel meeting a casting director under these circumstances is questionable and that there are more productive ways to spend your money.

*Per Diem* — Negotiated amount of money for expenses on location or on the road per day.

*Pictures* — The actor's calling card. An 8x10 glossy or matte print black and white photograph.

*Pilot* — The first episode of a proposed television series. Produced so that the network can determine whether there will be additional episodes. There are many pilots made every year. Few get picked up. Fewer stay on the air for more than a single season.

*Principal* — Job designation indicating a part larger than an extra or an Under Five.

*Ready to Book* — Agent talk for an actor who has been trained and judged mature enough to handle himself well in the audition, not only with material, but also with the buyers. Frequently refers to an actor whose progress in acting class or theater has been monitored by the agent.

*Resume* — The actor's ID; lists credits, physical description, agent's name, phone contact and special skills..

*Right* — When someone describes an actor as being right for a part, he is speaking about the essence of an actor. We all associate a particular essence with Brad Pitt and a different essence with Jim Carrey. One would not expect Pitt and Carrey to be up for the same part. Being right also involves credits. The more important the part, the more credits are necessary to support being seen.

*Scale* — See salary minimums of each union.

*Screen Actors Guild Membership Requirements* — The most prized union card is that of the Screen Actors Guild. Actors may join upon proof of employment or prospective employment within two weeks or less of start date of a SAG signatory film, television program or commercial.

Proof of employment may be in the form of a signed contract, a payroll check or check stub, or a letter from the company (on company letterhead stationery.) The document proving employment must state the applicant's name, Social Security number, the name of the production or commercial, the salary paid in dollar amount and the dates worked.

Another way of joining SAG is by being a paid up member of an affiliated performers' union for a period of at least one year, having worked at least once as a principal performer in that union's jurisdiction.

SAG Initiation Fee as of 7/03 is $1,406. This seems like a lot of money (and is) but the formula involved makes some sense. It's the SAG daily minimum, $678 times two, plus $50 for the biannual dues. For information on how to join 323-549-6772 or www.sag.org.

This money is payable in full, in cashier's check or money order, at the time of application. The fees may be lower in some branch areas. SAG dues are based on SAG earnings and are billed twice a year. Those members earning more than $5,000 annually under SAG contracts will pay 1.5% of all money earned in excess of $5,000 up to a maximum of $150,000. If you are not working, you can go on Honorary Withdrawal which only relieves you of the obligation to pay your dues. You are still in the union and prohibited from accepting non-union work.

*Screen Actors Guild Minimum* — As of 7/03, SAG Scale rates is $678 daily and $2,352 weekly for employment in films and television. Overtime in SAG is considerably higher than in AFTRA.

*Showcases* — Productions in which members of Actors' Equity are allowed by the union to work without compensation are called Showcases in New York and 99-Seat Theater Plan in Los Angeles. Equity members are allowed to perform, as long as the productions conform to certain Equity guidelines: rehearsal conditions, limiting the number of performances and seats, and providing a set number of complimentary tickets for industry people. The producers must provide tickets for franchised agents, casting directors and producers.

*Sides* — The pages of script containing your audition material. Usually not enough information to use as a source to do a good audition. If they won't give you a complete script, go early (or the day before), sit in the office and read it. SAG rules require producers to allow actors access to the script. Sometimes the script is still being written and is unavailable.

*Stage Time* — Term used to designate the amount of time a performer has had in front of an audience. Most agents and casting executives believe that an actor can only achieve a certain level of confidence by amassing stage time. They're right.

*Submissions* — Sending an actor's name to a casting director in hopes of getting the actor an audition or meeting for a part.

*Talent* — Management's synonym for actors.

*Test Option Agreement* — Before going to network for a final back for a pilot/series, actors must routinely sign a contract that negotiates salary for the pilot and for series. The contract is for five years with an option for two more years. All options are at the discretion of management. They can drop you at the end of any season. You are bound by the terms of your contract to stay for the initial five years plus their two one-year options.

*Top of Show/Major Role* — A predetermined fee set by producers which is a non-negotiable maximum for guest appearances on television episodes. Also called Major Role Designation.

*The Trades* — *Daily Variety* and *Hollywood Reporter* are daily newspapers covering show business news. *Back Stage West* published weekly lists information about classes, auditions, casting, etc. and is particularly helpful to newcomers. *Ross Reports* published monthly lists names and addresses of casting directors, studios, advertising agencies, studios and networks in both New York and Los Angeles. All are available at good newsstands or by subscription.

*Under Five* — An AFTRA job in which the actor has five or fewer lines. Paid at a specific rate less than a principal and more than an extra. Sometimes referred to as Five and Under.

*Visible/Visibility* — Currently on view in film, theater or television. In this business, it's out of sight, out of mind, so visibility is very important.

# 🔆 17 🔆
# Indexes

# ✒ Index to Agents & Agencies ✒

# Index to Agents for Kids and Young Adults

# ⚔ Index to Agents for Stand-ups/Voiceovers ⚖

# ◣ Index to Photographers and Teachers ◢

# ⚞ Index to Resources ⚟

# ⩗ Index to Web Addresses ⩘

# ☜ Index to Everything Else ☞

# ⊿ Endnotes ⊵

1. "Top Agent [Jane Sindell, CAA] Talks About Decision to Quit," December 2, 1997

2. "Acting Is One Thing, Getting Hired Another," May 25, 1997

3. "Acting Is One Thing, Getting Hired Another," May 25, 1997

4. "The Careerist's Guide to Survival," April 25, 1982

5. "The Careerist's Guide to Survival," April 25, 1982

6. "Ten-Percenter Power on the Rise," November 10, 1993

7. "Seismic Shifts for H'w'd Reps," June 14, 2000

8. "Agents Get Tough Grades from Pic Producers," October 3, 2001

9. "Company Town: Agency Shuffle Lights a Fuse," August 10, 1999

10. "Seismic Shifts for H'w'd Reps," June 14, 2000

11. "Ford Ponders Agency Home," January 10, 2000

12. "Out from the Shadows," January 13, 2000

13. William Morrow & Co., New York

14. "Top Agent Talks About Decision to Quit," December 2, 1997

15. "Hollywood's No. 2 Agent Views His Status and His World" March 2, 1994

16. "After Denver, His List of Things to Do in Movies May Grow," December 2, 1995

17. "The Full Mickey," November 28, 1997

18. "J. Lo: Ex-manager Violated," July 3, 2003

19. "Vardalos' Ex--manager Dealt Lawsuit Setback," September 17, 2003

20. "Bitter Shandling-Grey Break-up Strikes a Nerve in Hollywood," January 23, 1998

21. "It's Garry Shandling's Suit," February 17-23, 1998

22. McGraw-Hill, New York

23. "It's Garry Shandling's Suit," February 17-23, 1998

24. "SAG Study Unwraps Package Myth," April 25, 1985

25. "TV Talk," September 18, 2000

26. Silman-James Press, 2002

27. "Showcase Hell," January 9, 1998

28. "Pearls of Wisdom from Liz," March 31, 1996

29. "Do, Re, Me Me Me!" November 10, 1997

30. "CAA: Packaging of an Agency," April 23, 1979

31 ."Studios Rate the Reps," Oct. 3, 2001

32. "Tenacious Tenpercenters," April 7, 2003

33. "Julia Roberts Leaves ICM," April 30, 2003

34. "Agents Get Tough Grade from Film Producers," October 3, 2001

35. "Talent Agency Shows Stellar Teamwork in Hollywood, No Less," January 26, 1996

36. "Agents Are Casting About in a Torrent of Change," September 17, 1999

37. "The Biz: William Morris Snags Jim Wiatt, Former ICM Exec," August 10, 1999

# Complete your Library of Callan Career Books

order online at www.swedenpress.com or by mail.

## How to Sell Yourself as an Actor

*(From New York to Los Angeles and Everywhere in Between)*

It's not enough to be able to act, you need to translate that skill into gainful employment. How to Sell Yourself as an Actor is the first and last book an actor needs to stay on a successful career track.

On any given day, 85-90% of the members of the Screen Actors Guild are out of work. This complete actors marketing guide is filled with nuts and bolts information that can help you become one of the working 15%. Not only a philosophy about acting as a profession and lifestyle, but a guide for actually procuring work.

ISBN 1-878355-15-5
$18.95 + $3.85 priority mail U. S.

## The New York Agent Book

*(How to Get the Agent You Need for the Career You Want)*

No matter where you live, finding and evaluating a business partner is an essential part of an actor's life. Veteran actress K Callan's definitive agent book takes the mystery out of the process. She tells you how to agent yourself until you're marketable enough to attract an agent, what agents look for, what you should look for when you're agent shopping, how to shop, how to choose and she includes profiles of New York agents, their histories, and some of their clients
.

ISBN 1-878355-16-3
$19.95 + $3.85 Priority Mail U. S.

## Directing Your Directing Career
*(A resource book and agent guide for directors)*

Actress-author K Callan's best-selling resource book and agent guide for directors includes an analysis of directing as a realistic career choice, the need to focus one's energies on a particular part of the marketplace, how to know when you are ready to move to New York or Los Angeles, how you can be a working director in your own marketplace, relationships with agents and managers, what agents are looking for and how and when to approach them.

ISBN 1-878355-11-2
$18.95 + $3.85 Priority Mail U. S.

## The Script Is Finished, Now What Do I Do?
*(A resource book and agent guide for the scriptwriter)*

The complete marketing and agent guide for scriptwriters no matter where you live. *The Script Is Finished* features a realistic overview of the business emphasizing action and the need to focus your writing for a particular market. Callan's interviews with agents reveal what they are looking for and insights as to when and how to query them. The book no scriptwriter should be without.

ISBN 1-878355-14-7
$18.95 + 3.85 Priority Mail U. S.

# Order by Mail Today
Sweden Press
Box 1612
Studio City, CA 91614

✂···········································································

| # | Title | Price | Total |
|---|-------|-------|-------|
|  | The New York Agent Book | $19.95 |  |
|  | How To Sell Yourself as an Actor | $18.95 |  |
|  | The Script Is Finished, Now What Do I Do? | $18.95 |  |
|  | Directing Your Directing Career | $18.95 |  |
|  | The Los Angeles Agent Book | $19.95 |  |
|  | Priority Mail | $3.85 for 2 $4.95 for 4 |  |
|  | Total |  |  |

| Name |
|------|
| Street |
| City, State, Zip |
| Phone          E-mail |

# About The Author

Actress-author K Callan began writing her series of show business reference books in 1986 in answer to her own question: *If every agent in the world wanted you, how would you make an intelligent decision?*

Now, all these years and thirty-something books later, Callan still calls agents, researches the business for actors, writers, and directors, and delights in learning more about the process of the business on stage and off.

Callan is a member of the Academy of Motion Picture Arts and Sciences, the Academy of Television Arts and Sciences, and a past Board Member of the Screen Actors Guild.

Her acting career began in school plays in Texas and has continued through off-Broadway, films, and television. Her most visible television role to date was playing Superman's mom on ABC's hit series *Lois & Clark: The New Adventures of Superman.*

Callan's mothering career, in addition to her own three grown children, includes the likes of Michelle Pfeiffer in *Frankie & Johnnie,* Tom Hanks in *Bosom Buddies,* and Geena Davis in *Sara.*

Her big break came in 1971 with her first film, *Joe.* Her portrayal of Peter Boyle's subservient wife brought her glowing reviews in the *New York Times.* Other films include *A Touch of Class* with Glenda Jackson and George Segal, *American Gigolo* with Richard Gere, and *The Onion Field* with James Woods.

A regular on three network television series and a guest star in scores of television movies, miniseries and episodes, Callan also makes time to get back to the theater and is a member of the Classical Contemporary American Playwrights housed at Inside at The Ford in Los Angeles.

In addition to this latest expanded and updated edition of *The Los Angeles Agent Book,* Callan has written such other successful how-to tomes as *How to Sell Yourself as an Actor, The New York Agent Book, Directing Your Directing Career, The Life of the Party,* and *The Script is Finished, Now What Do I Do?*